BLUE RIDGE MUSIC TRAILS
OF NORTH CAROLINA

Blue Ridge Music Trails of North Carolina

is a project of the North Carolina Arts Council,

an agency of the North Carolina Department of Cultural Resources.

Wayne Martin, Executive Director, North Carolina Arts Council

The project is supported with a Federal Transportation Enhancement

Grant through the North Carolina Department of Transportation.

Published in association with the Blue Ridge National Heritage Area, Angie

Chandler, Executive Director, and the North Carolina Folklife Institute.

Project Manager: Steve Kruger

Blue Ridge Music Trails *of* North Carolina

Music Trails *of* North Carolina

A GUIDE TO MUSIC SITES,
ARTISTS, AND TRADITIONS
OF THE MOUNTAINS AND
FOOTHILLS

FRED C. FUSSELL

with Steve Kruger

Photographs by CEDRIC N. CHATTERLEY

THE UNIVERSITY OF NORTH CAROLINA PRESS

Chapel Hill

Portions of this work are adapted from Fred C. Fussell,
Blue Ridge Music Trails: Finding a Place in the Circle (2003).

The paper in this book meets the guidelines for permanence
and durability of the Committee on Production Guidelines
for Book Longevity of the Council on Library Resources.
The University of North Carolina Press has been a member of
the Green Press Initiative since 2003.

Library of Congress Cataloging-in-Publication Data
Fussell, Fred.
Blue Ridge music trails of North Carolina : a guide to music sites, artists, and
traditions of the mountains and foothills / Fred C. Fussell, with Steve Kruger ;
photographs by Cedric N. Chatterley.
pages cm
"Portions of this work are adapted from Fred C. Fussell, Blue Ridge Music Trails:
Finding a Place in the Circle (2003)."
Includes bibliographical references and index.
ISBN 978-1-4696-0821-1 (pbk : alk. paper)
1. Folk music—North Carolina—History and criticism. 2. Folk music—Blue Ridge
Mountains Region—History and criticism. 3. Musical landmarks—North Carolina—
Guidebooks. 4. Musical landmarks—Blue Ridge Mountains Region—Guidebooks.
5. North Carolina—Guidebooks. 6. Blue Ridge Mountains Region—Guidebooks.
I. Kruger, Steve. II. Chatterley, Cedric N., 1956– illustrator. III. Fussell, Fred. Blue Ridge
Music Trails. Adaptation of (work): IV. Title.
ML3551.7.N8F87 2013
781.62′1307568—dc23
                                                                    2012042540

17 16 15 14 13   5 4 3 2 1

A PLACE IN THE CIRCLE

Traditional mountain dance always starts in a big circle.
The circle of joining hands is a symbol of the community.
It's a part of America—we come from all places. It's
very important for a person to have a sense of place,
to belong to somewhere, to come from somewhere.
You come from someplace and everybody else does,
too. Knowing that gives you a sense of tolerance, of
openness, and of hospitality. I don't come from the best
of everything. I come from where I come from—and I'm
proud of it. In everyplace, there is everything. You're
not an outsider to the world if you know where you're
from. Instead you're a part of the world. You can start
from anywhere and go anywhere, but if you don't know
where you are when you begin, you're awash. There are
not a lot of places left that have a sense of place, but
Appalachia's one of them that does. It's a wonderful
place to visit. Maybe visitors who come here can take
something of that sense back home and establish it
where they come from—and appreciate their place.
— JOE SAM QUEEN, traditional mountain dance leader,
  Waynesville, North Carolina

CONTENTS

For additional venues, musician profiles, events, and updates on the Blue
Ridge Music Trails, please visit www.BlueRidgeMusicNC.com

A young listener looks over the shoulder of a dobro player on the front porch of the Barn in Rockingham County.

Preface Entering the Circle

The Appalachian Mountains in western North Carolina are the heart of a unique regional music-making legacy. This is a place where traditional music and dance are performed and celebrated as in no other place in America. Regular weekly square dances featuring live music are still popular in many mountain communities. Local radio stations still broadcast live performances of traditional music performed by local musicians. Fiddlers' conventions featuring local players occur on many weekends during the spring and summer, and in the Blue Ridge Mountains of western North Carolina, homemade music competes favorably with the popular commercial offerings that dominate the music scene in most other regions of the United States. The National Heritage Fellowship, our nation's highest honor for traditional artists, has been awarded to more musicians from western North Carolina than from almost any other state. Among these notable eleven banjo players, fiddlers, and singers are two of the people who are perhaps most responsible for bringing Appalachian music to the world's attention, Doc Watson and Earl Scruggs. Watson and Scruggs passed away in 2012. They were mourned by their fans all over the world, but especially by the people of their home state. They have left behind a rich legacy and a strong living tradition.

Traditional mountain music remains an integral component of community celebrations and holiday festivities. Fiddle bands play at molasses makings and at small-town festivals; singers gather to perform shape-note hymns and have dinner on the church grounds; and residents of small communities gather at more than one hundred local venues to enjoy traditional music played by their friends and next-door neighbors. All of this musical activity flourishes in a region that is also one of the most popular destinations in America. Hundreds of thousands of travelers visit the North Carolina mountains every year to enjoy vacations and getaways. In springtime, visitors hike the winding hillside trails, enjoy the grandeur of High Country vistas along the Blue Ridge Parkway, or fish for trout in the cold, clear waters of mountain streams and rivers. In summer, residents of warmer climes come seeking relief from the low-country heat. Visitors crowd the narrow mountain roadways in autumn to enjoy the spectacle of colorful foliage. In winter, families and groups arrive by the busload to ski and to play in the snow at mountain resorts.

And while they're in the area, many visitors stop to have a look at one or two of the numerous roadside attractions that vie for their attention.

Some pan for gold and jewels near Spruce Pine and Marion, sifting carefully through buckets of mountain dirt in search of semiprecious stones and anything else that glitters. Others search for and select that perfect Christmas tree from among the many thousands that dot the High Country hillsides. Still others watch woolly worms climb up lengths of cotton twine or shop in mountain gift shops and craft galleries.

Visitors who sense that there's something more to this beautiful place and seek a more meaningful connection with mountain people and with authentic mountain culture are often at a loss as to how to achieve it. It's not easy—or at least it doesn't seem to be—for strangers in an unfamiliar community to meet local residents and experience the essential life of the place they're visiting.

The soundtracks of popular television programs and motion pictures have introduced mountain music to people from outside the region who might otherwise never have heard it. Yet mountain residents are sometimes frustrated by the way outsiders perceive mountain culture. Comic strips and TV sitcoms set in Southern Appalachia depict stereotypical images of mountaineers and their music. Many visitors to the region, particularly for the first time, expect to encounter sights reminiscent of scenes from TV shows, like Jed Clampett dancing to the banjo picking of Earl Scruggs on *The Beverly Hillbillies*, the Darling Family gathering for an impromptu performance in the Mayberry jail on *The Andy Griffith Show*, or the banjo virtuosity of the blind mountain boy in the movie *Deliverance*. The popular movies *Songcatcher* and *O Brother, Where Art Thou?* have added more characters to the list.

An authentic experience of mountain music in the community is far richer than shows like these portray. Mountain residents continue to sing traditional ballads that have been handed down for generations, ballads that reach far back into history. And even though those ballads may speak of people they've never seen and places they've never been, the traditional singers hold on to them. They're aware of the rarity and the importance of such songs. And, furthermore, they simply like to sing them.

Many music makers in western North Carolina have grown from infancy to old age knowing traditional music as an integral part of their everyday lives—not exclusively through CDs or radio or television, but as living music played by living people, both at home and out in the community. This is music to be played in public and shared with others. Mountain people are rightfully proud of the musical heritage that distinguishes the region. Many are very much aware, both as individuals and as members of traditional communities, that they have inherited an unparalleled and

Forming the circle at the Mountain Street Dance in Waynesville.

precious cultural legacy. The responsibility to maintain and transmit that legacy to future generations inspires the preservation and sharing of these traditions.

The traditional musicians of western North Carolina—farmers, teachers, postal workers, barbers, architects, pharmacists, students, nurses, merchants, technicians, and other ordinary folks—love nothing more than to get together, socialize, tell corny jokes, eat good food, and make music. They play in community centers, coffee shops, barbecue restaurants, music stores, fast-food joints, shopping malls, community festivals, street fairs, barbershops, school auditoriums, and town parks. They play traditional bluegrass, old-time, country-and-western, gospel, and blues, and they play with gusto and enthusiasm. And they will often share their time-honored traditions and practice-honed skills with those who are interested, all the while swapping tunes, techniques, and lyrics with their fellow players. They make their music with a fine humor and with light hearts, but at the same time they're serious about it. They pick, strum, frail, and bow strings of steel pulled tight across instruments of spruce, ebony, walnut, cherry, rosewood, mahogany, and maple. They beat pairs of metal or wooden spoons together in the palms of their hands, and they scrub their fingers across the ribs of metal or wooden washboards. They blow harmonicas. They tap out a rhythm with their dancing feet. They unabashedly sing out with high-pitched tenor voices, creating the distinctive harmonies that are the backbone of American country music. They know that their music is distinctively southern, distinctively Appalachian, distinctively American, distinctively *theirs*—and theirs to share.

The circle, both literal and symbolic, is important to mountain musicians. They gather naturally in a circle when they come together to make music. The greater the number of players, the larger the circle grows. Local dances often begin with a circle or round dance. Everyone present can participate in a round dance, and the joining of hands within the circle reinforces the sense of community.

It is my hope that the information provided in this book—tips, leads, directions, maps, and images—will help people discover traditional mountain music. In the process, visitors will learn more about rural communities and perhaps—if they are fortunate—find their place in the circle. The music is there. The music makers are there. Hear the music. Dance the dance. Gather round, folks, and listen. Circle up. You'll be glad you did.

FRED C. FUSSELL

How to Use the Guidebook

We welcome you to Blue Ridge Music Trails—a gateway to the musical traditions of the Blue Ridge Mountains—connecting traditional music venues in North Carolina to the Blue Ridge Parkway and to major roads and byways of the region. This trails project takes its name from the largest of the Southern Appalachian mountain ranges, the Blue Ridge Mountains, and from its close association to the Blue Ridge Parkway, the 469-mile scenic route that links the region.

This book and the accompanying website (www.BlueRidgeMusicNC.com) are the most comprehensive guides to traditional music in western North Carolina. Each chapter starts with a regional overview and a theme that provides historic context for the region. An in-depth, insiders' view into traditional music—one you're unlikely to find outside of this comprehensive volume—is provided by author Fred Fussell and folklorist Steve Kruger and illustrated by powerful documentary photographs by Cedric Chatterley. Through transcribed interviews, musicians tell the stories of their lives and explain what music means to them and to their communi-

The Orchard at Altapass on the Blue Ridge Parkway in McDowell County.

Accepting donations for the Hog Stomp at the Old Helton School.

ties. Their voices speak on behalf of the thousands of residents who play and support traditional music in the Blue Ridge Mountains.

The guidebook divides Western North Carolina into six regions, starting with the northernmost region bordering Virginia, and then flowing south. Within each region, the music and dance venues are grouped under the counties in which they take place. Maps illustrate the locations of the communities where sites and venues are located. Since the maps cannot show all secondary roads in the mountains, the Blue Ridge Music website includes links to Google Maps for more detailed directions to many, though not all, of the sites.

Finally, when you see this icon ● in the guidebook, you can listen to music that corresponds to the text on the accompanying CD, whether it's a song by a musician profiled, a tune about an event that took place in North Carolina, or a number recorded at a Blue Ridge Music Trail venue.

As you explore the trails, keep in mind that even though all the events listed in the guidebook occur on a regular basis, some are staged weekly, some monthly, and some annually, and some events happen at the same time. Don't expect to move through all the music venues on one trip. Instead, use the guidebook to plan your visit to a region around scheduled events.

Traditional music aficionados have described western North Carolina as the "busiest nook" in America for singing, fiddling and banjo playing. If you're already a fan of traditional music, you might want to explore one of the more intimate events, such as the jam session at Zuma Coffee or the Alleghany Jubilee. The first-time visitor might enjoy the larger events, such as MerleFest and the Mount Airy Bluegrass and Old-Time Fiddlers' Convention, to sample the traditional music experience in a festival setting. No matter which venues you visit, you'll experience traditional culture of the region and feel closer to the folkways of the mountains. The following are a few more tips to deepen your Blue Ridge music experience.

CONNECT ON THE BLUE RIDGE MUSIC WEBSITE

BlueRidgeMusicNC.com is your up-to-date guide to Blue Ridge music. This is where you will find additional venues listed by region, as well as up-to-date news and tidbits about traditional music in western North Carolina.

An events calendar with a robust search capability will help you match a date with a region to find events. The easy-to-use navigation will take you to videos that feature interviews with musicians, audio files with music samples, and a variety of resources to help plan your trip.

You'll also find profiles of musicians and stories about music festivals and seasonal itineraries. Plus, it's easy to share our content and provide your own.

One of the magical elements of a Blue Ridge music experience is the opportunity to talk to musicians in informal settings. Their music is interwoven with who they are, and most would be happy to share a minute or two with you. (Read "Jam Protocol" on pages 161–62 to find out how to join a session.)

Share your experience. If the venue allows, use your phone to take pictures and videos. We invite you to post them on www.BlueRidgeMusicNC.com; or send us an email at NCArts@ncdcr.gov.

Living traditions change constantly as the local community changes. Traditional music is no exception. New sites emerge when informal or private music gatherings move to public spaces, or when one or more determined individuals decide to create something new in their communities. Music events in the Blue Ridge sometimes alter their schedules or locations, so it's wise to contact sites in advance to verify the accuracy of the information. Also, don't forget to bring cash, as many venues are not set up to accept credit cards.

Plan to visit the companion website, for up-to-date information on venues and more. Additionally, many venues not included in this guidebook are listed on the website, and new venues that meet the selection criteria will be added.

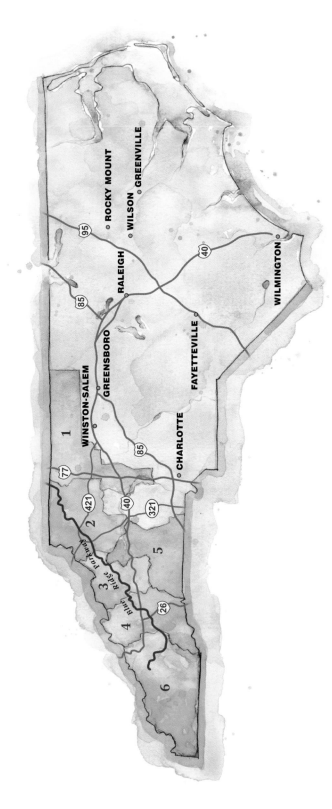

North Carolina has been an early leader in cultural tourism, gaining national attention for developing cultural trails that feature the state's significant arts assets: Blue Ridge music, Cherokee arts and culture, literary heritage, and African American music. Each of the numbered regions shown here corresponds to a chapter in this guidebook.

BLUE RIDGE MUSIC TRAILS
OF NORTH CAROLINA

Traditional Music in Western North Carolina *by Wayne Martin*

CELEBRATED HISTORY

Most stories about the origins of the rich music traditions of western North Carolina begin with the Scotch Irish settlers who moved down the great Wagon Road into the Piedmont region of Virginia and North Carolina and fanned westward into the Appalachians. The music traditions they brought with them survived because they were handed down orally from one generation to the next. The Scotch Irish influence is said to be the heart of modern Appalachian music, so much so that the fiddle and banjo music heard today is sometimes linked directly to the drones of bagpipes and the old Celtic melodies of the British Isles.

Tens of thousands of settlers are estimated to have traveled the Great Wagon Road into Virginia and North Carolina, so there is more than a little truth in this version of the evolution of mountain music. In reality, the story is far richer; a number of groups besides early settlers from of the British Isles shaped the music we hear today. African Americans brought the banjo and contributed greatly to repertory and style through work songs, blues, and gospel music. Recent scholarship also reveals that the Cherokee developed one of the earliest fiddle music traditions in the region. Even the dulcimer, the iconic symbol of Appalachian music, is not from the British Isles but is of German origin.

The conventional narrative also emphasizes the physical and cultural isolation of mountain people, a "trapped in amber" perspective that acknowledges outside musical influences with the advent of commercial recordings and radio in the early decades of the twentieth century. Again, the true story is more interesting. Touring minstrels, medicine show performers, and even circuses were bringing new musical influences to mountain communities as early as the antebellum era. Soldiers from western North Carolina traveled far from home to fight in America's wars, and mountain natives migrated to other states or regions to find work in coal mines, in logging camps, and, later, in textile mills. Those who eventually returned brought back new songs and musical styles that had a great impact on local music traditions.

For generations of settlers, music was a way to bring neighbors

Bascom Lamar Lunsford with the Lovingood sisters, circa 1940. Lunsford spent much of his life collecting and performing the traditional music of western North Carolina. He also organized the Mountain Dance and Folk Festival and wrote the song "Good Old Mountain Dew." Courtesy of Bascom Lamar Lunsford Scrapbook, Southern Appalachian Archives, Mars Hill College.

together at community social gatherings, to express faith and religious belief, or to ease the burden of physical labor at work gatherings. In the late nineteenth and early twentieth centuries, though, mountain music assumed a new value as an important part of the perceived cultural heritage of the region.

Collectors and musicians native to western North Carolina were hugely important in making this change. One of the earliest and most visible of these was Bascom Lamar Lunsford, a fruit tree salesman turned teacher turned lawyer. Lunsford was himself a fine banjo player and singer and began collecting songs as a way to gather new material for his own performances. He came to realize the cultural value of the songs he loved and saw the music and dance of western North Carolina as an older, rural based heritage that, ironically, would gain greater visibility in Asheville, the most populous city in the region. In 1928 he founded the Mountain Dance and Folk Festival and emphasized the presentation of the traditions he venerated:

> In the very beginning ballad singers, fiddlers, mountain dancers, old and young, came from the Valley of the Cheoah, Laurel River, Bear Wallow, Watauga River, Soco Gap, Oconalufty [sic] River, Sandymush, Rabbitham, and South Turkey Creek, or some 20 other mountain counties or communities where the old ballads have been sung at their best for years, where group dancing based on older figures and movements, and childhood games and singing games, all spirited and moving, were never talked out by a sophisticated society as had been done elsewhere.*

* Loyal Jones, *Minstrel of the Appalachians: The Story of Bascom Lamar Lunsford* (1984; reprint, Lexington: University Press of Kentucky, 2002).

During the string band recording boom in the 1920s and 1930s, record companies often played up the rural origin of the music. The Hill Billies were a popular early string band that included members from North Carolina, Virginia, and Tennessee. They were named by record producer Ralph Peer and donned overalls and kerchiefs for this publicity photo from 1926. Courtesy of the Blue Ridge Institute and Museum of Ferrum College.

Lunsford also participated in some of the first commercial recordings of southern folk musicians. In the 1920s, still early in the development of the recording industry, most major record companies were headquartered in the urban Northeast. Once they found a market for rural-based string band music, however, the record companies set up field studios in southern cities. Atlanta was a major recording center, but Asheville, Charlotte, and Winston-Salem also served as field sites that attracted hundreds of local musicians who auditioned for the chance to make records.

Western North Carolinians had a major impact in the early days of the recording industry. Samantha Bumgarner, a banjo player, fiddler, and singer from Jackson County teamed with a neighbor, Eva Davis, in 1924 to record some of the first mountain string band music issued commercially.

Lunsford appeared soon afterward with his own recordings, including his original song "Old Mountain Dew," which was later shaped into the now well-known "Good Old Mountain Dew."

Bumgarner and Lunsford were followed by other fiddlers, banjo pickers, harp blowers, guitarists, and singers from the mountains and western Piedmont of North Carolina—including Charlie Poole and the North Carolina Ramblers, DaCosta Woltz's Southern Broadcasters, J. E. and Wade Mainer and the Sons of the Mountaineers, and the Carolina Tar Heels, to name just a few, groups who made recordings that are today considered to be among the finest documented performances of American folk music.

The record companies often marketed these musicians as "hillbillies" playing "old-time" ballads, songs, and dance tunes that hearkened back to a rural, self-sufficient America. In fact, the term "hillbilly music" came to be applied to all white performers whose repertoire was folk-based, whether they lived in the mountains or not.

Collectors and scholars from outside of western North Carolina also influenced the growing awareness of the value of western North Carolina's music traditions. Foremost among these was English ballad hunter Cecil Sharp, who journeyed to the Southern Appalachians between 1916 and 1918. Sharp and his collaborator, Maud Karpeles, collected over five hundred distinct ballads, most with origins in the British Isles, from Appalachian singers living in five states, with North Carolinians contributing the greatest number. In August 1916 Sharp wrote in excitement about his success in Madison and Buncombe counties, North Carolina:

> Last week I went to Hot Springs, where I got thirty beautiful songs from a single woman. The collecting goes on apace, and I have now noted 160 songs and ballads. Indeed, this field is a far more fertile one upon which to collect English folk songs than England itself. The cult of singing traditional songs is far more alive than it is in England or has been for fifty years or more. I do not know how I shall tear myself away from the mountains and leave so much work undone when . . . If I could only have stayed here and collected until Christmas, I could have done a tremendous lot, collected probably over a thousand tunes.*

Besides Sharp, other scholars and song collectors who journeyed to western North Carolina in the first half of the twentieth century included Frank C. Brown, faculty member at Duke University and editor of *The Frank C. Brown Collection of North Carolina Folklore*; Robert Gordon, first

*Michael Yates, "Cecil Sharp in America," Music Traditions, January 22, 2000, http://www.mustrad.org.uk/articles/sharp.htm.

Frank and Anne Warner found a rich oral and musical tradition on Beech Mountain. Here, Ray Hicks dances to music provided by Frank Proffitt and Buna Hicks. Courtesy of the Warner Family.

director of the Archive of Folk Song for the Library of Congress; Dorothy Scarborough of Columbia University; and Alan Lomax with the Library of Congress. Like Sharp, these scholars and researchers found the region to be rich in folk song, and Gordon and Lomax recorded instrumental music traditions as well.

Frank and Anne Warner also traveled to western North Carolina during this period to record folk music. On their first trip to Watauga County in 1938, the Hicks and Proffitt families of Beech Mountain made an immediate and deep impact upon the Warners. Anne Warner remembers,

> Everyone was making music that afternoon. The sound, and the people, gave us a feeling we have never lost. Like the Proverbial stone tossed into still water, our first visit to the Beech caused ever-widening circles—not just in our lives, but the lives of so many mountain people and, in a sense, the world—since some twenty years later the song, "Tom Dooley," which Frank Proffitt sang to us that day, would spark the world-wide interest in American folk music which was so much a part of the sixties and beyond.

Inspired by earlier collectors and by the reissue of early hillbilly commercial recordings in an influential box set curated by artist and record collector Harry Smith, titled *Anthology of American Folk Music*, folklorists such as Alan Lomax and Ralph Rinzler continued to search western North Carolina for musicians in the 1950s and 1960s. Doc Watson, who made his debut onto the national scene with the support of Rinzler, is perhaps the best-known of those who were "discovered" in this era. Others from the region who achieved recognition outside of North Carolina include Frank Proffitt, Tommy Jarrell, Fred Cockerham, Etta Baker, Dillard Chandler, and Dellie Norton. These musicians were documented on sound recordings and presented at folk festivals and in concerts around the country.

That most of these singers and players made music as an avocation rather than as a profession, and that much of their music-making within their home communities was integrated into social and work events rather than presented as formal stage concerts, only added to western North Carolina's reputation for sustaining rich folk music traditions. The region was viewed as a place where extraordinary music was heard as a part of everyday life within the smallest towns and rural crossroads.

In explaining the evolution of guitarist and singer Doc Watson from a local guitar player busking on the streets for tips into one of America's best-known folk musicians, folklorist Ralph Rinzler wrote in 1971 that "western North Carolina has long been recognized as one of the richest repositories of folk song and lore in the southeastern United States." British folk song scholar A. L. Lloyd echoed that praise in 1977 when he asserted that the "northwest corner of North Carolina is still probably the busiest nook in the United States for domestic music, singing, fiddling, and banjo-picking."*

TODAY

So what is the current state of traditional music in the region? One doesn't have to dig very deeply to arrive at one obvious conclusion: there are a multitude of music venues in communities in the mountains and foothills of North Carolina. In fact, the same types of sites that were gathering places for musicians of past generations are still in place today. Fiddlers' conventions abound throughout western North Carolina, with some events tracing their beginnings back to the 1920s. In addition, local musicians continue to gather in neighbors' homes and in venues such as small stores, old school houses, and even barbershops to play informally.

Within some communities, particular families continue to be recognized for carrying on local music traditions over generations. Around Mount Airy, it includes the Lowes and the Sutphins; in Cherokee, the Sneeds; and in Madison County, the Freemans and the Chandlers, among others. Many of the songs and tunes played in past generations are still performed by musicians today, along with the addition of new pieces drawn from a variety of sources.

* Ralph Rinzler, foreword to Doc Watson, *The Songs of Doc Watson* (New York: Oak Publications, 1971); Doc Watson Family, *Tradition*, Rounder Records, 1977, liner notes.

Audrey Hash Ham of Ashe County continues the fiddle-making tradition she learned from her father, the influential fiddler Albert Hash.

Yet major changes in the traditions of music-making in western North Carolina have also occurred. Almost completely gone are the community work gatherings like cornshuckings, molasses-makings, and woodcuttings that required the cooperation of neighbors and often included string band music and a dance as a reward for the day's labor. Instead, the places in small and rural communities where you are most likely to hear traditional music are fiddlers' conventions, festivals, hometown opries, and coffee houses. Rather than showcasing just local musicians, as would have likely been the case in earlier eras, music venues these days often feature a mix of local players and musicians who live outside the community, the county, and sometimes the state.

Also changed is an old social code that even a few decades ago relegated women to making music in the home and church and preserved most public performances for men. Today, women musicians participate in roughly equal numbers at most public music venues that present traditional music. The contributions of women musicians from the region, such as banjo player and songwriter Ola Belle Reed, old-time fiddler Ora Watson, guitarist Etta Baker, and ballad singer Sheila Adams, to name a few both past and present, are also more widely acknowledged and embraced.

Public understanding of the development of music traditions in western North Carolina has also grown. As we said, the old notion that present-day mountain music is a legacy from the British Isles that was brought by the first white settlers and handed down in a pure form through many generations is fading. Taking its place is a more complex picture of interaction and cultural exchange between European Americans, Cherokees, African Americans, and mixed-race communities. For example, study of the brilliant fiddle playing of Cherokee musician Manco Sneed has uncovered sources that indicate that Cherokees have been playing fiddle music in western North Carolina for over two hundred years.

The contributions of African American musicians have likewise come to public light. Lesley Riddle of Yancey County, who collaborated with A. P. Carter to both document and contribute songs that could be recorded by the Carter Family, is now celebrated by the town of Burnsville through an annual festival. A surge in interest in the origins of the banjo have led scholars and musicians to twice organize a Black Banjo Gathering in Boone to explore and present the African American roots and branches of banjo music in western North Carolina and beyond.

A final difference from the past is the number of youth learning and playing traditional music of all stripes. In the 1960s and 1970s, young people from the region whose musical interests were shaped by community music traditions often gravitated to more contemporary genres such as blue-

Young students learning traditional mountain music at a regional JAM program gathering at the Stecoah Valley Cultural Arts Center in Graham County. Photograph by Robin Dreyer. Courtesy of the North Carolina Arts Council.

grass, gospel, and southern rock. The energy for preserving and perpetuating old-time fiddling, banjo playing, and ballad singing came more from outsiders than from natives. In fact, some predicted that the older musical forms would become wholly revivalist traditions that had little relevance to people born in the region.

That has turned out not to be the case. Youth in the region today are participating in a new wave of interest in traditional music and, for the first time ever, have unprecedented web-based access to archival materials that document musicians from western North Carolina. In addition, there are after-school resources like the Junior Appalachian Musicians program in public schools, traditional music "camps" where skilled musicians teach technique and repertory, and websites like YouTube and Facebook, where music instruction and performances can be shared with others who have similar interests.

As a result, young players are learning old-time fiddling and banjo playing, ballad singing, and blues, as well as continuing to play country music, gospel, and bluegrass. In addition, they are creating new forms of roots music influenced by singer-songwriters, Americana musicians, and even hip-hop artists. This youth movement is fueled both by the children of long-time residents of the region and by young people from other states who have moved to western North Carolina to be near the mountains, to participate in a vibrant youth culture found in communities like Asheville and Boone, and to experience a lively music scene.

The music traditions of western North Carolina share much with those of northern Georgia, eastern Tennessee, southwestern Virginia, and eastern Kentucky. Still, the traditional music of western North Carolina is distinctive in several ways.

DEVELOPMENT OF THE BANJO

No other place in America has had more influence on the development of the banjo than western North Carolina, a somewhat surprising realization given the instrument's origins. Enslaved Africans and African Americans in the Low Country and Piedmont regions created the first banjos in the antebellum South, instruments likely constructed from gourds. It was also slaves and free blacks who first combined the banjo with the fiddle to create a new ensemble tradition that would galvanize southern music and become a root of many American musical forms heard today, including mountain music, bluegrass, country, blues, and even jazz. Some southerners heard banjo and fiddle played by people of color, but many others in the South and beyond were introduced to this music through minstrelsy. A stage adaptation of music heard on the plantation with vocals, dance, and humor added, minstrelsy became the rage beginning in the 1830s and took the concert halls of America and Europe by storm. Many banjo pieces played today originated on the minstrel stage or were popularized by minstrel performers.

It is not a mystery how the banjo first came to western North Carolina. Slaves and free blacks and mixed-race residents, as well as some European Americans who played the instrument, likely brought it with them when they settled the mountains. What is harder to explain is why the people of western North Carolina took so strongly to the banjo. Over generations they developed a wondrous diversity of playing styles, ranging from what nowadays is referred to as clawhammer, where the strings are struck with the back of the fingernail followed by a brushing motion, to the method where two or three fingers are used to pluck the strings in a syncopated pattern. The banjo has proved so popular and adaptable in western North Carolina that it has become essential to instrumental music played for dances and as accompaniment for singing. In fact, a large repertory of songs such as "Wish I Were a Mole in the Ground" and "Little Turtle Dove" are so closely associated with the instrument that they are known as "banjo songs."

The list of extraordinary banjo players from western North Carolina is a long one and includes Samantha Bumgarner, Bascom Lamar Lunsford, Frank Jenkins, Charlie Poole, Ola Belle Reed, Frank Proffitt, Fred Cockerham, Tommy Jarrell, and Snuffy Jenkins. Without question, however, the musician who has had the greatest impact in innovating and popularizing the banjo is Earl Scruggs. Born in the rural crossroads community of Flint Hill near Shelby, Scruggs devised a new style of three-finger picking that, when introduced into the 1940s string band headed by Bill Monroe, created an immediate sensation and became one of the defining characteristics of bluegrass music. Scruggs brought a high level of creativity, precision, and artistry to banjo playing and through his long recording and touring career has carried the instrument to the forefront of American roots music.

AN UNBROKEN BALLAD SINGING TRADITION

Ballad singing is a folk practice that, by all rights, should be extinct in America. The tradition flourished in a time when the written word was rare in many rural communities. Ballads took the place of newspapers and books as a way to communicate events and occurrences and, in a larger sense, to ponder the human condition. Now, with the wide range of media available to citizens, it is surprising that there is one place, Madison County in North Carolina, where the ballad tradition is so important to its residents that the old songs are still learned and performed.

Doug Wallin (1919–2000) (left) and Jack Wallin (1923–2005) came from a large extended family of prolific and well-documented ballad singers and musicians from Madison County, including their parents, Berzilla Wallin and Lee Wallin; Cas Wallin; Dellie Norton; and Dillard Chandler. Their descendants still sing. Photograph by Rob Amberg. Courtesy of the North Carolina Arts Council.

The documentation of ballad singing in Madison County reaches back to 1916, when Cecil Sharp visited singers in and around the communities of Hot Springs, Alanstand, and Sodom Laurel. Jane Gentry of Hot Springs was an especially rich source of older ballads. Sharp documented nearly seventy songs from Gentry, more than he collected from any one singer, including fine versions of older British ballads such as "Lamkin," "The Cherry Tree Carol," "The False Knight on the Road," and "The Grey Cock."

Sharp surmised that many of the ballads he heard had their origins in the British Isles and were introduced to western North Carolina by early settlers. While he focused his full attention on documenting ballads with an English or Scottish pedigree, he soon discovered that singers in Madison and surrounding counties also knew story songs that were not from the "old country." The ballad "Poor Ommie," for example, documented from the singing of William Riley Shelton, recounts the murder of a young woman from Randolph County and demonstrated to Sharp that ballad creation was an ongoing process in North Carolina. However, it is unclear whether he realized that the verses of "Swannanoa Town," though documented from white singers, originated as an African American call-and-response work song.

Unaccompanied ballad singing rapidly diminished in the Southern Appalachians during the twentieth century. However, Madison County singers continued to learn and sing ballads. Cas Wallin, Doug Wallin, Jack Wallin, Dellie Chandler Norton, Berzilla Chandler Wallin, Dillard Chandler, Betty Smith, and Evelyn Ramsey, excellent singers all, grew up in the tradition but also traveled outside of Madison County beginning in the 1960s to share their songs with new audiences. Singers like Sheila Adams and Joe Penland followed in their footsteps, and an even younger generation of singers, including Donna Ray Norton, Melanie Rice, Denise Norton O'Sullivan, and Dee Dee Norton Buckner, are active performers today.

BIRTHPLACE OF TEAM CLOGGING

String band music in western North Carolina has evolved in large part as a response to a community predilection in the region to gather and dance. Early white settlers brought folk and popular dances with them, and they encountered long-standing dance traditions among the Cherokee. African Americans who came to western North Carolina also influenced Appalachian dance, most likely through solo dance steps often referred to as buck-dancing.

Square dancing, with its focus on integrating participating couples into a larger group dance, is a long-standing tradition that served as community entertainment, as a mechanism for socialization, and as a courting ritual.

The Soco Gap Square Dance Team. Courtesy of the North Carolina Office of Archives and History, North Carolina Department of Cultural Resources.

As tourism became a prominent industry in western North Carolina, demonstration square dance teams formed to entertain visitors to the mountains.

Sam Love Queen of Haywood County emerged as a key figure in the transformation of dance in western North Carolina during the mid-decades of the twentieth century. Queen grew up going to dances and learning the art of the square dance caller. In the 1930s, he collaborated with Bascom Lunsford to create a competitive dance category at the Mountain Dance and Folk Festival. Queen's group, the Soco Gap Dancers, was a frequent prizewinner at the event. The Soco Gap Dancers combined aspects of traditional big-circle dancing with individual flatfooting and buckdancing. Queen's dancers were stage performers who would improvise individual steps while executing figures that were associated with square dances.

Sam Queen is given credit for popularizing a double shuffle step that his team used to great effect on stage. When the visiting Queen of England witnessed a performance by the Soco Gap team at the White House in 1939, she remarked on the step's similarity to English clog dancing. Whether this is indeed the origin of the term "clogging" or the story is apocryphal, both this step and its name have become a defining characteristic of modern-day exhibition dancing. In fact, most groups engaged in this tradition today refer to themselves as "cloggers" or "clogging teams."

Western North Carolina continues to be a hotbed of traditional dance. Sam Queen's grandson, Joe Sam Queen, calls a community dance in front of the Haywood County courthouse in Waynesville on Friday nights in the summer. Just down the road in Maggie Valley is the Stompin' Ground, a performance space for precision clogging created by Haywood County native Kyle Edwards. At fiddlers' conventions and hometown opries throughout the region, live fiddle music continues to inspire local residents to show off their clogging, flatfooting, and buckdancing steps.

THE OLDEST FOLK FESTIVAL IN AMERICA

When Bascom Lunsford added a traditional music and dance component to Asheville's Rhododendron Festival in 1928, he was attempting to bring wider visibility to these traditions. However, he could have scarcely foreseen that the festival format that he created would emerge as a widely adopted model for presenting the living cultural traditions of communities, regions, or nations.

In the early years of the festival, Lunsford issued personal invitations to fiddlers, banjo players, ballad singers, and other traditional artists in western North Carolina and gave each a performing slot on the platform that was erected in Pack Square in the center of the city. Dance teams from Buncombe and surrounding counties were also invited to attend and compete for prizes. Lunsford's event drew enthusiastic audiences, and it soon broke away from the Rhododendron Festival to become an annual occurrence known as the Mountain Dance and Folk Festival.

Sarah Gertrude Knott, a Kentuckian who was influenced by Frederick Koch and Paul Green in North Carolina during the era when these dramatists explored the concept of "folk drama," attended the Mountain Dance and Folk Festival in 1933. Knott appropriated Lunsford's model and created the first national folk festival the following year. Lunsford was a supporter of Knott's endeavor and brought performers from western North Carolina to the National Folk Festival on a regular basis.

Samantha Bumgarner and her neighbor Eva Davis made some of the earliest commercial mountain music recordings. Bumgarner played at every Mountain Dance and Folk Festival from 1928 to 1959. Courtesy of the Southern Folklife Collection, Wilson Library, University of North Carolina at Chapel Hill.

Traditional Music in Western North Carolina

The Mountain Dance and Folk Festival is presently held in the Diana Wortham Theatre in downtown Asheville on the second weekend in August. The Shindig on the Green, a companion series that culminates with the festival, occurs on Saturdays in the summer and is attended by thousands. In a nod to Lunsford's original vision, performers are presented on an outdoor stage in Pack Square Park. In addition to the stage performances, scores of musicians turn out to jam nearby on sidewalks and in storefronts.

A FIDDLE AND BANJO ENSEMBLE TRADITION
KNOWN THROUGHOUT THE NATION

Situated in the shadow of Fishers Peak in the Blue Ridge Mountains of Surry County, the tiny community of Round Peak has produced some extraordinary old-time musicians. Many of the families who live there can recall older relatives who played the fiddle or banjo and helped evolve a repertory and style of playing that was unique to the community. However, few people growing up in Surry County prior to 1970 would have predicted that that Round Peak string band music would one day be emulated throughout the United States and beyond.

Mandolin player Verlen Clifton remembers that music-making in the Round Peak community was both informal and inclusive. "When I was growing up, I can't remember what you'd call 'bands' around our neighborhood," he recalls. Instead, local musicians would gather in people's homes to play for dances or meet at stores and gas stations for impromptu music sessions.

Guitarist Paul Sutphin, Clifton's neighbor, described Round Peak as a poor community where residents created their own entertainment. "A lot of fellows had them a banjo and they'd sit around tobacco barns at night and go to playing. And on Christmas Day they'd have an all-day-long dance. And they'd make music and I'd stand and watch them old men breaking up Christmas."

Opportunities to perform in public encouraged Round Peak musicians to organize themselves into string bands. Fiddlers' conventions, once small community gatherings, became regional events where groups competed for recognition and prize money. Around the same time, local radio stations, in particular WPAQ in Mount Airy, began hiring bands for live performances.

In 1963, Clifton and Sutphin joined with Round Peak musicians Fred Cockerham, Kyle Creed, and Earnest East to form the legendary Camp Creek Boys. For ten years the group played hard-driving dance music that captured first prize at numerous fiddle contests across the region. They also recorded an album that, when released in 1967, grabbed the attention of

Benton Flippen
(1920–2011) (left) and
Andy Edmonds, one of
the younger musicians
carrying on the Surry
County string band
tradition.

listeners across the nation and inspired many young urban musicians to travel to Surry County to seek them out.

The following year saw the release of an LP featuring Tommy Jarrell, another native of Round Peak, with fellow musicians Fred Cockerham and Oscar Jenkins. Jarrell had learned fiddle and banjo prior to World War I and had chosen not to update his style or repertory to keep up with newer musical trends. Upon his retirement in 1966 and the subsequent death of his wife, he returned to his music. Jarrell welcomed young people from outside his community who wanted to learn, and over the years he was visited by hundreds of aspiring fiddlers and banjo players. As these younger players formed communities among themselves, Jarrell's versions of Round Peak tunes began to be played throughout the country.

The Mount Airy Bluegrass and Old-Time Fiddlers' Convention, which started as a local fund-raising event, drew players from outside the area who had been influenced by Jarrell, members of the Camp Creek Boys, and another Surry County old-time fiddler, Benton Flippen. Over the years, increasing numbers of musicians from across the country attended and eventually transformed the Mount Airy fiddlers' convention into one of the largest gatherings of old-time musicians in the country, with participants from all fifty states and from other countries, including Japan, Canada, the United Kingdom, and France.

LARGEST AMERICANA MUSIC FESTIVAL

Doc Watson's stature grew throughout his career, and no Southern Appalachian musician is now more publicly acclaimed. Watson also enjoyed immense respect from fellow musicians who marveled at his individual creativity yet admired how his music retained its connection to family and region. Doc Watson had the uncanny ability to arrange traditional songs and tunes in ways that give this older repertory a new vitality and relevance. Amazingly, he could also achieve the opposite effect. In his hands, a contemporary song with no direct connection to the mountains was transformed into a performance that was as evocative of the Blue Ridge as an old ballad.

The Merle Watson Memorial Festival came together quickly in 1988 when Doc Watson's music friends and colleagues rallied around him to pay tribute to his son, who had lost his life in a tractor accident. That first festival featured bluegrass and country musicians Earl Scruggs and fiddler Jim Shumate, Tony Rice, Chet Atkins, Grandpa Jones, Marty Stuart, John Hartford, Mark O'Conner, Jerry Douglas, and George Hamilton IV, among others. The lineup of subsequent festivals has followed this format and has always included professional touring artists who know or admire Doc Watson.

Doc Watson at the age of sixteen holding one of his first guitars. Courtesy of David Holt.

MerleFest, as the event is now named, attracts audiences approaching 80,000. The festival's popularity, and the incentive to meet and possibly perform with Doc Watson, proved attractive to musicians of all stripes, and the scope of the festival expanded early on to include performers in more commercially based music genres. Dolly Parton, Vince Gill, Hot Tuna, John Prine, and Willie Nelson have been among the featured artists. Perhaps as a by-product of this eclectic musical mix, the festival has become a proving ground for groups that are attempting to break into the professional arena with their own brand of roots-inflected music. Old Crow Medicine Show and the Carolina Chocolate Drops are two in recent years that have utilized MerleFest to help launch their careers.

The music that younger generations of musicians are creating and presenting at MerleFest integrates the elements of singer-songwriting, alternative country, blues, bluegrass, rock and roll, and even hip-hop. The term "Americana" has been applied to this genre, and MerleFest has emerged as the largest and perhaps the most influential Americana festival in the country.

CONTINUING TRADITION OF LIVE RADIO

The advent of radio and commercial recordings in the early decades of the twentieth century are two factors often cited for the decline of distinctive local community music traditions in the South. Repertory, song texts, and styles of playing and singing, once influenced mainly by community musicians and passed down orally through generations, were increasingly replaced by performers who were heard on records or on radio.

In the years between 1930 and 1960, live radio was a particularly strong influence, with professional bluegrass and country music performers broadcasting daily on local radio stations and performing shows in surrounding communities on nights and weekend. Groups like the Monroe Brothers, Wade and J. E. Mainer, the Stanley Brothers, and Flatt and Scruggs, among many, built their careers through live radio. In the process, they shaped the music of tens of thousands of musicians who listened to their broadcasts.

Ralph Epperson, who designed and constructed station WPAQ in Mount Airy and took it on the air in 1948, was happy to give professional bluegrass and country musicians a performance slot when they traveled through town or performed nearby. However, Epperson was both knowledgeable and passionate about local music traditions and he resolved to present musicians from the region through a weekly live show called the *Merry-Go-Round*. Many of these local musicians were highly accomplished and could be heard at square dances and fiddlers' conventions and in churches in communities near Mount Airy. However, relatively few made a full-time living through music. Most worked on farms, in textile mill factories, or in other blue-collar occupations and played music on night and weekends.

Over sixty years since its initial broadcast, the *Merry-Go-Round* continues to showcase old-time, bluegrass, and gospel performers from North Carolina and Virginia. Along with WSM in Nashville, the home station of the *Grand Ole Opry*, WPAQ may be the last AM radio station that presents live old-time and bluegrass performers on a weekly basis. Unlike the Opry, which has focused on transforming performers into national country music celebrities, WPAQ's allegiance to the local community has been credited for preserving, rather than eroding, distinctive regional music traditions. It is no accident that WPAQ is located in an area where string band music has retained a recognizable style and repertory.

NATIONAL RECOGNITION OF WESTERN
NORTH CAROLINA MUSICIANS

Eleven ballad singers, old-time fiddlers, and banjo players from western North Carolina have been awarded a National Heritage Fellowship, our nation's greatest honor in the traditional arts. The National Endowment for the Arts created the Fellowship in 1982, and the combined number of North Carolina recipients for these musical genres exceeds that of any other state in the union. This recognition is evidence of the national reputation of western North Carolina as a center of traditional music within the Southern Appalachians.

The recipients include musicians who were living in North Carolina when the award was given as well as those who were born in the state and learned their music in North Carolina before moving to another state. Awardees include:

1982 Tommy Jarrell, Surry County: Old-time fiddler, banjo player, and singer
1983 Stanley Hicks, Watauga County: Banjo and dulcimer player and maker
      Ray Hicks, Avery County: Storyteller and harmonica player and singer
1986 Ola Belle Reed, Ashe County: Banjo player and songwriter
1987 Wade Mainer, Buncombe County: Banjo player and singer
1988 Arthel "Doc" Watson, Watauga County; Guitar and banjo player and singer
1989 Earl Scruggs, Cleveland County: Banjo player
1990 Doug Wallin, Madison County: Ballad singer
1991 Etta Baker, Burke County: Guitarist
1992 Walker Calhoun, Qualla Boundary: Singer, dancer, and banjo player
2007 Mary Jane Queen, Jackson County: Ballad singer and banjo player

A BRIGHT FUTURE

Awareness within western North Carolina of the value of its music traditions is growing. The music heritage of the region was a primary justification for the creation in 2003 of the Blue Ridge National Heritage Area, which encompasses twenty-five counties. The Blue Ridge National Heritage Area promotes traditional music events and has built a traditional artist directory, which currently includes 250 entries of active musicians in the region.

Traditional Music in Western North Carolina

A young
fiddler on
the porch of
the Barn in
Rockingham
County.

Local arts councils in the western counties are also an important part of a new infrastructure to present and sustain traditional music. These organizations produce concerts, festivals, and other special events that showcase local performers. One, the Surry Arts Council, built the Old-Time Music Heritage Hall in Mount Airy to honor local musicians who have shaped string band music locally and across the nation. Arts councils are also sponsors of after-school programs in the region that utilize local fiddlers, banjo players, and guitarists to teach youth to play. Western North Carolina currently supports fourteen of these programs, more than in any other state.

Finally, new music venues that feature traditional, roots, and Americana music are sprouting up across the region. The number of community music

Traditional Music in Western North Carolina

events and sites that are publicly accessible has increased over the past decade. Many of these are described in this guidebook or on the accompanying website for the project. Two major music venues, both focused on North Carolina banjo players, are working towards completion. The Earl Scruggs Center will open in 2013 in the renovated courthouse in Shelby. The town of Eden in Rockingham County has purchased the Nantucket Textile Mill, where Charlie Poole worked, and is planning a center to explore and present the development of the banjo in America.

Judging by participation, by attendance at music venues, and by a growing public awareness of its importance, traditional music in western North Carolina is currently in a very healthy state. Even though the region is a far different place than when Ralph Rinzler and A. L. Lloyd visited, their assessments continue to ring true. Western North Carolina may still be the "busiest nook" in America for singing, fiddling, and banjo playing.

Western North Carolina enjoys a national reputation as a music-rich region within the Southern Appalachians, and its traditions of old-time string band music, ballad singing, and bluegrass are known and admired throughout the world.

Sprout Wings and Fly

The western border of Surry County is the highest section of this region, and the Surry County line hugs the edge of the Blue Ridge Escarpment. Here, in and around the small community of Round Peak, a style of fiddle and banjo music developed that would eventually make this area famous. During the days before the radio and the phonograph became commonplace in most mountain households, musicians learned the greater part of their music from family members and nearby neighbors. Musicians in specific areas of the mountains and foothills learned sets of songs and how to play them in ways that were traditional only to the places where they and their families worked and lived.

In the communities around Round Peak and Low Gap near Mount Airy, a local mode of homemade music developed—a string band tradition that was based on driving rhythms and a close, syncopated, almost bluesy interplay between the fiddle and the banjo, which was often, but not always, fretless and played clawhammer style.

One of the earliest groups to be recorded playing the Round Peak style was DaCosta Woltz's Southern Broadcasters, a band that cut several records for the Gennett label in the 1920s. This group counted among its members a fiddler named Ben Jarrell. His son, Tommy Jarrell, would later become one of the most well-known and influential old-time musicians in the history of American music.

Other influential old-time musicians who came from Surry County include Paul Sutphin, Kyle Creed, Ernest East, and Fred Cockerham, who joined together to form a popular band called the Camp Creek Boys. The Camp Creek Boys, along with other Surry County artists like Benton Flippen and Mac Snow, helped keep the older style of music alive by playing often on Mount Airy's regionally popular radio station, wPAQ. Their exciting musical skill and energetic presentations enabled them to successfully compete with bands that played a newer style of mountain music called bluegrass.

Beginning in the 1960s, scores of young, mostly urban musicians—so-called revivalists—began visiting the area hoping to learn the distinctive regional style of playing from

DaCosta Woltz and the Southern Broadcasters. From left to right: Woltz, Price Goodson, Ben Jarrell, and Frank Jenkins. Courtesy of Richard Nevins.

its many old-time practitioners. Often, they also recorded them. Upon hearing those recordings, aspiring musicians from around the nation were captivated and began flocking to Surry County to learn to play in that style. The fiddler Tommy Jarrell, especially, with his larger-than-life personality, good humor, intricate bowing style, and distinctive singing voice, welcomed many visitors into his home. Jarrell soon became the focus of attention and adulation for many young revivalist fiddle and banjo players. As a result, Round Peak– or Surry County–style tunes such as "Old Bunch of Keys," "Breaking Up Christmas," and the so-called Surry County national anthem "Sally Ann," can be heard at jam sessions today throughout the nation.

The old tunes are also kept alive in the region where they originated, played now by the descendents and younger friends of the well-known Round Peak musicians of the past. Surry County remains a place of pilgrimage for old-time music fans seeking to experience the kind of community and events that gave the world such beautiful and distinctive music. For a modern-day traveler happily witnessing or even participating in a late-night jam session at the Mount Airy Fiddlers' Convention, the words that

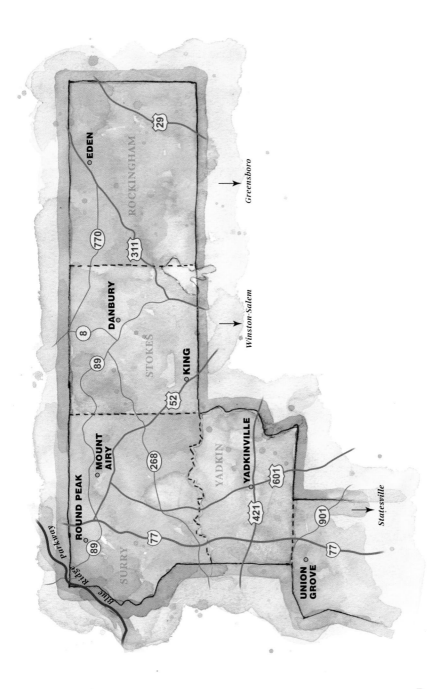

EDEN

ROCKINGHAM

29

770

311

→ Greensboro

DANBURY

8

89

STOKES

KING

52

→ Winston-Salem

MOUNT AIRY

268

YADKINVILLE

ROUND PEAK

YADKIN

601

89

77

421

→ Statesville

SURRY

901

77

Blue Ridge Parkway

UNION GROVE

Region 1

THE PLACE

This region is where the rolling land of the North Carolina Piedmont meets the easternmost foothills of the Blue Ridge Mountains. Rockingham County, the easternmost county on the Blue Ridge Music Trail, and neighboring Stokes County, to its immediate west, lie directly south of the Virginia border, stopping just short of the suburban areas that surround Greensboro and Winston-Salem.

A few decades ago, much of the land in this region was agricultural, planted in bright-leaf tobacco. And even though today the region remains mostly rural, fewer and fewer people here raise tobacco. While passing through, modern travelers can still see many of the small barns where tobacco leaves were once cured and stored before being taken to auction.

The isolated Sauratown Mountains rise up in Stokes and Surry Counties and run westward from Hanging Rock near Danbury to the distinctive Pilot Mountain. In the shadow of Pilot Mountain flows the Yadkin River. The Yadkin River valley, in Yadkin and Surry Counties, is the cradle of North Carolina's newly established and rapidly growing wine industry.

Beginning in the early twentieth century, textile mill operators in the region utilized the rivers of the Piedmont and the foothills to turn water wheels and turbines, powering machinery that turned cotton into thread and cloth.

Mill towns, including Spray and Draper in Rockingham County, grew around the new factories. These and other towns attracted poor families from the mountains seeking employment, and many great musicians, including Spray's own Charlie Poole, spent their working days operating looms and spinning frames in the cotton mills of the North Carolina Piedmont.

Mount Airy, located in the center of Surry County, is the largest town in the region, and is the home of mountain music institutions like radio station WPAQ, and the Mount Airy Fiddlers' Convention.

One of the many beautiful views in Hanging Rock State Park. Photograph by Steve Kruger.

Tommy Jarrell and his father Ben before him sang so often might reflect the mood of the impromptu gathering:

I'll eat when I'm hungry,
Drink when I'm dry.
Get to feeling much better,
Gonna sprout wings and fly.

REGION 1 AT A GLANCE

Fiddles for sale at the Charlie Poole Festival.

SURRY COUNTY

MOUNT AIRY BLUEGRASS AND OLD-TIME FIDDLERS' CONVENTION
Mount Airy

One of the more significant of the music festivals that are held in the Blue Ridge every summer is the annual Bluegrass and Old-Time Fiddlers' Convention at Mount Airy. Established in 1972, this event is now more than four decades old. Because the fame of Surry County musicians has spread

Fiddler Ernest East (1916–2000), here with Andy Cahan, played with the Camp Creek Boys and helped to develop the powerful string band music we now associate with Surry County. Photograph by Rob Amberg. Courtesy of the North Carolina Arts Council.

throughout the nation and beyond, the convention is attended every year by hundreds of musicians and thousands of mountain music fans. Originated by G. F. Collins, who with Kyle Creed, Paul Sutphin, Verlen Clifton, Earnest East, and Fred Cockerham formed the legendary band called the Camp Creek Boys, the Mount Airy Bluegrass and Old-Time Fiddlers' Convention is seen by many of the participants as a kind of annual homecoming.

During its early years, the Mount Airy Fiddlers' Convention was mainly a local event, but gradually outsiders began to show up to hear the performances of their mentors and to take advantage of the opportunity to associate with the Surry County players they admired. As more and more revivalist musicians emulated the local musical styles, the Fiddlers' Convention gained participants who wanted to perform alongside the old-timers. Even now, after many of the original master artists have died, the younger musicians continue to gather at Mount Airy.

This two-night event is sponsored by the Mount Airy American Legion and the local VFW. Appropriately, it's staged at the Mount Airy Veterans Memorial Park, a broad, grassy, ten-acre field that contains the festival stage, a huge camping area, and parking for three thousand cars. The park is surrounded on three sides by low, wooded hills that provide the event with a feeling of isolation from the nearby town.

The single stage at this event is basically an open-sided truck trailer that's been outfitted with stage lights and a sound system. Participating musicians line up and socialize beneath a large backstage tent while they're waiting their turn to perform. Contestants compete in a number of categories, including bluegrass and old-time band, bluegrass and old-time fiddle, bluegrass and old-time banjo, guitar, mandolin, bass, dobro, dulcimer, autoharp, folk song, and dance. More than two thousand dollars in prize money is awarded each year, along with a long list of ribbons and trophies. There's a platform near the stage for dancing, and there's lots of open space out front on the grassy lawn where audience members can spread their blankets and set up their folding chairs. In the event of bad weather, the contests move over to a smaller, indoor space located in a metal building onsite.

As with other fiddlers' conventions in the region, a compelling feature of the Mount Airy Bluegrass and Old-Time Fiddlers' Convention is the preponderance of free-wheeling jam sessions that take place all around the campground—and all around the clock. Activities happening at the main performance stage are broadcast live over WPAQ 740 AM radio. This event attracts thousands of people from all around the region, the nation, and a number of foreign countries.

Camping is available at the festival site on a first-come, first-served

Musicians jam at
the campground
on the hill at
the Mount
Airy Fiddlers'
Convention.
Photograph by
Hobart Jones.
Courtesy of
the Surry Arts
Council.

basis, and the owners of the tents, campers, and recreational vehicles that
show up every year arrive as early as possible in the week to insure landing
their favorite parking spot. The festival grounds are well furnished with
restrooms, concession stands, and picnic shelters.

WHEN: Friday and Saturday, first weekend in June; music starts at 7 P.M.
on Friday and 9:30 A.M. on Saturday
WHERE: Mount Airy Veterans Memorial Park, 691 West Lebanon Street,
Mount Airy, 27030
ADMISSION: Fee charged for festival (children under 5 admitted free) and
camping
CONTACT: Gary Willard, 336-345-7388
WEBSITE: www.mountairyfiddlersconvention.com

MAYBERRY USA

Just south of the Virginia state line, down the mountain in Surry County, is the town of Mount Airy. This picturesque town is situated near the eastern edge of a region of North Carolina that, along with its neighboring southwestern Virginia counties to its north, comprises a section of the Blue Ridge where traditional music remains exceptionally strong and is most obviously a part of everyday life for many of the people who live there.

The town of Mount Airy is the hometown of comedian and actor Andy Griffith (1926–2012). As an actor starring in the television series *The Andy Griffith Show*, in which he portrayed the sheriff of a bucolic place called Mayberry, Griffith drew heavily from the character and traditions of his hometown in depicting the fictional town of the TV show, at times even incorporating actual places in Mount Airy as well as local music traditions into the series.

Because of that and the long-standing national popularity and celebrity of Andy Griffith and his television series, the Mayberry theme dominates commercial life in the town of Mount Airy. Mount Airy is obviously a much larger town than the fictional television village of Mayberry, but the name Mayberry appears frequently on business marquees, on café menus, and in storefront window displays.

Charles Dowell prepares breakfast at the Snappy Lunch Café, a Mount Airy institution established in 1923 and mentioned on the Andy Griffith Show. Charles Dowell started working at Snappy's in 1943 and owned the restaurant from 1960 until he passed away in 2012.

WPAQ SATURDAY MORNING *MERRY-GO-ROUND*
Mount Airy

One particular weekly radio program in the Blue Ridge—the WPAQ Saturday morning *Merry-Go-Round*—has an exceptionally long history of presenting the best of live traditional mountain music. In fact, Ralph Epperson (1921–2006), the late owner of radio station WPAQ in Mount Airy, maintained traditional music at the forefront of his radio programming for more than fifty years, and the tradition he began continues today. When Epperson's newly inaugurated radio station went on the air in 1948, live and recorded music performed by native Southern Appalachian musicians immediately became the cornerstone of his broadcasts. Through the years, a host of regional and national music legends, including Tommy Jarrell, Benton Flip-

A display case in the lobby of the historic Earle Theatre holds memorabilia from WPAQ, including transcription discs and Ben Jarrell's fiddle. Photograph by Hobart Jones. Courtesy of the Surry Arts Council.

pen, the Carter Family, Mac Wiseman, Lester Flatt and Earl Scruggs, and Bill and Charlie Monroe, have gathered before the microphones of WPAQ for the Saturday morning *Merry-Go-Round* broadcast. The program's popularity and long history of devotion to regional music has made it one of the longest-running live radio programs in the nation.

The Earle Theatre, formerly called the Downtown Cinema Theatre, where the *Merry-Go-Round* broadcast originates, is a vintage movie theater that seats up to 450 people. An ornate marquee on the theater's facade looms over the sidewalk of Mount Airy's Main Street, announcing the WPAQ *Merry-Go-Round*'s schedule, as well as other performances, concerts, and films.

The small lobby of the Earle Theatre is reminiscent of many that are found in surviving 1930s-era movie houses. The theater auditorium is comfortable, clean, and well maintained. Large black-and-white portraits of Surry County's musical legends, including Ralph Epperson and former WPAQ announcer Clyde Johnson, line the walls. A case holding late fiddler Benton Flippen's trophies sits at the foot of the stage. In front of the stage, at floor level, is a small open area for dancing.

On a typical Saturday morning, a technician at the rear of the auditorium greets visitors with a friendly nod as they enter the room. A few patrons are seated here and there, scattered randomly in twos and threes around the house. A group of musicians are playing an extended medley of bluegrass and old-time mountain tunes. They play banjos, fiddles, and guitars. The time is ten minutes before eleven and the final moments of the weekly Saturday morning jam session at the Earle Theatre are passing by. At eleven

BLUE RIDGE MUSIC ON THE AIR

The long tradition of broadcasting live and recorded regional music on the radio is a key factor in the continued widespread popularity of traditional music in the Blue Ridge. Musician after musician who grew up in the region acknowledge that as youngsters they learned their very first old-time songs "off WPAQ or the *Grand Ole Opry*." Caldwell County native Glenn Bolick and his family were radio fans when Bolick was a youngster (see profile, page 63). "We had a battery-powered radio at our house before we got electric power," said Bolick. "We listened to the *Grand Ole Opry* on the radio sometimes on Saturday night. Hickory had a station back in those days. The Blue Sky Boys, Bill and Earl Bolick, were distant cousins of ours, and they were on the radio."

Whether the programming is recorded or live, vintage or contemporary, radio stations featuring traditional music and musicians are an important and popular aspect of the music scene in the Blue Ridge region today.

A scan of your radio dial while you're driving through western North Carolina will reveal what the local folks are talking about when they speak of finding "real good" music on the radio. Station WPAQ in Mount Airy can be heard on 740 AM, and there are many other stations that regularly feature mountain music.

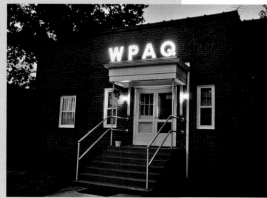

Benton Flippen (1920–2011) (left) and Verlen Clifton warm up in preparation for a live radio performance. Flippen played at the station's dedication in 1948 and was playing live when WPAQ started streaming on the web almost sixty years later.

WPAQ in Mount Airy first broadcast live local musicians in 1948.

o'clock, the WPAQ Saturday morning *Merry-Go-Round* radio show will begin another edition of its live broadcasts.

After a short pause, the house lights dim, a bright red "on the air" electric sign lights up on the proscenium, and the emcee welcomes the theater and radio audiences to the program. He quickly introduces the trio of musicians, and they immediately take off with a bright rendition of "Boil Them Cabbage Down." Just like that, another episode of Appalachia's longest-running live radio program is on the air. The music is fine, the scene is friendly and comfortable, and the famous pork chop sandwich of the Snappy Lunch Café waits for you right across the street. It's a good day.

WHEN: Saturdays, 11:00 A.M. to 1:30 P.M.

WHERE: The Earle Theatre, 142 North Main Street, Mount Airy, 27030

ADMISSION: Fee

CONTACT: The Earle Theatre, 336-786-2222; WPAQ, 336-786-6111; or the Surry Arts Council, 336-786-7998

WEBSITES: www.wpaq740.com or www.surryarts.org

TOMMY JARRELL FESTIVAL

Mount Airy

Attend any old-time jam in the country and you are likely to hear a fiddle tune popularized by National Heritage Award–winner Thomas Jefferson Jarrell (1901–1985). Tommy Jarrell's influence on modern old-time music is

A TRIBUTE TO RALPH EPPERSON

by Paul Brown

Ralph Epperson translated his love of mountain music into a focal point for community life: a radio station. He had an early understanding of what he wanted to do, and he pretty much stuck to his vision for more than five decades. That alone would be worthy of notice. But he loved not just mountain music in general. He loved specifically the music of his own community. He wanted to promote it, reflect it, and preserve it. His love of the music sprang not just from what he found to be its distinctive, alluring sounds. It also grew from his fondness for the people around him. Because he understood his community's uniqueness, the world received the phenomenon called WPAQ. It also received a priceless collection of recordings.

Working for Ralph was memorable to say the least. I quickly discovered that the station moved on what could be called Ralph time. Some of us young people wanted things to move more quickly. We wanted more aggressive marketing of what WPAQ was doing. Still others wanted a more modern approach to programming, featuring more country music. But Ralph had been in business for quite awhile. He'd been through ups and downs, and through many employees. He was a southern gentleman. In his quiet, good-humored, and gentlemanly way, he would hear us—and keep doing what he had been doing since 1948, at a speed that was comfortable to him.

He wanted people to have the chance to hear the Gospel. He believed in news coverage. He wanted to keep local musicians in the spotlight as much as possible. And so that's what WPAQ did.

Ralph was also a packrat and an obsessive recordist. He recorded as many local musicians as he could. He asked that we tape all the live Saturday morning *Merry-Go-Round* programs featuring local and area talent. We also taped large numbers of remote events such as fiddlers' conventions. He sent staff members out onto the grounds of conventions, where we would record jam sessions and interview musicians. Then we would play selections from all these adventures on the air.

Keep in mind, all of this was at a commercial radio station. It was distinctly out of the ordinary in the modern broadcasting environment. There was a certain heady feeling to it in particular during the 1980s when interest in the music, including among relatively young people, was still strong. I recall feeling excited and incredibly fortunate.

Working for Ralph also had an oddly dreamlike quality. It gave the sense of

Ralph Epperson, founder of WPAQ and champion of traditional mountain music.

being in the past and present at once, which it was. It had the feeling of mission, because the station had missions. No matter that the pay was low and the equipment often old and sometimes balky, the situation was by and large a good thing, because for those of us who were open to the idea of community service through radio, Ralph demonstrated the possibilities. And it was simply very cool to be doing what we were doing, watching Ralph's example of belief in his missions, and seeing and hearing the community respond.

Where Ralph was concerned, the more layers one peeled back, the more one would find. He was a massively knowledgeable radio engineer, a deep thinker, an explainer, and an enthusiast. He tirelessly encouraged musicians, young and old. And he gave us a place to play. He transformed his beliefs and his visions into reality that benefited all of us. The radio world—and the world at large—could use many more such people.

This piece was originally published in the Old Time Herald. *Paul Brown is a commentator for National Public Radio and a player of traditional Blue Ridge music.*

Tommy Jarrell, Chester McMillian, Mac Snow, and Blanton Owen make music for a dance, 1980. Photograph by Lyntha Eiler, Blue Ridge Parkway Project, American Folklife Center, Library of Congress.

partially due to his intricate fiddle bowing and clawhammer banjo playing accompanied by his rough but powerful voice. He was also known for his personality as a good-natured, good-timing ex-moonshiner. As he became widely known to fans of mountain music, Tommy Jarrell often welcomed younger generations of musicians—many from outside the region—into his home. These aspiring, and admiring, players of traditional music learned his style and his repertoire, and they helped to spread Tommy Jarrell's reputation as a musician of note far beyond Surry County.

Tommy Jarrell was born in Round Peak, a small mountain community that has produced many influential old-time musicians, including Fred Cockerham, Kyle Creed, and Charlie Lowe. Tommy's father, Ben Jarrell, was an outstanding fiddler and recorded in the 1920s with DaCosta Woltz's Southern Broadcasters. Tommy himself took up the banjo at age seven and the fiddle at thirteen, and was soon playing for dances and cornshuckings in the Round Peak area. He learned from his father but also picked up tips from older members of the community such as Civil War veterans Preston "Pet" McKinney and Zack Payne. As a young man, Jarrell raised tobacco. After a season in which his fertilizer bill exceeded his profits from selling his crop, he realized he could make a lot more money by making and selling homemade liquor. Later, after marrying and starting a family, he took a job operating a motor grader for the North Carolina Highway Department, where he worked for forty-one years. In retirement he returned to his music, which had not changed much stylistically since his youth. It was then that Jarrell made his first commercial recordings.

Sprout Wings and Fly

On the weekend before the centennial of his birth, the first Tommy Jarrell Festival took place in Mount Airy. It featured a dance, a film screening of the documentary film about Tommy Jarrell titled *Sprout Wings and Fly*, and performances by members of Surry County's old-time and bluegrass community, many of whom had known and performed with Jarrell during his lifetime. The event now occurs annually on the last weekend of February in the Old-Time Music Heritage Hall at the Earle Theatre in downtown Mount Airy to celebrate Jarrell's birthday on March 1. This venue also hosts a variety of square dances, the Voice of the Blue Ridge concert series, weekly jam sessions, and Surry County's Traditional Arts Program for Students (TAPS), which teaches traditional music to a younger generation of area musicians.

WHEN: Last weekend in February
WHERE: The Old-Time Music Heritage Hall at the Earle Theatre,
    142 North Main Street, Mount Airy, 27030
ADMISSION: Fee
CONTACT: Surry Arts Council, 336-786-7998 or The Earle Theatre,
    336-786-2222
WEBSITES: www.surryarts.org or www.TheEarle.org

STOKES COUNTY

STOKES STOMP
Danbury
Moratock Park in Stokes County is named after the ruins of the Moratock Iron Furnace, a Civil War–era blast furnace. The massive stone chimney still stands today. A community music festival has been held in Moratock Park every September since 1974. Now named the Stokes Stomp, this free event features local bluegrass, Americana, and blues music, a high school marching band competition, and a parade. Some festival-goers watch the event from the grassy hillside that's located next to the stage. Others enjoy food from vendors, sitting under the wooden shelter that hosts the Royce Memorial Bluegrass Jam during the summer. Visitors can browse through the tents of the craft vendors that are set up to the left of the stage. During the warmest part of the day, you can cool off by taking a dip in the Dan River, which slowly meanders through the park.

Moratock Park is near the historic town of Danbury, the county seat. Hanging Rock State Park is nearby. Hanging Rock's rugged, rocky cliffs rise high above the surrounding Piedmont, a part of the Sauratown Mountains,

Back-Step: Keep It Fresh and Keep It Alive

Chester McMillian has played with all the great musicians who lived in an area of North Carolina in Surry County called Round Peak—Tommy Jarrell, Kyle Creed, Fred Cockerham, and many others. His son, Nick McMillian, learned as a child to play the traditional Round Peak style of fiddle from his father and his grandfather, Dix Freeman. Nick's longtime girlfriend, Kelley Breiding, now rounds out their band, Back-Step, with her masterful playing of the old-time fretless banjo—a banjo that once belonged to Dix Freeman.

Chester: I was brought up in a family of musicians on both sides—my mama's side and my daddy's side. My daddy played old-time banjo. On Mama's side we had fiddle players *and* banjo players. Back then every little community had their own musicians. I grew up in the times when we didn't have televisions and very few people had radios, so you made your own music. WPAQ was the first radio station I ever listened to. Daddy went somewhere and bought a radio. It had a battery; I think maybe he put a car battery on it or something. Anyway, we listened to WPAQ, and they played music all the time. I remember playing on there myself in about 1956, on one of the remote programs they had. I remember Benton Flippen being on there. I think he was one of the first ones on WPAQ. That was the only thing we had to listen to back then. But, first thing, we made our own music. People started coming down because of it, like from the Smithsonian and all, to find out about our old-time music. They came down to visit old man Dan Tate when we was living in the Fancy Gap. That was in the late fifties. And then Tommy Jarrell started back playing again and he got to be real popular. So they started visiting him. Well, he started traveling around a little bit to different festivals and stuff like that. They called that "back in the hippy days." I played with old man Tommy Jarrell about fifteen years beginning back in the late sixties. Before that I played all kinds of music. We played bluegrass, played gospel, we even played some of this rock and roll, like Elvis stuff. Oh, yeah. But my roots are in the old-time music, and I like that. It's always been a part of my life.

Kelley: My mom played the piano, and my dad played the guitar, but they didn't really play any kind of traditional music. Mom played classical music on the piano and I played the piano when I was a kid. I didn't really discover this kind of music until I went to college at Western Carolina University. It was there that I got exposed to this music, through people in Asheville and in the counties to the west of there. Then I found my way over here to this area, and I found more old-time music—and I got hung up in it.

Nick: I have music on both sides of my family—on my mother's side and on my father Chester's side. My mother's maiden name is Polly Freeman. Dix Freeman was her father. He played the banjo with Tommy Jarrell. They played music together when they were kids. Ben Freeman, my great-grandfather, and Tommy's dad,

Ben Jarrell, were best friends. They hung out all the time. When they got to be older men, they still played together a whole lot. It feels good to play the music in the same way that my people in the past did. I learned to play the fiddle from my grandfather, Dix Freeman. When he got to be older, his banjo playing kinda slowed down, and so I was able to play the fiddle along with him. I learned most of the fiddle tunes that I play now while I played along with him. He really enjoyed it. But learning to play was not forced upon me. And even though it was never something that I felt like I *had* to do, it was real important to my grandfather and to my dad that I learn to play music. And it's something that I'm glad that I did. It made both of them very happy to be able to pass it down. I think it reminded granddad of a time that was kind of gone, I guess. He had such a good childhood with the music and all the things they used to do. But he felt like the music was changing and that it needed to stay more like it was when he was a kid. He tried to pass it down to me in such a way that it would live on like he thought it should.

Chester: To me, it [old-time music] has always seemed to be pretty popular. I've traveled, I guess, all over the United States. Let's see, I've been to four or five national folk festivals, to the Chicago Folk Festival, all up outside of Boston, down to festivals in Louisiana—and I don't know how many times I've been to D.C. to play at the Library of Congress and the Smithsonian. Back when I played with Tommy, my oldest daughter traveled with us. My kids always went, you know? I guess Nick was into music before he was born. It was an every weekend thing with me. I still had a job, but I always made time for music. The good Lord blessed me a whole lot. This music is something we take with us everywhere we go. It's just a part of us.

Nick: For old-time music, acoustic instruments are all you need. But we like to play a traditional kind of Western swing too; early country, Bob Wills' era stuff. Kelley is a marvelous singer, so she does that type of music. As far as me personally playing the fiddle, I only play music from right around here, around Round Peak.

I don't seek out a lot of new tunes, I just play what I learned from my grand-father. And I don't really do any other types of fiddle styles. I just try to preserve the way that he taught me. In old-time Round Peak–style fiddle playing, there's less chording than in bluegrass. A lot of times bluegrass fiddlers use a lot of chords and really long bow strokes. And a bluegrass fiddler is apt to be backing up singers—that's one difference. But even today when it's time for a bluegrass fiddler to play a turn out front, he's likely to play an old-time tune. However, the way I play the fiddle differs quite a bit from the regular bluegrass style. The way that I work the bow and get the rhythm from the motion of the bow is different. In bluegrass, it would be done more with noting, and slide noting, and long bow strokes. There'd be a lot more action by the fiddler on the fingerboard in blue-grass.

Kelley: One of the main differences between old-time and bluegrass music is based on the fact that old-time music is really dance music. It is meant for dancing, whether it be for a lone dancer or for a square dance. But bluegrass is more of a sit down, listening, kind of music. It's not really for dancing. Old-time music has a driving dance beat, whereas bluegrass has a different taste.

Nick: For instance, break-taking. That's where each instrument is spotlighted in turn, with the dynamics shifting from one instrument to the next—that's a bluegrass trait. Each instrument has a chance to take the lead as the song goes along. But in old-time music everybody plays at the same rate, and they all play together. The fiddle is the lead instrument, and everybody else plays what the fiddle plays.

Kelley: In old-time music there's a real sense of community all across the board—with the dancing, with the music, and within the band. With an old-time band all the players are of an equal part and parcel.

Nick: To me, what we play is the natural evolution of the Round Peak style of music. It was passed on to me from my grandfather, just like he learned it when he was a kid. I really try not to copy anybody. I try to do my own thing. Tommy Jarrell didn't play just like his father. He learned from him and then he took up the style and made it his own.

Kelley: I feel like if you try to copy some other person's music exactly, it's like you *antiquify* it. It's like you're making it into a museum piece. You're reenacting an exact style of music, and that's making it a dead thing. It's like you're putting it away and saying, "Well, this is over." But if you just let it live and play a style in the way it naturally goes, but not in an exact way, you keep it fresh and you keep it alive.

Demonstrators forge iron at the site of the Moratock Furnace during Stokes Stomp. Photograph by Steve Kruger.

an ancient and isolated chain that stretches across Stokes County, ending with Pilot Mountain, a distinctive monadnock in Surry County. From the top of Hanging Rock you can see the hazy skylines of Winston-Salem and Greensboro in the distance. These cities seem even farther away when you settle into your chair near the pristine forests and clear streams of Moratock to listen to an afternoon of bluegrass music.

WHEN: Saturday and Sunday, second weekend in September

WHERE: Moratock Park, Danbury, 27016. Immediately south of Danbury, off of NC 89 on Sheppard Mill Road. The park is across the river. Look for signs.

ADMISSION: Free

CONTACT: Stokes County Arts Council, 336-593-8159

Foothills Hayride

The Foothills Hayride is an effort by residents of Stokes County to connect all of the traditional music events in the county and to celebrate the unique musical heritage of the foothills region. The Hayride maintains a website and sponsors events such as the Stokes Stomp, dances, and a series of jam sessions that move seasonally around the county. The regular Foothills Hayride Jam takes place at Kings Music Center in King on Wednesday nights. Royce's Memorial Jam takes place in Moratock Park every second and fourth Saturday evening during the summer.

Down the road from Moratock Park is Priddy's General Store, which hosts "Pickin' at Priddy's" bluegrass concert series on Fridays in February and on Saturdays in October. Bring a folding chair since no seating is provided. Priddy's General Store was established in 1888 and has been run by the Priddy family since 1929. It offers a small selection of dry goods as well as refreshments, preserves, crafts, and souvenirs.

More information is available at http://www.foothillshayride.com or by contacting the Stokes County Arts Council.

WEBSITE: www.stokesarts.org/stokesstomp.html or
www.foothillshayride.com

ROCKINGHAM COUNTY

CHARLIE POOLE MUSIC FESTIVAL
Eden

The Charlie Poole Music Festival takes place annually on the second weekend in June in Eden. The festival celebrates the life and music of Charlie Poole, one of the first rural southern artists to enjoy widespread commercial success as a recording artist during the "hillbilly" music craze of the 1920s and 1930s. Eden is the modern name for three textile towns, Leaksville, Spray, and Draper, that incorporated as one city in 1967. Charlie Poole, who worked in textile mills in Leaksville and Spray, reputedly developed a unique three-finger banjo style of playing to compensate for an injury to the fingers on his right hand that he received while playing baseball. Poole possessed a powerful and expressive singing voice, one that crossed the established boundaries between traditional southern music and the popu-

Mill workers at the Granite Mill in Haw River, N.C., 1912. The mill towns that rapidly grew along the rivers of the Piedmont produced many fine musicians. Charlie Poole is on the far right in the last row. Courtesy of Kinney Rorrer/Pearl Spoon.

lar musical forms of the era. His distinctive music and his image as a fast-living, hard-drinking songster continues to influence old-time, bluegrass, country, and Americana musicians well into the twenty-first century. This festival memorializes Poole, who died at age thirty-nine on a drinking binge while celebrating his landing of a role in a Hollywood film.

A Friday evening concert kicks off the festival weekend spotlighting old-time and bluegrass music. The festival site is located across the street from the massive Spray Cotton Mill complex, no longer in operation. The festival is staged on and around the surviving ruins of a much earlier complex of mill buildings, and fragments of the old brick and stone foundations of the early-nineteenth-century mills that once operated there are visible all around the site.

Music competitions occur throughout Saturday afternoon and into the early evening. Categories in the competition include both junior and senior divisions. Cash prizes and ribbons are awarded to the winners of competitions in old-time and bluegrass fiddle, flat pick and finger-style guitar, clawhammer and bluegrass banjo, bluegrass and old-time band, and duet singing. A prize is also given for the best rendition of a Charlie Poole song, and a $500 grand prize is awarded to the winning old-time three-finger-style banjo player. Each year the program is a little different, but it often includes

Performers onstage
at the Charlie Poole
Festival.

workshops, lectures, and historical tours. In 2011, for example, a river adventure on Saturday morning, called the Charlie Poole River Ramble, centered around a scenic float on the Smith River. It began at the old Spray Cotton Mill complex, where Charlie Poole once worked. There was also a toy duck race on the nearby river—a tongue-in-cheek tribute to the still-familiar lyrics of the once popular Charlie Poole song titled "If the River Was Whiskey": "If the river was whiskey, / And I was a duck, / I'd swim to the bottom, / And never come up."

Campers and RVs are welcome to arrive ahead of time during the week before the festival to set up campsites. Food and craft vendors are on-site during the festival, and there's a special activities area for children. Occasional extemporaneous jam sessions occur near the edges of the festival grounds, and festival-goers can listen or join in the fun. The festival is produced by Piedmont Folk Legacies, a nonprofit organization that has also purchased the adjacent Nantucket Mill, which it plans to turn into the National Banjo Center, an educational site, museum, and performance space for teaching the public about the banjo, the instrument that Charlie Poole did so much to popularize.

WHEN: Second weekend (Friday and Saturday) in June
WHERE: Governor Morehead Park, 422 Church Street, Eden, 27288
ADMISSION: Fee
CONTACT: Piedmont Folk Legacies, Inc., 336-623-1043
WEBSITE: www.charlie-poole.com

THE BARN
Eden

Not many people create a music venue in their front yard. Several years ago, though, following a trip they made to a music hall a few hours away, Jerry Wilson and his wife, Debbie, who's a fiddler, decided their own community needed a similar place for folks to come together and make music. So they built a large wooden barn that's situated only a stone's throw from the front door of their small house near Eden. Now, on Tuesday nights, people of all ages gather to see and hear bluegrass and gospel bands play in the Wilsons' barn.

The Barn is a fairly intimate space with room for around a hundred people. There is a small dance floor, and several rows of folding chairs face the stage. Christmas lights strung from the rafters illuminate the photographs, antiques, records, and other items that decorate the walls. Inside The Barn, people two-step, waltz, and flatfoot to the music that rings out

◉ Kinney Rorrer

Kinney Rorrer taught history for thirty-two years at Danville Community College in Danville, Virginia, before retiring in 2006. He is the author of Ramblin' Blues: The Life and Songs of Charlie Poole. *Rorrer is also a musician—a member of a group called the New North Carolina Ramblers, so named in tribute to Charlie Poole's band, the North Carolina Ramblers.*

I was born in Eden, North Carolina—in what was then called Leaksville. Leaksville, Spray, and Draper were three separate towns back then. I was born in what's now the Leaksville section of Eden in 1946. January 4th. My parents were Clifford and Virginia Rorrer.

When I was in the eighth grade—I was about eleven years old then—my dad brought home from the mountains of Franklin County, Virginia, which is where he was born, a stack of old 78 rpm records, records that his uncles had made. One uncle was Posey Rorer, a fiddler, and the other one, an uncle by marriage, was Charlie Poole, a banjo player and singer. Charlie was married to Posey's sister, who was my dad's aunt. So Dad brought home that stack of old 78s, and I would lie on my stomach on the floor and play them on my sister's little record player. I would play those records while I was on the floor doing my homework. That may be why I didn't do so well in some of my classes. [Laughs.] I was listening to things like "Leaving Home" and "Flying Clouds" and those tunes. That was in 1957, 1958. So I would lie on the floor and listen, and I was just captivated! That sound! It's hard to explain. It just kind of grabbed me. I was really taken with the sound I heard on those 78s. I asked my dad how many records Posey and Charlie had made, and he said he thought about five or six. Well, as it turns out, Charlie made thirty-six records and Posey made fifty-five. [Laughs.] So I began looking for their records, trying to find copies that I did not have. Then my dad bought an old Victrola, which I still have. He paid five dollars for it. I would play those records over and over on that Victrola. I would put my ear right up against those slats—when you open the two doors on the front there are slats that house the internal horn—and I would put my ear up against those slats because I wanted to hear *every* note, *every* word.

My dad encouraged my brother and myself to learn that music. He played the fiddle around the house. He didn't play out in public. He'd sit on the couch at home and play some of Posey's tunes, tunes that Posey taught him. Tunes like "The Highway Man," "Green Mountain Polka," and "Don't Let Your Deal Go Down." Again, I was just captivated by that sound. Dad bought me a banjo when I was a teenager—a Maybelle banjo for ten dollars. He bought my brother a Stella guitar. I don't remember how much he paid for it, but it couldn't have been much. My brother, who has a much better ear for music than I do, would figure out what Charlie Poole was doing on the banjo and then he would show me. So I really learned with my brother showing me the chords, the notes, that kind of thing. So I just got hooked on the music, and I

never got over it. Not to this day. You know, it's a shame that dad didn't continue playing the fiddle, but after Posey died he just kinda let it slide until my brother and I got interested.

I must have been around eighteen, maybe seventeen, when my brother and I first played for our family reunions, but I didn't play in public that much. My dad would take us to see local musicians, and we'd play some with them. There was a service station there in Spray where they had music on Tuesday nights—a Sunoco service station—and he'd take my brother and me down there, and we'd watch those musicians play. Then there were some other musicians who played at a country store in Draper on Friday nights. It was that kind of exposure that I had to the music.

Once my dad took us to see Bascom Lamar Lunsford. That was in the spring of 1964. I have a picture of my brother and me sitting on Bascom Lamar Lunsford's front steps with Lunsford and his wife. In the picture I have my little banjo, my brother has his guitar, and Lunsford has his banjo and his wife has a guitar. Lunsford

Region 1

was really the first person who ever taught me a chord *by name*. My brother would show me "put this finger here, put that finger there" and that kind of thing. But I remember Lunsford showing me how to make a D chord to play "White House Blues." That was the first chord, *by name*, that I ever learned. I never forgot that.

Regarding the highlights of my personal experiences as a musician, I'd say playing at the Kennedy Center for their homegrown music series was a real treat. Our band, the New North Carolina Ramblers, played there. We also played at the Library of Congress. We played on the same stage where Jelly Roll Morton once played. That was a really neat feeling! The Kennedy Center videotaped our concert and then ran it on their website. That was cool. That was one of my highlights of playing music. We're going to England soon, to play at the Gainsborough Folk Festival. That should be neat. Over here, we sometimes take our American music for granted. People around here grow up with it and so they don't see anything special about it. But to Europeans and others it's something that they take a very strong interest in. And I'm glad they do.

I would love to see more young people take up an interest in this "homegrown" music of ours—the traditional, rural music that's so much a part of our heritage. It's Americana. It's great music. This music is so authentic, it's so real, and it's a true reflection of the people who worked in the mills, in the tobacco fields, in the coal mines—you just couldn't ask for anything more genuine. It has a great history, and it ought to be preserved. There's so much fakery now and so much plastic in our world, that it's nice to see something, like this music, that's real and isn't just a veneer. There's too much veneer in the world. This music really speaks. It would be so wonderful to see a lot more young folks get to be actively involved in it.

onto the porch and into the grassy yard. Outside, around the grounds, local musicians of all ages gather to talk and jam. Following the more formal performances, the stage is turned over to the local regulars. It is a friendly crowd, and the players enjoy spending time with friends and meeting new ones. On the second and fourth Saturdays of every month, the Wilsons host a covered dish dinner and a concert that features performances by Debbie's band, The Heart Strings, followed by an open jam session.

WHEN: Tuesdays and second and fourth Saturdays, 7 P.M.
WHERE: 151 Gant Road, Eden, 27289. Gant Road is located on NC 770
    (Meadow Road), about 6 miles east of Eden.
ADMISSION: Free, but donations are accepted
CONTACT: Jerry and Debbie Wilson, 336-706-2144

Dancers take to the floor at the Barn.

● FIDDLERS' CONVENTIONS IN WESTERN NORTH CAROLINA

The tradition of organizing fiddlers' contests goes back to 1924 in the small rural community of Union Grove. That year, H. P. Van Hoy needed money to buy supplies for the school where he taught. Realizing that the local community was full of good string band musicians, he and his wife, Ada, held a fiddlers' convention on the school grounds the Saturday before Easter. Half the proceeds were used for prize money for competitors and half went to the school. The contest caught on and became an annual affair.

During the 1960s and early 1970s, the fiddlers' convention transitioned from a local to a national event. People from across the country, some interested in traditional music and others who saw the festival as an opportunity to participate in a large, open-air party, were attracted to Union Grove. The audience expanded more than tenfold, prompting one of Van Hoy's sons to move the convention to his nearby farm. Crowds continued to grow, and eventually overwhelmed security and support services. Disruptive behavior by attendees caused Van Hoy to discontinue the event.

A branch of the Van Hoy family restarted the Union Grove Festival in 2012 after a hiatus of thirty years. The event is held Easter weekend at the Van Hoy Family Campground. In recent years, more and more fiddlers' convention have sprung up. Some are large outdoor affairs; others are small, one-day gatherings. It is possible to attend a convention almost every month of the year, and many diehard musicians do. Each convention tends to develop its own character and its own unique audience. They also tend to favor a particular sound in the contests and jam circles. For more details and a full listing of North Carolina fiddlers' conventions and jam sessions, visit www .BlueRidgeMusicNC.com. Here is a partial listing of fiddlers' conventions in western North Carolina:

Alleghany Fiddlers' Convention
Appalachian State Old-Time Fiddlers' Convention
Ashe County Fiddlers' Convention
The Charlie Poole Festival
Ellenboro Fiddlers' and Bluegrass Convention
Happy Valley Fiddlers' Convention
Mount Airy Bluegrass and Old-Time Fiddlers' Convention
Music Competition at Brevard Halloweenfest
Music Competition at the North Carolina Mountain State Fair
Stokes County Fiddlers' Convention
Surry County Fiddlers' Convention
Union Grove Fiddlers' Convention
Yadkin Valley Bluegrass Convention

Musicians jam while in the line for a competition at Mount Airy.

YADKIN COUNTY

YADKIN VALLEY BLUEGRASS CONVENTION
Yadkinville

Before the advent of large outdoor multiday fiddlers' conventions, most southern music contests were held indoors in public spaces such as courthouses and school buildings. These early contests in the first few decades of the twentieth century were often considered to be a way of preserving a romantic and disappearing Appalachian culture. For musicians, the contests were a way of earning relatively easy money, and contestants would often travel great distances to attend. A few early hillbilly recordings recreated these old-time music contests right down to the announcer.

These smaller early contests live on at locally oriented events like the Yadkin Valley Fiddlers' Convention. Begun in 1985, it has become a favorite among bluegrass and old-time-music fans and musicians alike. The convention is held annually at the Yadkinville Elementary School multipurpose center and is sponsored by the Yadkin Arts Council. The contest features local and regional talent. Bands and individuals are judged on items such as timing, choice of material, accuracy, and appearance. Prizes are awarded to the top five bluegrass and old-time bands as well as to the top three finishers in each of the following categories: fiddle, banjo, mandolin, lead guitar, acoustic bass, dobro, lead vocal, and young talent. For the past few years, a Friday-night concert featuring a well-known touring act has opened the festival.

WHEN: Friday evening and Saturday beginning at 12 p.m., third weekend in April
WHERE: Yadkinville Elementary School, 305 North State Street, Yadkinville, 27055
ADMISSION: Fee
CONTACT: Yadkin Arts Council, 336-679-2941
WEBSITE: http://yadkingrass.com

Feed Me on Cornbread and Beans

In the Southern Appalachian region, traditional food and traditional music are close friends. They're seen together all the time. In fact, they're practically inseparable. Mountain musicians will sometimes actually stop playing music long enough to eat. They sure don't stop very long for anything else! The combination of good homemade food and good homemade music can be found at dozens of music venues around the Blue Ridge. Almost without exception, every folk festival, fiddlers' convention, hometown opry, and dance venue in the Blue Ridge provides a bounty of food choices to go with the music, often paying deference to regional specialties. Typically, festival and event managers will contract with commercial vendors and community service organizations to prepare and serve specialty regional and other traditional foods at hometown celebrations.

As the lyrics to "Lonesome Road Blues" imply ("Oh, they feed me on cornbread and beans / Lord I ain't a-gonna be treated this-a way"), pinto beans have been a longtime sustenance (and favorite) food in Southern Appalachia. Traditionally eaten with a big square of baked corn bread and a thick circle of sliced onion, pinto beans may be the most frequently served of all the regional favorites in the Blue Ridge. They're prepared nowadays at festivals, at fiddlers' conventions, at street fairs, in restaurants, and at home.

To find truly regional cuisine, with or without music, drop in at the local cafés and restaurants scattered here and there in the smaller cities and towns of the Blue Ridge. Harold's Restaurant, located on Highway 115 in Wilkesboro, is one of many local eateries that offer a whole array of regional favorites from which to choose. For example, Harold's breakfast menu lists homemade biscuits with your choice of bacon, bologna, chicken fillet, country ham, egg, grilled chicken, hog jowls, jelly, livermush, sausage, steak, tenderloin, bacon and egg, boiled ham and egg, bologna and egg, country ham and egg, hog jowls and egg, livermush and egg, sausage and egg, or steak and egg.

Other traditional foods that are prepared with a regional

Food and music often go hand in hand. Participants in the shape-note singing at Morning Star Methodist Church in Canton take a break to share dinner on the grounds.

A heaping platter of Sims barbecue.

flair include barbecued pork and chicken and all of the related side dishes — roasted corn on the cob, chili, homemade ice cream, and a variety of home-baked cakes, pastries, and cookies.

REGION 2 AT A GLANCE

LANSING

194

16

221

18

SPARTA

ALLEGHANY

88

JEFFERSON

Mount Airy

WEST
JEFFERSON

ASHE

Blue Ridge Parkway

21

SUGAR
GROVE

194

TODD

WILKES

321

DEEP
GAP

16

18

268

WATAUGA

Blue Ridge Parkway

BOONE

105

WILKESBORO

421

BLOWING
ROCK

Blue Ridge Parkway

Historic Happy Valley Corridor

FERGUSON

115

Grandfather
Mountain

Winston-Salem

268

18

90

16

CALDWELL

LENOIR

64

DUDLEY
SHOALS

321

GRANITE
FALLS

Hickory

Region 2

THE PLACE

Alleghany, Ashe, and Watauga Counties sit perched in the very northwestern corner of North Carolina. Even the flat ground in most of this region is close to 3,000 feet in elevation, and the mountains rise to nearly 6,000 feet. The high altitude and steep slopes, combined with very few good roads, historically made it a very difficult region to reach from the eastern part of the state. This remoteness led the area to become known as the Lost Provinces. Today the region is known as the High Country. With the advent of good roads and modern communications, the High Country of North Carolina has become one of the state's most popular destinations.

The town of Boone, located in the southwestern corner of the region and Watauga County's seat of government, is home to Appalachian State University, the largest institution of higher learning in the state's Blue Ridge Mountains. With its proximity to Grandfather Mountain, the heavily visited town of Blowing Rock, the Blue Ridge Parkway, and several major ski resorts, Boone and the eastern part of Watauga County have become more heavily populated and developed than the rest of the region. The western side of the county, including the scenic Watauga River valley and the small town of Valle Crucis, is more rural, as is the New River valley in Ashe and Alleghany Counties to the north.

The High Country is also closely linked to the two foothill counties of Caldwell and Wilkes, both of which sit immediately "off" the mountain. In the past, the two county seat towns of Lenoir and Wilkesboro were the closest market towns to the mountains, and it was there that many mountain people went in search of jobs. A large furniture industry supported by a nearby railroad and plentiful hardwood forests flourished here.

A tobacco farm in Ashe County. Burley tobacco was once a cash crop in the mountains. These days, you are more likely to encounter Christmas tree farms in the High Country.

Today, the furniture industry is almost gone, and the once nearly depleted forests are making a comeback. Nearby, the Wilson Creek area has blossomed as a playground for outdoor enthusiasts who come to experience waterfalls, trout fishing, rock climbing, and miles of wilderness hiking trails.

Wilkes County has had a reputation for producing prodigious amounts of moonshine whiskey—a staple for some, a scourge to others. Many of the nation's greatest auto-racing pioneers, including the legendary Junior Johnson, got their start hauling illegal Wilkes County liquor in their souped-up, well-oiled machines, hotrods outfitted to outrun the Wilkes County sheriff or any federal revenue agents who might try to catch up with them as they sped along the county's curvy highways and winding back roads. Later, those same daring drivers would make the transition from bootleggers to the first stars of the NASCAR racetrack circuit.

CALDWELL COUNTY

SIMS COUNTRY BAR-B-QUE
Dudley Shoals

The main dish at Sims Country Bar-B-Que, as you might guess, is barbecue—pit-cooked barbecue. Located on Charlie Little Road in Dudley Shoals, Sims Country Bar-B-Que advertises itself as being "centrally located

A public mural in West Jefferson.

in the middle of nowhere." So before you try to find your way there without knowing exactly where you're going, save yourself some trouble and follow the driving directions in this guide. You *can* get there. It *is* possible. Lots of people have done it. It's easy—if you know how.

Hidden away from view until you've driven up, down, and around a half-mile of dirt driveway, Sims Country Bar-B-Que is suddenly revealed as you crest a gentle open ridge. Beneath a grove of huge trees that stand clustered on the edge of a broad, grassy slope sits a large, rustic, meandering building that can accommodate more than three hundred people. That's the restaurant. It's essentially one big room divided into two parts by a massive double-sided stone fireplace. The enormous dining area is furnished with lines of simple tables and wooden benches set up in long, end-to-end rows, boardinghouse style.

There are many things to do at this place, which is part restaurant, part park, part music stage, and part dance center. Some folks enjoy a leisurely walk around the edges of a nearby pond before dining or a stroll out onto the earthen walkway that runs a short distance into the water. The grassy banks of the pond are neatly kept and mowed. A few crumbs of bread tossed onto the surface of the water will often attract surprisingly large fish.

Between the pond and the main building, near a small creek, are several spots for tossing horseshoes. Horseshoe pitching is a popular pastime at Sims, especially for men and boys, and during the early evening hours the

Visitors of Sims Country Bar-B-Que compete in a game of horseshoes.

courts are very busy. Inevitably, some of the players are novices, so a word of caution is in order: The accuracy of the aim of some of the players can't be relied on. Meanwhile, inside, the food is ready when you are. It's a bountiful buffet that's continuously replenished, as needed, throughout the evening.

Here you'll find *real* barbecue, not just any kind of meat that's cooked outdoors and over (or even near) a burning flame. Traditionally prepared, authentic, real southern barbecue has to be cooked over a pit. "Pit-cooked" is the operative term here. If it ain't pit-cooked over wood, it ain't barbecue.

Don't worry about how to spell barbecue correctly. There's no universally accepted spelling of the word in the South. It can be "bar-b-cue," "barbe-cue," "barbeque," "B-B-Q," or "bar-b-que," but the spelling doesn't matter. What does matter is that it's cooked over a pit!

Three generations of the Sims family are involved in the management and operation of this colorful place. Keith Sims, along with his wife, Shirley, and others in the family, including Susan Sims Bumgardner and Joe Sims, provide a family-oriented spot to enjoy good food accompanied by traditional music and dance. The menu board reads: "Coffee, Soft Drinks, and the Best Iced Tea Around! (No alcohol is served or permitted)."

For a set price (one price for adults, less for children), patrons get the all-you-can-eat buffet, served cafeteria style. The buffet is the only choice there is at Sims, but it's a good one. It includes barbecued beef, pork, and chicken; baked beans; coleslaw; cornbread fritters (fried cornbread patties); pickles; potato chips; and loaf bread. Pitchers of iced tea, coffee and soft drinks and desserts are extra. And don't forget—it's all-you-can-eat!

Once you've loaded your tray with that enormous plate of food and something to drink, look around and select a table that's as close as possible to the dance floor and music stage. Then settle in. There's a full eve-

THE MOLASSES FESTIVAL AT SIMS COUNTRY BAR-B-QUE

Molasses, made from ground sorghum (also called cane), is an important sweetener in rural Appalachia. The dark, sticky confection graces many a mountain table and is used in baking and cooking, or it's poured over biscuits, hotcakes, or anything else. Molasses boils are one of many annual agricultural rituals that marked the changing of the seasons. Cane stalks are ground to extract juice in a mill powered by mule, horse, or, today, often a tractor. The juice is then boiled down until only the sweet, sticky molasses is left. The whole process takes a long time, and requires a lot of helping hands, so making molasses is a social occasion, one that often involves making music too. On the second Saturday in October, Sims Country Bar-B-Que hosts its annual Molasses Festival. A variety of demonstrations, displays, and other activities that are all related to the heritage of Southern Appalachia are presented during

the day. These include molasses making, apple butter and apple cider making, flatfoot dancing, mountain music, hayrides, crafts, cloggers, and (you guessed it) barbecue! Festival hours are 9 A.M. to 4 P.M.

Boiling down molasses.

ning ahead of you—eating more tasty barbecue than you should, drinking lots of iced tea, meeting and socializing with nice people, listening to hours of fine bluegrass and old-time music, and watching—and perhaps participating in—lively mountain dancing.

WHEN: Fridays and Saturdays, opens at 5 P.M.; music starts at 7 P.M.
WHERE: 6160 Petra Mill Road, Granite Falls, 28630. *From Hickory and I-40*: Travel north on US 321 toward Granite Falls. After crossing the Catawba River Bridge, turn right at the stoplight onto Grace Chapel Road. Travel 7 miles, then turn right onto Bowman Road. Bear right at the stop sign onto Dudley Shoals Road. Turn right onto Charlie Little Road. At the stop sign, turn left onto Petra Mill Road. The driveway for Sims will be on your right. *From Lenoir via US 321*: Travel to Granite Falls on US 321. Turn left at the stoplight onto Pinewood Road. Turn

left at the stop sign onto Dudley Shoals Road. Travel 5.5 miles, then turn right onto Charlie Little Road. At the stop sign, turn left onto Petra Mills Road. Turn right into the Sims driveway.

ADMISSION: Free, but fee charged for food
CONTACT: Joseph Sims, 828-396-5811
WEBSITE: www.simscountrybarbque.com

HERITAGE DAY AND KILN OPENING AT BOLICK FAMILY POTTERY
Between Blowing Rock and Lenoir

In northern Caldwell County, not far from Blowing Rock, are the Bolick Family Pottery Shop and the Traditions Pottery Shop. The woodlands, fields, and pastures surrounding the Bolick complex are nestled within a beautiful mountain hollow that's forested with hardwood trees and nice thickets of mountain laurel. It's a picturesque and relaxing place to hear some good easy-going and traditional mountain music. A bumper sticker on a pickup truck that's usually parked nearby reads, "I'm a potter, that's why my eyes are glazed," and a sign tacked high up on a nearby shed declares, "This is a work free, smokin', pickin', chewin' area."

Glenn Bolick's love of traditional ways and history is evident at the annual Heritage Day held every summer. Festivities at the pottery include old-time and bluegrass music, clogging, flatfooting, buckdancing, mountain crafts, and heritage demonstrations—blacksmithing, ox handling, a sawmill demonstration, quilting, colonial knotting, children's games, and pottery making—and the opening of a wood-fired pottery kiln that Bolick patterned after a style used by the pottery-making Owens family, his wife's forebears. Glenn Bolick blows a hunting horn, and a crowd gathers to watch

Glenn Bolick helps his son-in-law, Mike Calhoun, fire the pottery kiln.

A steam-driven sawmill is often cranked up on Heritage Day.

the newly-fired pieces being removed from the kiln and displayed for sale. The Bolick's Heritage Day and Pottery Kiln Opening combines a variety of mountain cultural traditions and heritage practices into a celebratory occasion that is informative and festive for both community members and visitors to the region.

WHEN: Last Saturday in June

WHERE: Bolick Family Pottery, Blackberry Road, Lenoir, 28645. The Bolick and Traditions Pottery Shops are located side by side on Blackberry Road, about 3 miles south of Blowing Rock (or 15 miles north of Lenoir) off US 321. Turn at St. Mark's Lutheran Church and follow the unpaved road downhill for about half a mile. The potteries are identified with signs.

ADMISSION: Free

CONTACT: 828-295-5099

WEBSITE: www.traditionspottery.com

⬤ Glenn Bolick: Sawmill Man

Glenn Bolick is a musician, a potter, a sawmiller, and an inventor. A visit to his place on Blackberry Road in Caldwell County treats guests to a rare look at an operating antique sawmill, a lesson on contemporary stoneware-pottery-making processes, and a taste of old-time mountain music.

I'll start with my grandfather and this old house that I live in. This house is a hundred and twelve years old. I grew up just across the way over there, and I spent a lot of time here in this house with my grandparents. My grandfather and grandmother would sing together—gospel hymns—using the *Christian Harmony* songbook. They sang three-part harmony. They didn't have a guitar, or a banjo, or nothing playing with 'em. That's the first remembrance that I have of any kind of music.

I was born in 1939, June the thirtieth. I was the sixth child of ten. My parents sang shape-notes at the Baptist church. They'd teach the shaped notes to us, the do-re-mi. I didn't really learn it like I should have. But I've always loved singing. As I grew older, we had a battery-powered radio at our house. And we had one of those crank-up record players—a talking machine, we called it—that we listened to different artists on. We listened to the *Grand Ole Opry* on the radio sometimes on Saturday night when I was a child.

We're part of that same family of Bolicks that came from Germany in 1753. They didn't get out anywhere much then, and nobody much came in here from somewhere else. It was mostly just the local folks, so that's who they married—each other. It's like Jeff Foxworthy says, "Our family tree don't fork all that much." My great-grandfathers were brothers, so I think that would make Mama and Papa second cousins.

We didn't get to go to dances until we got grown and left home. When I was a teenager in the fifties, they had some dances at Blowing Rock with live bands that would play all kinds of music. Rock and roll was going strong then, and I liked it pretty good. But I got over it. I got back to the old traditional stuff. I had always had a guitar and banjo, you know, just messing around with them. I had my banjo in my car one day when we had come home here for the weekend. We stopped to visit my grandmother. She saw that banjo in the car, in the back seat, and she said, "Lord, there's an old banjer! Let me see that thing." So I got it out and handed it to her. She went to tuning on that thing, and she tuned it up in one of the older styles of tuning. Then she played "Fly Around My Pretty Little Miss" and she sung it. After I saw her do that, I just had to play in her style. That's the way I learned it, after I saw her do it that way.

My wife is Lula Owens, and her folks were in pottery. I married into the pottery business. We worked for her dad at his pottery for ten years before we come back here. I got a chance to buy this old farm, and we started our pottery business here in 1973. My family had just done sawmilling and farming and digging roots and herbs.

Courtesy of the photographer, Jeremy Stephens.

That's the way we grew up. I wrote a song about my dad, and his dad and granddad, about them all being sawmillers. I call it "The Sawmill Man." Each generation used a different power system to run the sawmill with, from a water wheel to a steam engine to a kerosene burner to a diesel, which I now use myself.

My daughter Janet and my son-in-law Michael have a shop of their own here. They call it the Traditions Pottery. My daughter started making pottery when she was very young. They both wanted to do pottery. They opened a shop at Blowing Rock, and after a couple of years up there, they built their own shop down here. So they have their own business. We fix our clay together. We dig it and process it together. We work together a lot. I think the two shops complement one another.

The musicians who play here do it just for the enjoyment of it. They're not paid. People come to enjoy the music, but once they're here, they can go in the shop and look around, buy pottery. Our Heritage Day was started very small, with mostly family and friends. The first year we had some quilts, a fellow brought his oxen and wagon, his wife churned butter, and we had all different kinds of old-timey things— blacksmithing, log skidding with mules, the sawmill going, and so on. We cook pinto beans in there on the wood cookstove—about thirty pounds of beans—and we bake cornbread. Last year my sister-in-law made fried pies. A niece made homemade ice cream. The whole family is involved in it. People like it 'cause it's so laid back. I don't have a lot of rules and regulations. We just ask that they don't have any alcohol or use any bad language. It's a family event, and we want to keep it that way.

The Yadkin River at the Jones Farm, site of the Happy Valley Fiddlers' Convention.

HAPPY VALLEY OLD-TIME FIDDLERS' CONVENTION
Yadkin Valley

Of the many smaller fiddlers' conventions taking place across the Blue Ridge region, the event in Happy Valley stands out for its natural beauty and historic setting along the banks of the Yadkin River north of Lenoir. The serpentine NC 268 follows the upper valley of the Yadkin, hugging the base of the Blue Ridge Escarpment. The three-day gathering occurs on Labor Day weekend on a working farm near the community of Yadkin Valley, itself a significant site in the history of Appalachian music. In a field behind the main stage, a small white fence encircles the final resting place of Laura Foster, whose murder is the subject of the famous ballad "Tom Dooley."

Like other fiddlers' conventions, many attendees are musicians who come to jam and compete in the old-time and bluegrass competitions held on Saturday. Their campsites stretch along the woods below the main stage, and old-time and bluegrass jam sessions can be heard most of the day and into the night. Others come mainly for the bluegrass, old-time, gospel, and blues groups that perform Friday and Saturday night and all day Sunday under the big tent. Throughout the weekend, festival-goers can also sample local cuisine such as barbecue, livermush, and ham biscuits provided by churches, civic organizations, and the North Carolina Cattlemen's Association. Some beat the heat by taking a swim in the river, which flows along the edge of the property. Others participate in workshops and children's activities, or visit with local artisans and luthiers who spread out their crafts and handmade fiddles, banjos, and guitars under a tent near the main stage.

WHEN: Friday–Sunday, Labor Day weekend
WHERE: Jones Farm, 3590 NC 268, Lenoir, 28645. The farm is located

Feed Me on Cornbread and Beans

approximately 20 miles from US 421 in Wilkesboro and 10 miles from US 321 north of Lenoir. Look for the signs.
CONTACT: Caldwell County Chamber of Commerce, 828-726-0616
WEBSITE: www.happyvalleyfiddlers.com or
www.ncartstrail.org/happyvalley

WILKES COUNTY

MERLEFEST
Wilkesboro
Every year during the last weekend in April, the small town of Wilkesboro, population 3,044 in 2010, rapidly grows by seventy-five thousand or more as throngs of music lovers from around the United States and beyond arrive for MerleFest, one of the premiere musical events in the nation. This internationally acclaimed festival is an annual four-day musical extravaganza that's staged in memory of Merle Watson, the late son and former playing partner of festival founder Doc Watson, the acclaimed master of Blue Ridge–style guitar and vocals. Merle Watson was fatally injured in a tractor accident in 1985. Beginning on Thursday afternoon until late Sunday afternoon, the one hundred and fifty acre campus of Wilkes Community College is literally flooded with music.

Reflecting the eclectic musical interests of Doc Watson, whose own repertoire included bluegrass, old-time, blues, rockabilly, country, and jazz, MerleFest features a broad range of musical events and styles presented at fourteen different stages scattered around the campus. There's traditional mountain music—old-time, bluegrass, and gospel. There's Delta and Piedmont blues. There's country, jazz, Cajun, Western, singer-songwriter, and Americana. And there's dancing, too—clogging, flatfoot, free-style, square, circle, contra, and swing.

The expert staging of MerleFest is a testament to the experience and skill of the folks who produce and manage this extraordinary event. Even though there may at times be as many as twelve stages running simultaneously, several of which are quite large and located outdoors, there is little or no carryover of sound from one to the other. It's a technical and logistical feat worth admiring.

The main stage at MerleFest is positioned at the southern edge of a large grassy field that will accommodate many thousands of music fans, most of whom bring along their own folding chairs, snacks, soft drinks, water bottles, blankets, rain gear, and sunscreen. There's a reserved seating area down front for those who want the convenience of having their seat pro-

Clyde Ferguson Jr.: God Gave Me the Love of Music

Clyde Ferguson Jr. is a music educator and gospel and blues bassist. He was raised under the musical tutelage of his blues-playing father, Clyde "Pop" Ferguson in Caldwell County.

I was born right here in Lenoir, North Carolina, and I've spent all my time here—except when I went off to college. After that, I came back and taught school here. I've won several national championships with my school music programs. But my history with music began long before that.

My dad is Clyde Ferguson, also known as "Pop" Ferguson. My mom was Margaret Ferguson. My mom and dad had separated when I was born so I actually didn't grow up with him. But I knew him. I'd get to go see him and hear him play. So I started to learn about traditional music from the blues era because that's what my dad played. I remember once when I was about nine I got to go visit him, and he played a song that was really awesome. I remember tears running down my face because it was so awesome. It was fantastic.

My dad was self-taught. His father—my grandfather—was a Holiness minister. He was all fire and brimstone and by the book. According to him, if you did anything at all wrong, it was gonna send you straight to Hades. The family didn't own a guitar back then, and there were no instruments in the church, so my grandfather—Gordon Ferguson—would send my Pop over to his sister's house to borrow a guitar for the church service. Her son had a guitar. So Pop would go get the guitar from his cousin—he's walking—and on the way back he would sit down on this certain tree stump by the road and strum that guitar. Man, he loved the way those strings sounded. Then, after church was done, he'd take the guitar back. He'd stop again at that same stump and sit and strum that guitar. Just strum it. He really liked that sound.

Back when Pop was young they used to have carnivals that would come around, and the carnival people would stay in people's homes. There were no other accom-

modations for black folks back then. There was a man named Mister LaVette who was with the carnival, and Mister LaVette was also a part-time minister. So my granddad would welcome him into his home. Well, he played guitar in open tuning. Back then they called it vestapol. So he showed Pop how to tune a guitar like that and Pop thought that was

Clyde "Pop" Ferguson (center, bottom row) with a group from Lenoir in the early 1940s. Pop still tours with his son, Clyde Jr., on bass. Courtesy of the Ferguson family.

just it! He thought he was really going then! At about that same time, there was a radio show that came on every Wednesday night called *Jam-Up and Honey*. And Pop loved the theme song for *Jam-Up and Honey*. The two men on the show were also involved in Vaudeville. They'd do blackface, and over the radio they sounded as if they were black, but they were not. They were actually two white guys. But Pop really liked their music and thought that their guitar sounded different from anything he's ever heard before. So he got to messing with the tuning of his guitar and actually ended up tuning it to standard tuning. And he learned to play that song. That's how he learned to play.

In our home when I was small we had a phonograph that played old 78 records. Also we had a strong church background. There were always great musicians at the church where we attended. From that, and from those records, I just knew somehow that I was supposed to have been living back during the swing era. Even when I went on to school at Shenandoah Conservatory for Music in Winchester, Virginia, and at Mitchell College, I never really developed a love for modern music. I had a great love for that gospel sound and that strong bluesy sound that we would hear in the church. I always say that God gave me the love of music in order to reach other people, and especially children. I taught in the public school classroom for twenty-six years. Through music I was able to reach a lot of students, and I like to think I was able to help many of them express themselves through the music we were making together.

After Pop and I were apart for a few years, we reunited in 2006, and I wanted to figure out what I could give him for Christmas to celebrate our being back together. I decided that he had everything he needed, except we had never played music together. So his Christmas gift from me would be that I would play the guitar for him. I enrolled in a guitar class at the community college and I also hired a private teacher. For the next ten weeks I did nothing in my spare time but work on learning to play blues guitar. So Christmas day came and I played for him. When I finished playing, Pop said, "That's good boy, but I believe that song goes like this." Then he took the guitar out of my hands and he blistered it. My feelings were hurt at first, but on New Year's Day I went to his house carrying a bass guitar that I had purchased. Then I proceeded to play a tune that I had worked on. Pop then said, "Wow! Make that again," while reaching for his guitar. And the rest is history. Since then we have probably missed no more than forty-five to sixty days that we have not played together or shared some ideas on our music.

These days, when Pop and I go out playing music, we try to grab the essence of the musical tradition and relay that to the people—give them an idea of what that pure music was like. Sometimes it's really hard. And it's not a money-making thing because people can't listen to just that for a very long time. We can't make a whole show out of it.

My dad is a real character. He makes up things as he goes. He tells about the guitar that plays in his head. Once we were playing at the Carl Sandburg Festival and he looked over at me with his eyes all out of focus. He said, "Do that again." So I repeated what I was doing on the bass, and he played the most wonderful solo I've ever heard. I thought, "Wow!" So, when the show was over, I said, "Where'd *that* come from, Pop?" And he said, "From that guitar in my head!" And even now, when we're *really* playing, just he and I, that guitar turns on in his head and we connect— and we do things that we've never done before. It happens at that moment and maybe never again. When my dad was young, he would do some funny blues stuff, you know, back in those days. Even now, at eighty-three years old, he has a tremendous ear. I don't ever challenge him. If I say, "Pop, that's in the key of A." He'll say, "No, boy, that's in G." I say, "OK." His ear is *exact*.

I wish I could find a magic wand that would cause more people to be receptive to and understand the importance of this kind of music—the traditional music. Pop and I play and people enjoy us a lot, but we just can't seem to get far enough out. When we go places and play music that's, say, from 1940 on back, people really embrace it. So my big thing now is to somehow help to keep the blues alive.

Jam-Up and Honey was a blackface comedy duo that appeared on WSM's radio broadcasts of the Grand Ole Opry beginning in the early 1940s and lasting through the late 1950s. The duo consisted of Howard Evans and Lee Davis "Honey" Wilds. Wilds organized the first Grand Ole Opry–endorsed tent show in 1940. For more than a decade he ran the traveling show, with Jam-Up and Honey as headliners.

Musician and artist Willard Gayheart's rendering of MerleFest pays homage to Merle Watson, Merle's son Richard, and Doc Watson, pictured left to right. © Willard Gayheart.

vided for them. High-quality loudspeakers mounted on poles are placed at intervals throughout the audience area to insure good acoustics for all. A huge Megatron screen positioned alongside the main stage provides a great view of the performers onstage for everyone, some of whom can be seated as far as 100 yards away from the stage.

A series of workshops are offered in guitar, banjo, fiddle, blues, dobro, bass, vocals, and several of the technical aspects of recording and producing music. Contests for various instrument players take place during the festival, and a picking tent and a dance tent are on-site. Children's activi-

AMERICANA MUSIC

MerleFest is known the world over as a place to hear the best in bluegrass and other forms of strictly traditional music, but it is also billed as an Americana Festival. "Americana" is a term that encompasses everything from the very oldest traditional music to contemporary music that draws on the sounds and influences of traditional music, but it may also incorporate original songwriting and elements of rock and roll, country, and other popular music forms. The tendency for Americana music to move across genres can be traced in part to the folk revival of the 1960s and especially to the singer-songwriter and country rock movement of the 1970s, when artists like Emmylou Harris and the Nitty Gritty Dirt Band collaborated with traditional artists and made a new sound while drawing on deep roots.

During the 1990s and early 2000s, the term "alternative" or "alt" country was applied to a new wave of artists who were influenced by the work of older country musicians and whose music was produced independent of the slicker, more commercialized styles that were coming out of Nashville at the time. This also led to new critically acclaimed albums by some of those older musicians, like Johnny Cash and Loretta Lynn. The resurgence of a widespread interest in truly traditional southern music came about in part with the success of the motion pictures *Oh Brother, Where Art Thou* and *Cold Mountain*, and several others. The producer of the soundtracks for those films, T Bone Burnett, also produced albums for Steve Earle, Elvis Costello, and an album that paired Led Zeppelin front man Robert Plant with bluegrass artist Allison Krauss.

The integration of singer-songwriter and popular music into southern and Appalachian styles of music has put a new spin on many of the old songs

and as a result has brought traditional music to new and wider audiences. Some players of Americana have actively sought out the roots of the music they play by visiting older artists in the southern mountains. And many of the artists who are influenced by North Carolina's

The Avett Brothers performing at Merlefest. Courtesy of the photographer, Ashley Melzer.

traditional music have increased their visibility by playing at MerleFest and at other Blue Ridge venues. Gillian Welch, for example, who moves deftly between bluegrass, indie folk, and country, won one of the first songwriting contests ever held at MerleFest. Old Crow Medicine Show, the Avett Brothers, and the Carolina Chocolate Drops all got their start in North Carolina, and they all owe part of their widespread success to the large crowds who first heard them at MerleFest. Many other music sites along the Blue Ridge Music Trails are increasingly featuring singer-songwriters and younger musicians who draw their material and their inspiration from a combination of traditional and popular music.

New musicians emerging today in hotbeds of Americana music such as Asheville may eventually displace some of the older, more traditional acts at events like MerleFest. But that's part of the continuing interaction that has occurred for a very long time between popular and more local musical traditions all around the Blue Ridge. These days, it's not uncommon to hear songs by Americana artists being played by bluegrass bands, showing that influence can run in both directions.

ties include a petting zoo, playgrounds, storytelling, sing-alongs, and face painting. There's a large sales tent stocked with CDs of music by festival performers as well as other musicians who have appeared at MerleFest over the years. An "Expo Center" features a selection of musical instruments and musical accessories for sale. The Heritage Crafts Tent offers handcrafts and demonstrations by regional artisans and a festival gift shop stocked with t-shirts, caps, children's items, and other festival necessities. The Food Tent area features a variety of foods, and seating at dining tables for hundreds is located adjacent to the main stage area. Portable flush toilets are readily available throughout the festival grounds.

Alcoholic beverages are not allowed at this event, and all coolers and bags are screened at the festival entrance in an effort to strictly enforce that rule. In addition, the Wilkes Community College Campus is a 100 percent tobacco-free site.

MerleFest was started in 1988 to benefit the establishment and maintenance of a memorial garden at Wilkes Community College. The Eddy Merle Watson Memorial Garden for the Senses is designed to appeal to the senses of smell and touch and contains a collection of diverse plant species chosen for their strong fragrances or unusual textures. The garden complex

● Uwe Krüger: Not a Stranger Anymore

Brothers Jens and Uwe Krüger are natives of Germany who grew up in Switzerland. The Krügers started singing and playing instruments at a very young age. Growing up in post–World War II Europe, music was a critically important part of life for them as children. The brothers first came to the Blue Ridge in 1997. Joel Landsberg, a native of New York City, joined the brothers in the early 1990s. Together, they've established the incomparable sound that the Krüger Brothers band is known for today. They live in Wilkes County, North Carolina.

My mother was a kindergarten teacher, and she had a song for everything. We sang a lot at home. We mainly sang old German folk songs. She was from Germany—East Prussia. My dad was from Northern Germany. For them, music was a way of keeping our culture alive. In Switzerland, [German music] was not very highly regarded. As Germans in Switzerland, we were guest workers—much like the Mexicans are here today. It was hard for us. We wanted to sing those German songs because they meant a lot to our family.

When I was about ten years old, we met a boy whose daddy was an American GI. He had married a German woman and became a kindergarten teacher in Switzerland. As a teacher, he taught his students to speak English with the help of American folk songs. By then, Jens and I were already playing banjo and guitar. We were doing the sort of Dixieland tunes that my uncle played with his band up in Germany. We played songs like "You Are My Sunshine" and "My Bonnie Lies Over the Ocean." [Laughs.] People really liked that. Our parents liked it, and the Swiss people liked it, because, you know, it was not German. It was like a neutral ground for us. So, when this man heard us play, he said, "Well, you have to come to my house."

He had this huge collection of old Folkways records, the whole *Anthology of American Folk Music*, the Pete Seeger *America's Favorite Ballads*, Woody Guthrie, Lead Belly, and all those old records. My dad got me a little tape recorder, which back then was a big investment, and I would sit for hours in front of [the man's] record player and copy those songs onto cassette tapes. So, my brother and I started playing that music. We fell in love with it. My dad gave me a phrase book—an English-German dictionary—and I sat down and started translating those songs. Just like you're supposed to do, right? [Laughs.] I started learning how to speak English that way.

When you're a boy of eight, nine, or ten years old, you think Western! The American West was a dream world for us, a place where everything was better—the outlaws, the cowboys, and all that. So, we learned to play American folk music. The melodies sounded really like German music to us, but with different words. One of the first songs I learned was "Tom Dooley"—the Kingston Trio version. Then I learned "Oh Mary, Don't You Weep Don't You Moan" and all the Pete Seeger material, you know? "The Fox Went Out on a Chilly Night" [laughs], and "This Land Is Your Land!" Those songs really left an impression on me.

From left to right: Jens Krüger, Uwe Krüger, and Joel Landsberg. Courtesy of Uwe Krüger.

In 1973, we had our first paying gig, Jens and I. I was just twelve or thirteen. I played guitar, he played banjo. We had a washtub bass player and a washboard player instead of a drummer. We were called the Undertaker's Skiffle Company. Skiffle was a kind of music that was pretty wild and woolly. We were fascinated with the idea that you could play music any which way you wanted to, with just these acoustic instruments. It was a natural way of doing it for us. We kept that band together all the way until I was eighteen or nineteen. We played every weekend, all over Switzerland.

One Christmas, we got two records. I got *Hello, My Name Is Johnny Cash*, and my brother got a sampler with bluegrass on it, *Bluegrass from the Hills*, or something like that. It was one of those cheap samplers, but it had "Foggy Mountain Break-down" on it. The first time my brother heard that song, he went nuts! [Laughs.] He started spinning around like a Tazmanian Devil! All around the living room—honestly! He said, "That's what I want to do!" He was playing a tenor banjo then, so he put a thumb-screw on it and added a fifth string so he could play bluegrass.

We left home when I was eighteen and my brother was sixteen, and we became street musicians. Our home had fallen apart, pretty much. My mom passed away when I was thirteen, and my dad didn't take it very well, so we just left. We were street musicians for a couple of years, and we traveled all over Europe. We had our first blue-grass band then. Two brothers from New York joined us—a mandolin player and a bass player—and we actually got a CBS recording contract with our band, Rocky Road.

Back where we grew up, Russian tanks were only eight hours away, and Russian rockets eight minutes. All of Europe back then pretty much identified with Western culture. And America was the beacon of freedom, the beacon of hope, the beacon of success, the beacon of—it was the place that you wanted to be like, a place where everybody ran around in blue jeans and basketball sneakers.

After World War II, European cultures had to reinvent themselves. And what was there to look up to? American culture. The U.S. State Department had programs back then where they used American music almost like propaganda. They were sending a lot of it out on the Voice of America radio shows. And, of course, I listened to that. I was not supposed to, but I could understand English so I did. I had a little AM radio that was my grandpa's—an old fifties German tube radio, which I kept in a small cabinet. At night, when I was supposed to be asleep, I'd get into that cabinet, close the door, and turn on the radio. I'd listen to Voice of America or the American Armed Forces Network. They played everything, but mainly country music. The GIs who were over in Germany mostly came from the South, so they played a lot of bluegrass. I remember the first time I heard "Run, Ol' Molly, Run." I will never forget that! It was the best-sounding thing ever.

Traditional music in Europe is very restrictive. You play the music where you're from and that's it. You're supposed to play just like your grandpa did. You don't change anything. You have no freedom whatsoever. You adhere to these strict boundaries. But Jens and I, being immigrants from Germany, could never really fit into the Swiss culture. German culture had been raped by the Nazis, so we found a new home in American folk music. The music from the South was the most accessible to us because, I believe, that people all over the world, when they live in the mountains, share certain traits in their lives. And good folk music tells about those things. When I first discovered Doc Watson, that's exactly what happened. He talked about life the way *I* would talk about life. And the way my dad would talk about life. He was straightforward.

America has something that looks very familiar to me, especially here in the Appalachian Mountains. When I first came here in 1997, it was like I had *touched the ground* for the very first time in my life. I felt at home. That had never happened to me before, and probably will never, ever happen to me again. I wrote a little song about that feeling. It's called "Carolina in the Fall." It's about how I felt that day. For the first time in my life, I was not a stranger anymore.

Here you can be whoever you are. The standoffishness that you sometimes see here is basically shyness. People here are often very careful about who they associate with, and they want to check you out first. That's exactly the same as it is in Switzerland. It's like they're all the same people. They're always a little bit wary of newcomers. They don't talk much at first. Then, if they see that they like you, you have their hearts. And that's exactly what has happened to us here. We are really lucky. We have found some really good people here.

includes a series of distinctive relief brick wall panels. The various features of the garden are labeled in Braille.

Limited tent and RV camping is available on campus. Public parking is located near the campus, and there's a free shuttle bus from there to the festival site, although most people walk the short distance to campus.

WHEN: Thursday–Sunday, the last week in April; gates open at 2 P.M. on
   Thursday and at 9 A.M. on Friday, Saturday, and Sunday
WHERE: Wilkes Community College, Wilkesboro, 28697. Located off
   NC 268 immediately west of US 421 (accessible from Exit 286-B)
ADMISSION: Fee
CONTACT: 1-800-343-7857
WEBSITE: www.merlefest.org

WHIPPOORWILL ACADEMY AND THE TOM DOOLEY MUSEUM
Ferguson

The Tom Dooley Museum is part of the Whippoorwill Academy and Village, a complex of restored buildings created and cared for by Edith Carter. The museum, housed in an old hewn-log cabin, features artifacts, photographs, paintings, and written information on the story of Tom Dula, who was hanged in 1868 for the murder of a young woman named Laura Fos-

Whippoorwill Academy and Village features a restored
schoolhouse, store, smokehouse, and cabin.

⦿ THE LEGEND OF TOM DOOLEY

Many Americans—maybe most—have probably never heard an honest-to-gosh traditional Appalachian ballad from the lips of a traditional singer from the Blue Ridge. One popular version of a traditional mountain ballad, however, seems to have remained widely known, even though it was popularized back in 1958. It's "The Ballad of Tom Dooley."

According to traditional North Carolina ballad singer Bobby McMillon, the Tom Dooley story is based on a murder that was committed by Tom Dula (sometimes locally pronounced "Dooley"), a Confederate army veteran from Wilkes County. The song gained national popularity after it was adapted, recorded, and then performed on national television by a folk revivalist group, the Kingston Trio. Their rendition of the song was based on a ballad that Frank Proffitt of Beech Mountain, North Carolina, had recorded in the 1930s or 1940s. According to Frank Proffitt Jr., his father learned about the Kingston Trio's rendition one Sunday evening when he saw them perform the song on *The Ed Sullivan Show*. It was quite a shock to him. The version they sang that night was:

> Hang down your head, Tom Dooley,
> Hang down your head and cry;
> Hang down your head, Tom Dooley,
> Poor boy, you're bound to die.
>
> I met her on the mountain,
> There I took her life;
> Met her on the mountain,
> Stabbed her with my knife.
>
> Hang down your head, Tom Dooley,
> Hang down your head and cry;
> Hang down your head, Tom Dooley,
> Poor boy, you're bound to die.
>
> This time tomorrow,
> Reckon where I'll be;
> Hadn't a-been for Grayson,
> I'd a-been in Tennessee.
>
> This time tomorrow,
> Reckon where I'll be;

Down in some lonesome valley,
Hangin' from a white oak tree.

Hang down your head, Tom Dooley,
Hang down your head and cry;
Hang down your head, Tom Dooley,
Poor boy, you're bound to die.

According to Bobby McMillon, after that song reached the height of its national popularity, a local story was circulated around southwestern North Carolina that the basis for the song was "that there was a guy named Bob Grayson who was in love with Laura Foster. And Tom was in love with Laura, too. And they got in a fight, and somehow Laura was accidentally killed. They said Tom was hanged because of a misunderstanding. That was the story that came out when the Kingston Trio popularized the song."

"In reality what happened," McMillon continued, "was that before he went to the war, he [Tom Dula] had an affair with a girl named Anne [Foster] Melton. Old man Wade Gilbert, he's the one who told me the story of Tom Dooley, said his grandmother was with Anne Melton the night she died. While Tom was gone to the [Civil] war, Anne Melton married. When he come back and saw that she was married, he started seeing some of the other ladies in the community. One of them was Anne's cousin, Laura Foster. She lived up here in Caldwell County. But [Tom Dula] kept up the affair with Anne Melton while he was at the same time seeing Laura Foster. It's been said that Anne Melton was jealous of Laura Foster.

"One morning Laura took her daddy's mare and disappeared. The day that she disappeared, he

Tom Dooley is buried on private land near the Wilkes-Caldwell county line. Dooley has two tombstones. One mentions his alleged crime and has been chipped away by souvenir seekers. The other alludes to his military service during the Civil War.

[Tom Dula] had walked all the way to Caldwell County. He left his home the morning that Laura Foster was killed, and he went down to the river. Then she took her daddy's horse and she come down to the river. Somebody saw her leaving home that morning, and she told them she was running away from home to marry Tom. Two days later the mare come home, but she never did.

"They went hunting for her and couldn't find her for several months. The body was finally found in a shallow grave in the woods down there close to where she was killed, in Wilkes County. Tom, in the meantime, had left the state. He went to Tennessee to work for a man named James Grayson. That's how the Grayson name got in it. Tom had worked for him for several days when two deputies came out of Wilkes County hunting for him. They actually came hunting for him before her body had ever been discovered.

"Grayson took the deputies and some other men, and they located Tom. By the time they brought him back, they'd found her body. They accused him of the murder. They had one trial in Wilkesboro, the county seat, and I don't remember for what reason, but they threw it out. Then they bound it over to the court in Statesville, a couple of counties away, probably because they couldn't get a fair trial in Wilkes County, and they found him guilty.

"Most people in this area believe he was hanged in Wilkesboro on the Tory Oak, which goes back to the Revolution, but he wasn't. The second trial was in Statesville, and Anne Melton was in jail there, too, accused with him. That jail's still standing. The night before they hanged him, he wrote a note exonerating Anne Melton from having had anything to do with it. But I think if she didn't do it, she had a hand in it.

"Tom was a fiddle player, and they say [on the day of the hanging] that he sat on his coffin and rode it from the jail to the place of execution, a-playing the fiddle. They said when he got there he looked up at the scaffold and said, 'Boys, if I'd a known you was gonna hang me with a new rope, I'd a washed my neck this morning.' Then he got up and made his little speech. He held out his hand and said, 'Gentlemen, you see this hand as it trembles? I never hurt a hair on that girl's head.' And that was it. His sister and her husband, they was there, so they claimed the body and took it back to Wilkes County for burial."*

*From author's personal interview with Bobby McMillon, December 1, 1999.

ter. There's a historic marker at the intersection of Highways 268 and 1134 in Wilkes County that calls attention to the murder and Dula's subsequent capture and punishment. Dula's grave is located about a mile from the Whippoorwill Academy on the Tom Dooley Road, overlooking the Yadkin River. Laura Foster is buried about seven miles away, in Yadkin Valley, Caldwell County.

The enduring legend of Tom Dooley has generated several books, a video program, the museum exhibit at Whippoorwill Academy, and the hit recording "Hang Down Your Head Tom Dooley." Additional information on the Tom Dooley saga is available at the Old Wilkes County Jail, a local history museum that's located behind the old county courthouse in Wilkesboro.

WHEN: Saturdays and Sundays, 3 to 5 P.M., and during the week by appointment, April–December; open by appointment only January–March.

WHERE: 11929 NC 268, Ferguson, 28624 (approximately 12 miles from Wilkesboro and 20 miles from Lenoir)

ADMISSION: Fee

CONTACT: Edith Carter, 336-973-3237

WKBC *HOMETOWN OPRY*
North Wilkesboro

A sign on the outside of a windowless one-story building in North Wilkesboro proclaims it to be the home of the WKBC *Hometown Opry*. This building houses the Main Street Music and Loan Company, a pawnshop that's also a lively Wilkes County musical institution. From here, on the second Friday morning of each month, local radio station WKBC broadcasts a live bluegrass show called the *Hometown Opry*.

The WKBC *Hometown Opry* is a community-based, homegrown kind of event where the crowd is friendly, welcoming anyone who shows up from out of town. One of the first things you'll notice when you enter the shop are the many guitars, fiddles, and banjos that fill virtually every spot of open space along the walls. This is not too surprising since Main Street Music and Loan is, after all, a pawnshop, and all the merchandise that crowds the walls is for sale.

During the show, *Opry* host Steve Handy will often invite audience members from the community to come forward to make announcements or he will talk to them informally from the broadcast table. It's a friendly, laid-back event. Sometimes the store owner and jokester Mike Palmer will give Steve a start by lowering a rubber snake in front of him from a fishing line

Herb Key: I Didn't Think *Anybody* Could Build a Guitar

Herb Key has played music for most of his life. He has also spent more than thirty years making, repairing, and restoring musical instruments. He currently performs with the Elkville String Band, a group that was originally formed as the house band for the Wilkes Playmakers' annual production of Tom Dooley: A Wilkes County Legend.

I was born a long time ago—1936, actually. I was born here in Wilkes County, up near Moravian Falls at a little community around Cub Creek Church. We were members of the church there. We walked to church back then. Lots of people did. I was born in a house up there that my brother still lives in. My dad built that house. My dad was a carpenter. He built it before he really got to be that good, but he did pretty well. And he remodeled it over the years. I helped him do a lot of that. That's where I got my start in woodworking.

When I was little my mother had a guitar she played a little bit, and my dad could play. But he didn't really want me to play music. You know back then we had folks that wouldn't work, and Dad knew a lot of musicians that wouldn't work—Charlie Poole, for instance, was one of 'em. I became interested in music pretty early on. My grandmother had one of those windup Victrolas, and she had some records that I recall. One in particular was Mother Maybelle playing "The Wildwood Flower." I was five, six, maybe seven at the time, and I'd sit on the floor, and my grandmother would put that record on and play it for me. I was *so* fascinated by the sound of that guitar. She wouldn't let me wind up the Victrola myself, she was afraid I'd break the spring. So she'd wind it up as many times as I wanted to hear it, and play it for me. I was just fascinated! We had the radio we listened to, and the Victrola, and that was about the only connection we had to music. I had an uncle who played, and he'd come around occasionally and show me a few things. So that's how I got started trying to play music.

In high school we had a little band, and I played in that—pretty much old-time music. I played bass in that configuration. There was a radio station here in the fifties, and it's still here, WKBC. So we got to playing on the radio—on Saturdays. At that time, they had an auditorium and people would come in and listen to the live broadcasts. There was a box on the wall like a mailbox, and people would mail in their requests. So we'd get those letters out, open then up, and read them on the air. And we'd play the request. It was really a pleasant thing. I remember we'd always get these requests for me to sing this particular song. I can't remember now what song it was, but the requests came from "Brown Eyes." The letters were signed "Brown Eyes." You know, "Please dedicate this song to Brown Eyes." Well, it turned out that Brown Eyes was my mother. She was just trying to help me along.

Later on, the next big influence on me was Doc Watson. That was in the sixties. I just couldn't believe how he could play a guitar. Mother Maybelle was great, but that's a different style. They call it the Carter scratch. But Doc was playing with that straight pick, and I was fascinated with that.

The band I play with now is the Elkville String Band. We were formed, I guess, about ten or twelve years ago to perform for the play, *Tom Dooley*. That's what the band was originally formed for. It was Drake Walsh, who's Dock Walsh's son, myself, Jerry Lankford, Nicole Vidrine, and Bill Williams. So after the play happened, we just sorta kept going. Now Drake has passed, and we've made some other changes in the lineup, but we're still trying to keep it going.

There's a little community up the river from here called Elkville. That's where Tom Dooley came from. We used that name then and still do. There's a fiddlers' convention

up near there now where Laurie Foster's grave is, and they've asked me to come play there several times, but it seems like I've always had some conflict or other. So I've never been to it.

There was a local guy here in the late sixties named Jack Williams. He's passed on now. He was a local repairman, and I got to hearing about him. I heard he'd built a guitar. At that point I didn't think *anybody* could build a guitar. That was just beyond comprehension—to me. He was primarily a fiddle repairman and a banjo repairman. So I decided I'd build a banjo, 'cause that's what he was building, mostly. He helped me. You know the pearl inlay like goes on the fingerboard? I used a Gibson hearts-and-flowers pattern and I made the inlay out of pearl buttons! And I made 'em with a file. I didn't know anything about a jeweler's saw or any of the modern methods of making inlay. But I did a pretty good job. The banjo turned out good.

Later, I was in another band, and Larry Pennington was also in that band. The

High Country Ramblers was the name of it. The High Country Ramblers became rather popular. We all dressed in matching pants and shirts, even wore string ties sometimes. We actually won first place at the Galax Fiddlers' convention, as well as many others. We recorded a few things, but looking back now I wish we had done more. Larry Pennington was reaching his zenith on the banjo, and Wayne Henderson was burning that guitar up. Both these great friends were just beginning to be recognized. Larry went on to win many more ribbons and helped to get [the band] Big Country Bluegrass on its feet. Johnny Miller—he used to play with Ola Belle Reed—was doing some unmatched fiddling, and Raymond Pennington played a great mandolin. And he sang a high part that would almost kill your chickens. Paul Gentle played a great rhythm guitar. I played bass.

By the late sixties, I had heard about Wayne Henderson, and I met him at a fiddlers' convention. And we struck off as friends right off the bat. Wayne was a real likeable guy and still is. He was building guitars then, he'd built just a few. So I connected with him. You know, Wayne's early guitars—he didn't have anything to do it with—he scraped the wood down with pieces of broke glass. He had a plane that he used to make the joint for the tops that he'd hold between his knees, a big ol' long jack plane. We became friends, and I got to pickin' with him more. And that's how I got connected in with instrument repairing and building. You had to sorta figure out how to do it yourself. At that time I worked at the furniture factory, and they had a triple drum sander, so Wayne got me to take the tops down there and get the thickness sanded down. I did that for him a lot. I don't do a lot of building myself. Most of my work is restoration of older instruments. I always try to use whatever kind of wood was used at first. A lot of the older ones have red spruce tops, or Appalachian spruce. There's still a little of that around. Usually they have mahogany for the sides and backs, and ebony for the fingerboards and bridges. The older ones were sometimes Brazilian rosewood.

I first heard Doc Watson back in the sixties before he got really real popular. I didn't know him personally back then. I got to see him at fiddlers' conventions here and there, and got to hear him on the radio. But then I went to his house and we became pretty good friends. He used to come to the shop right much. He liked honey and I keep bees, so I took him a quart of honey every once in a while. You know, I admired Doc's music abilities and his determination and outlook on life. I have a brother who's blind, so I understand a little of what he faced. He was handicapped but he never let that stop him or bother him.

Instruments for sale at Main Street Music and Loan, home of
the WKBC Hometown Opry. Photograph by Steve Kruger.

that's tied to the ceiling. It isn't the first time he's ever pulled this prank, but
it seems to work every time.

Main Street Music and Loan isn't a large place—there's room for fewer
than one hundred folks—but when you add in the devoted following of
fans who listen at home and those who watch the show on a local TV station, it draws a very respectable audience. Those who are dedicated enough
to actually brave the early start time and show up in person are in for some
good music and some good company in a fun environment. After the show,
there are lots of places in town to grab some breakfast and maybe have another cup of coffee.

The show at the Main Street Music and Loan often features such talented musicians as Blue Ridge Music Hall of Famers Eric Ellis and David
Johnson. The Wilkes Heritage Museum and Blue Ridge Hall of Fame are
located down the street in the old Wilkes County Courthouse, so while
you're nearby, take that in as well.

WHEN: Second Friday of the month, 7 to 9 A.M.

WHERE: Main Street Music and Loan, 302 Main Street, North Wilkesboro, 28659

ADMISSION: Free

CONTACT: 336-667-2274

WILKES HERITAGE MUSEUM AND THE BLUE RIDGE MUSIC HALL OF FAME
Wilkesboro

The historic town of Wilkesboro, with a population slightly over 3,000, is located along the south bank of the Yadkin River and situated directly opposite its slightly larger sister town of North Wilkesboro. Wilkesboro is the county seat of Wilkes County.

The Wilkes County Courthouse, built in 1902, now houses the Wilkes Heritage Museum and the Blue Ridge Music Hall of Fame. If one had to select a small local history museum anywhere to serve as a model of excellence, it would be the Wilkes Heritage Museum.

Using a varied collection of intriguing artifacts and vintage images, the museum on the ground level of the historic courthouse tells the story of Wilkes County's settlement and industrial development, in addition to interpreting its history in the areas of agriculture, education, law, entertainment, moonshining, medicine, stock-car racing, and transportation. And it's all done in a simple, factual, and interesting way.

The former courtroom on the second floor is now home to the Blue Ridge Music Hall of Fame, developed to preserve and celebrate the musical heritage of the Blue Ridge Mountains region from northern Georgia to northern Virginia. The displays interpret the history of the musical forms that are traditional to the region and highlight many of the most outstanding artists who have performed that music. As the name implies, there is also on display a roster of musicians who have been inducted into the Hall of Fame since its founding in 2008. Inductees include nationally known musicians, traditional dancers, regional musicians, songwriters, pioneer artists, gospel musicians, music scholars, luthiers, side men, recording producers, and promoters. Emmylou Harris, Ralph and Carter Stanley, Ola Belle Reed, Mike Seeger, Doc Watson, and Earl Scruggs are just a few of the recent Hall of Fame inductees.

Two other buildings are part of the Wilkes Heritage Museum complex and available for guided tours. The historic Old Wilkes County Jail (built in 1860) is a short walk from the courthouse and is also maintained by the Heritage Museum. There, visitors can stand in jail cells that held Tom Dooley and his purported accomplice, Anne Melton, during their first trial in

● STORY OF A SONG: OTTO WOOD THE BANDIT

On New Year's Eve in 1930, one of North Carolina's most famous outlaws was killed in a barrage of gunfire. Otto Wood was born in the Dellaplane community of Wilkes County. He spent most of his short life traveling across the country as a bootlegger, a bandit, and a fugitive. As the song would later say, "He loved the women, he hated the law and he just wouldn't take nobody's jaw." Wood committed his first crime (stealing a bicycle) as a teenager. He did time in the Old Wilkes County Jail, also the temporary home of another North Carolina music legend, Tom Dooley. In 1923, Otto shot and killed a pawnbroker in Greensboro named A. W. Kaplan. Allegedly, the argument arose when Kaplan sold a watch Wood had pawned containing a photograph of his beloved mother. Though he was sentenced to thirty years in prison, Wood managed to break out of the North Carolina State Prison four times, quite a feat considering he had a lame foot and had lost a hand in a hunting accident as a teenager.

Otto Wood's mugshot, taken between jailbreaks in the 1920s.

Despite his crimes, Wood was beloved by many people in western North Carolina. In a time of severe economic hardship, he was a Robin Hood character, a generous man who robbed only the rich and was kind to all who remembered him. His exploits are still vividly recalled around Wilkes County to this day. Thousands of people attended Otto Wood's funeral, and the citizens of Salisbury, where he died, raised money to send his body to his mother in West Virginia.

Two songs about Wood were pressed the year after his death. Walter "Kid" Smith and the Carolina Buddies recorded perhaps the most enduring version on the Columbia label just two months after he was laid to rest. The song has gone on to be recorded by Doc Watson. It is also a favorite of Wilkes County musician Herb Key.

Step up, buddies, and listen to my song
I'll sing it to you right, but you may sing it wrong,
All about a man named Otto Wood,
I can't tell you all, but I wish I could.

He walked in a pawn shop a rainy day,
And with the clerk he had a quarrel, they say.
Pulled out his gun and he struck him a blow,
And this is the way the story goes.

They spread the news as fast as they could,
The sheriff served a warrant on Otto Wood.
The jury said murder in the second degree,
And the judge passed the sentence to the penitentiary.

CHORUS: Otto, why didn't you run?
Otto's done dead and gone.
Otto Wood, why didn't you run
When the sheriff pulled out his 44 gun?

They put him in the pen, but it done no good,
It wouldn't hold the man they call Otto Wood.
It wasn't very long till he slipped outside,
Drawed a gun on the guard, said, "Take me for a ride."

Second time they caught him was away out west,
In the holdup game, he got shot through the breast.
They brought him back and when he got well,
They locked him down in a dungeon cell.

He was a man they could not run,
He always carried a 44 gun.
He loved the women and he hated the law,
And he just wouldn't take nobody's jaw.

He rambled out west and he rambled all around,
He met the sheriff in a southern town.
And the sheriff says, "Otto, step this way,
'Cause I've been expecting you every day."

He pulled out his gun and then he said,
"If you make a crooked move, you both fall dead.
Crank up your car and take me out of town,"
And a few minutes later, he was graveyard bound.

◉ Christine Horton: I Have Many Regrets

Christine Horton is an old-time piano and keyboard player. She is the daughter of traditional musicians who taught her to play when she was a child. She lives in the community of Ferguson in Wilkes County.

At one time my ancestors owned this whole valley. That was years ago when this community was known as Elkville, not Ferguson. This place here is real near where Tom Dula courted Laura Foster. My daddy was a musician, and my granddaddy was the champion fiddle player of this whole community. His name was Rufus Horton. My daddy played the guitar some and the fiddle. I hate to brag on him—and he didn't know *all* the songs—but he played the smoothest violin that you've ever heard in your life. His name was W. E. Horton. He'd play "Over the Waves" waltz and a lot of fast tunes, and you could just feel yourself dancin' to hear him play such smooth music. My father, my mother, and I all played, and we would all sing together. Had we had some money and could have gone to Nashville or somewhere like that, we could have, maybe, perhaps, been something like the Carter Family.

I played mainly piano. I didn't play the fiddle; I was too sorry to learn. My mother could sing from a page of music that she'd never seen before. She could look at that song on the page and know what the sound was and what the note was and every-thing. She could sing that song to you and never have to go near a piano to hear it. My mama tried to teach me to read notes, too, but I said, "You're talkin' monkey stuff to me. I'm not gonna fool with that." But I would watch her play a song, and then I could go back and play it myself.

Music, years ago, was a form of entertainment at home. We would go to people's

houses to play music, and they would all come to our house. Boys would bring their girlfriends and get me to play music for them. They'd give me candy to play for 'em. One man who ran a hosiery mill would bring me sacks of socks when I would play. Oh, I had red, blue, and every color of socks you can imagine, coming and going. Entertainment back then was what you could make for yourself, years ago when there wasn't any electricity and there wasn't any television.

I started out making money by playing music when I was thirteen. Back then people were nice. They were well behaved. We played at the VFW hall in North Wilkesboro. I was playing for ten dollars a night, and ten dollars back then could buy you a lot of stuff. By the time I was fourteen, everybody was getting radio programs, playing on WKBC. A lot of people out of Ashe County came down there to play on the radio. Del Reeves even sung there. So I sat down and I wrote me a little letter to WKBC. I addressed it to the manager, and I said I'd like to come down for an interview, to see if I can get me a radio program myself. Well, he wrote me back and said to come on down at a certain time and on a certain day. I walked in there and I played "Lovesick Blues" for him. That song had just been released by Hank Williams. He asked me when did I want my radio program. I told him, "Right now." So I played there for two or three years. But that didn't really make me no money.

I have many regrets. Many. One time my father took me to play for Bill Monroe. He had a tent show set up in Wilkesboro. And Bill Monroe said for him to bring me over to Nashville. But we never got to go. My father died and then my mother had a stroke and I had to take care of her. We didn't have any money to do anything with and I was the only child. We was always looking for a dollar, and there wasn't much of a dollar to be found. Well, I was forty years old, lacking a few days, by the time my mother died. After that I'd say, "I'm gonna leave, I'm gonna leave." I'd say, "I'm gonna get in the car and I'm gonna drive off." But when you're by yourself and there's nobody to go with you, nobody to know where you are, or to know when you're coming back or anything, you can't go. So I just didn't. I kept putting it off.

I had more ambition about playing music back when I was young than I do now. I only play two or three times a year now. I still have a lot of ambitions, but I am seventy-five years old. I'd like to find some decent good place to play, but you can't find that too much now. I'm too lazy to learn all these new songs, so I play old things like "The Tennessee Waltz," old square-dance tunes, and a few slow ones. My most requested song is "Last Date." I told somebody not long ago that I haven't learned a new song since that song came out. I don't know. I just like the old ones.

Wilkes County. Another famous inmate was the outlaw Otto Wood. You can read graffiti carved in the walls by past prisoners and see some excellent pieces of period furniture in the jail-keepers quarters. The Captain Robert Cleveland Home (c. 1779) is a two-story log structure that interprets the story of early colonial settlement in western North Carolina.

A listing of scheduled appearances by nationally and regionally known musicians who appear from time to time at the Wilkes Heritage Museum and the Blue Ridge Music Hall of Fame is available on the museum's website.

WHEN: Tuesdays–Saturdays, 10 A.M. to 4 P.M.
WHERE: 100 East Main Street, Wilkesboro, 28697
ADMISSION: Fee
CONTACT: 336-667-3171
WEBSITE: wilkesheritagemuseum.com

ALLEGHANY COUNTY

THE ALLEGHANY JUBILEE
Sparta

On Saturday evenings year-round in Sparta, the seat of Alleghany County, there's a dance on Main Street. By 7 P.M., small groups of people can be found standing around outside in front of the old Spartan Theater, waiting impatiently for the band to strike up its first tune of the evening. While waiting for the music, some find a seat inside the theater and change from their usual footwear into their stark-white, steel-tap-bottomed dancing shoes. Others quietly converse over a cup of coffee. The scene is the weekly Alle-

Dancing the two-step at the Alleghany Jubilee.

The sign on the window of the Alleghany Jubilee.

ghany Jubilee—where flatfooting, clogging, buckdancing, and especially the mountain two-step are the order of the evening.

Every Saturday evening a hundred or more dancers from all around northwestern North Carolina and southwestern Virginia converge upon the historic Spartan Theater to energetically dance to the music of some of the region's most popular musical groups. For a small admission fee, it's a great show and a wonderful opportunity to see real traditional dancers, who, for the most part, are regulars who come often and are well practiced in local dance and music traditions.

The Spartan Theater is a narrow storefront building located on downtown Sparta's Main Street. The building houses a snack bar, dance floor, and performance stage. Adorning the walls of the hall are snapshots of patrons dancing, eating, and having fun; group portraits of various bands that have appeared there over the years; a few reproductions of William Harnett paintings depicting vintage musical instruments; several large plywood silhouettes of dancing couples; and a variety of other mountain music– and dance-related decorations.

By far the greater part of the room is its cavernous open center, which is meant for dancing. Three groups of vintage folding theater seats are fixed in rows near the rear of the long, rectangular room, creating two narrow aisles that lead to the dance floor. Additional rows of seats and chairs line the side walls and, at the far end of the room, is the bandstand—a raised wall-to-wall platform that's crowded with a sound system and the usual stage paraphernalia—microphone stands, stools, speakers, lights, and drapes.

On a typical night, at 8 P.M. sharp, the band, which has been quietly tuning up onstage for twenty minutes or so, lets go with a fast-paced mountain

● BLUEGRASS TRAILBLAZERS OF THE BLUE RIDGE

In the late 1940s, a new sound came over the airwaves, what folklorist Alan Lomax would later call "folk music with overdrive." It had close vocal harmonies, punctuated by instrumental breaks of virtuosity and improvisation, all set to a driving beat, and soon mountain musicians everywhere were taking it up. What came to be called bluegrass music drew from older regional folk traditions but also incorporated the sounds of contemporary commercial country music, jazz, and blues. Its history today is told mostly in terms of the front men, men like Bill Monroe, Flatt and Scruggs, and the Stanley Brothers. But the lesser-known sidemen and session musicians they hired, the Blue Grass Boys, the Foggy Mountain Boys, and the Clinch Mountain Boys, did just as much to craft that early sound by drawing on their own creativity, their knowledge accumulated from the musical communities they grew up in, and their time spent listening to early radio stars like Fiddlin' Arthur Smith. North Carolina produced some of the most influential of these musicians.

Some famous examples include Earl Scruggs (1924–2012), who got his big break as a banjo player for Bill Monroe's band in the late 1940s, and George Shuffler, a multi-instrumentalist and singer who played with the Stanley Brothers for years and developed the "cross-picking" style of guitar. Carl Story (1916–95), born in Lenoir, was known more for his singing as the "father of bluegrass gospel" but served a brief stint as a fiddler for Bill Monroe. Clyde Moody (1915–89), from Swain County, was the first guitar player for the Blue

Grass Boys and went on to become a country music star, known as the "Hillbilly Waltz King." But some of the instrumentalists are less well

North Carolina Heritage Award–winner Jim Shumate was the first fiddler to record with Flatt and Scruggs and one of many North Carolina musicians who influenced the early development of bluegrass music.

known to those who aren't aficionados of bluegrass music. Two of the most important fiddlers in early bluegrass hail from the northwestern corner of the state.

In 1939, Art Wooten (1906–86) became the first fiddler in Bill Monroe's new band, the Blue Grass Boys. He missed the first recording session but was there for the band's first appearance on the *Grand Ole Opry*. He returned in 1941 to lay down fiddle on the second Bill Monroe session, which included classic fiddle tunes like "The Orange Blossom Special" and "Back Up and Push." He joined the Stanley Brothers in 1948, playing fiddle and singing harmony on many of that group's classic early sessions for Columbia Records. He also toured occasionally with the Foggy Mountain Boys. According to Bill Monroe, "[On] the old time fiddle numbers, he was hard to beat."

Jim Shumate was born in northern Wilkes County and learned to play the fiddle from an uncle who lived nearby. He spent his teenage years working in the furniture factories until he had a lucky break. Bill Monroe was traveling through the area and happen to hear Shumate on Hickory's WHKY. Impressed, he called and offered the young man a job. Shumate played with the Blue Grass Boys from 1943 to 1945, while Howdy Forrester was serving in World War II. He is credited with inventing the iconic "fiddle kickoff," a way of leading into a song with a few staccato notes and a short instrumental. Shumate is also credited with introducing Bill Monroe to Earl Scruggs in 1945. After Flatt and Scruggs left to form their own group in 1948, they hired Shumate to play on their first recording session. He can be heard on one of their earliest and best-known recordings, "My Cabin in Caroline."

Life for a touring bluegrass musician in the early days was tough. Pay was scanty and bands worked hard, remaining on the road, away from home, for long periods of time. They were essentially hired hands employed by the band leaders, and turnover was high. Often members would spend a few years with a well-known act and then strike out on their own, as Flatt and Scruggs did. Others made their way home and worked outside of music. Still, many of those musicians like Shumate and Wooten continued to play on the local and regional bluegrass circuit and helped mentor and inspire the next generation of musicians in their home communities.

● JUNIOR APPALACHIAN MUSICIANS (JAM) PROGRAM

At the Sparta Elementary School on Wednesday afternoons, you will hear the sounds of the next generation of old-time and bluegrass musicians coming into their own. Children as young as seven and eight years old, wielding fiddles, mandolins, banjos, and guitars, cluster in small bands or in circles around their instructors. Helen White, a guidance counselor for the Alleghany County schools, founded the Junior Appalachian Musician (JAM) program in 2000. The idea was to make learning mountain music an option for all kids through subsidized instruction and instrument rental fees. That would in turn inspire pride and interest in the young people's own heritage and would help provide a healthy place where the community could come together, all while injecting new life into the region's traditional music scene. JAM students learn in a small-group setting, with a heavy emphasis on playing by ear, as opposed to relying only on sheet music or tablature. The classes are taught by some of the region's most talented artists, many who grew up playing old-time or bluegrass. Students also learn about the history of the music, take field trips to music venues, and spend time with musical elders from the community.

JAM ensembles and bands perform around the region, even at the beginning level. The musicians who go through the whole program acquire up to ten years of experience, and some go on to make records and take home prizes at fiddlers' conventions. The idea has proved popular, and JAM and other similar programs have spread across the mountain regions of North Carolina, South Carolina, and Virginia. The Stecoah Valley Arts Center in Graham County hosts a JAM program, and if you come to the Jones House Jam in Boone, you may get a chance to hear students from the JAM program, which meets on Thursday afternoons before the jam begins.

The North Carolina Arts Council

JAM students performing at the Stecoah Valley Cultural Arts Center in Graham County. Photograph by Robin Dreyer. Courtesy of the North Carolina Arts Council.

favorite—"Old Joe Clark," for example—at considerable volume, fiddle and banjo in the lead. Just as suddenly, sixty or more dancers immediately hit the floor, white bucks flashing, and begin rhythmically shuffling around in partnered pairs, dancing the mountain two-step. Their shoes are fixed with hard steel taps on heel and toe, and the dancers loudly stomp on the hardwood floor with great zeal in unison with the rhythm of the old-time fiddle tune. For the uninitiated, it's a stunning moment.

On Tuesday nights at the theater, there's another bluegrass and old-time picking session with dancing. The public is welcome to join in and dance or to simply enjoy listening to the music.

There's lots of on- and off-street parking nearby. Coffee, soft drinks, and snacks are available for purchase.

WHEN: Tuesdays, 7 to 10 P.M.; Saturdays, 8 to 11 P.M.
WHERE: The Spartan Theater, 25 North Main Street, Sparta, 28765
ADMISSION: Fee, but children under 12 admitted free
CONTACT: 336-372-4591
WEBSITE: alleghanyjubilee.com

ASHE COUNTY

OLA BELLE REED MUSIC FESTIVAL
Lansing

Born in the mountains fifty years ago,
I've trod the hills and valleys through the rain and snow,
I've seen the lightning flashing I've heard the thunder roll,
I've endured, I've endured how long can one endure.

Ola Belle Reed seated with "hollerer" Leonard Emanuel and blues musician "Peg Leg" Sam Jackson at the 1975 North Carolina Folklife Festival. Courtesy of the photographer, Bill Boyarsky.

Barefoot in the summer on into the fall,
Too many mouths to feed, they couldn't clothe us all,
Sent to church on Sunday to learn the golden rule,
I've endured, I've endured how long can one endure.

I've worked for the rich, I've lived with the poor,
I've see many a heartache, there'll be many a more,
Lived loved and sorrowed, been to success's door,
I've endured, I've endured how long can one endure.
—Ola Belle Reed, "I've Endured"

During the Great Depression, thousands of families left the mountains to seek employment in mill towns and industrial cities in the Piedmont, the Ohio Valley, or the North. Yet they maintained their connections to home by returning frequently to visit and by continuing to play the music they first learned in the mountains. Ashe County native Ola Belle Reed (1916–2002) was one of those who moved north but still kept her family's musical traditions strong. She was born into a large family, many of whom were instrumentalists and singers, including a grandfather who was both a Primitive Baptist preacher and a fiddle player. Ola Belle took up the clawhammer banjo as a young girl and developed a powerful singing voice. After she and her family migrated to Maryland, they formed a family band called the North Carolina Ridge Runners, playing at parks, picnics, and music halls, usually for appreciative crowds of fellow Appalachian migrants. Later the Reeds helped organize the New River Ranch, a music park near Rising Sun, Maryland, where some of the biggest names in bluegrass and country music performed for audiences in the urban mid-Atlantic states.

Ola Belle Reed sang traditional songs and hymns, but she became best known for her original songs. Many of those have become standards, for example, "High on a Mountain," "My Epitaph," and "I've Endured." In 1986 she received a National Heritage Fellowship from the National Endowment for the Arts, the country's highest honor for traditional artists. The Ola Belle Reed Music Festival held in her hometown of Lansing celebrates her accomplishments and legacy. The festival takes place in a park located along the route of an old logging railroad that once ran from nearby town of Todd into Virginia. On Friday and Saturday regional musicians perform and hold workshops on music and dance, featuring a nice balance of traditional old-time and bluegrass music.

Camping is available on-site.

WHEN: Schedule of events varies; check website or call for details.
WHERE: Lansing Creeper Trail Park, Lansing, 28643. In Lansing, look for Teaberry Road. Go across the low-water bridge. (Don't worry! It's safe, even for big RVs.) Take the first right across the bridge onto H Street, and you will see the festival grounds.
ADMISSION: Free, but donations are encouraged
CONTACT: 336-977-1320; for camping information, call 336-384-4311
WEBSITE: www.olabellefest.com

OLD HELTON SCHOOL HOG STOMP
Sturgills
Every Thursday evening in Sturgills there's a social gathering, dance, and jam session that's locally called the "Hog Stomp." This friendly and fun

A jam session at the Old Helton School.

event is held at the Old Helton School, a small brick and frame building that serves as a community center for the northern area of Ashe County. Once led principally by the fiddler Dean Sturgill and the late tobacco farmer and bluegrass banjo player Larry Pennington (1946–2003), this weekly event is truly a community-based entertainment venue. It's very popular with local folks, and the small classroom turned concert hall is frequently filled to overflowing by 7 P.M.

Despite the fact that there are numerous participating musicians—as many as fifteen at times—the event is more a performance than it is a jam session. The musicians stand while they play, and there's a very clear delineation between the performing musicians and the appreciative audience members who show up to listen and dance to the music.

The musicians group together at one end of the room as they play. A variety of second-hand chairs and sofas, two deep, line the walls around the room. A small closet-sized kitchen on the end of the room opposite the players holds a pot of fresh coffee, home-baked cakes, and store-bought cookies brought by local ladies in attendance.

While the musicians play, a small number of individual dancers may occasionally flatfoot dance inside the circle of listeners. Otherwise, most who are there simply sit comfortably to the side, watch the musicians, and listen to the music.

The music at the Old Helton School is typically presented in two sessions, each lasting about an hour or a little more. If the weather's not too cold or rainy, the musicians will often move their second set outdoors to an adjacent parking area or on the elongated concrete porch that borders the south side of the building. There the music and dancing continues until around 10 P.M.

WHEN: Thursdays, 7 to 11 P.M.
WHERE: Old Helton School on Old Helton School Road, Lansing, 28643. From Lansing, head north on NC 194 approximately 4 miles to the Sturgills community. Pass by the intersection of the road that goes to Whitetop (Helton Creek Road) and then take the next driveway on the right (just before you reach a new concrete bridge). The Old Helton School is located at the end of the driveway.
ADMISSION: Free, but donations are accepted
CONTACT: Rita or Jerry Moore, 336-384-4707

Near Lansing

Phipps General Store is a small, simple white wooden building set alongside Silas Creek Road, which winds through the picturesque rolling countryside near the north fork of the New River in Ashe County. It is still in the family who operated it when it was a functioning general store. On Fridays, Rita and Jim "Dawg" Wood, open the doors for a jam session that can be one of the most lively in the region. During the summer, people might be playing out on the porch or on the grass. In the winter, pickers sit in straight-back chairs and warm up by the woodstove. Like the Helton School, it is a local social event, and it also draws regulars from surrounding counties. Spectators sit and chat in benches by the old counter, or in chairs surrounding the musicians, occasionally getting up to flatfoot, if the music has a good dance beat. It often does. The Phipps Store jam is unusual in that it is enthusiastically attended by both old-time and bluegrass musicians. The session can favor one style or the other depending on who shows up. If the weather is warm, there may be two separate jams or people will take turns playing. Often the music is reminiscent of what some call the "transitional sound" that emerged in northwestern North Carolina and southwestern Virginia in the 1950s and 1960s. Most of the musicians at that time had grown up with a local old-time music style, but they were also influenced to varying degrees by early bluegrass. A band competing at a fiddlers' convention at that time (before there were separate categories for music type) might have had a bluegrass banjo player and an old-time fiddler, or vice versa. For many, then and now, it is all mountain music. That spirit is alive and well at Phipps. On any given night you can hear good mountain music played by people of all ages, and visitors are welcome to participate. The store also sells refreshments and local artwork and hosts a musical "breaking up Christmas" party around the 5th or 6th of January, depending on the weather. This is a nod to an old tradition in the southern mountains, where in each community there would be a house party every night for twelve days after the 25th.

WHEN: Fridays, 7 to 10 P.M.

WHERE: 2425 Silas Creek Road, Lansing, 28643. *From Jefferson*, go 4.4 miles on North Main/Old Hwy 16. Turn left on North Fork New River Road and go .5 miles. Cross the river bridge, turn right on Silas Creek Road, and go 3 miles. *From Lansing*, take Piney Creek Road (which will turn into Bart Hurley Road) for 3.9 miles. The store is located at the corner of Bart Hurley and Silas Creek Roads.

CONTACT: Jim and Rita Wood, 336-384-2382

Contrary to its name, the New is one of the oldest rivers in North America.

TODD NEW RIVER FESTIVAL AND MORE
Todd

Todd is one of many mountain towns whose fortunes have waxed and waned along with the timber industry. During the last decades of the nineteenth century and into the beginning of the twentieth, expanding rail lines opened up the last corners of North Carolina to logging operations. Todd was the last stop on the Virginia Creeper line. Even though it had existed earlier as a small trading community known as Elk Crossroads, it really blossomed during the heyday of timbering. By the height of the timber boom in the early twentieth century, Todd was larger than the town of Boone. However, two catastrophic floods—one in 1916 and another in 1940—washed out the railroad tracks that served the logging industry. The floods and depleted resources forced a decline in the economies of all the timbering boomtowns in the North Carolina mountains, and Todd was no exception. Today, the picturesque village is spread out along one last short stretch of that nearly forgotten railroad, the only clue to the town's industrial past.

During recent years, the town of Todd has evolved into a visitor destination. Two historic structures in the town—the Todd General Store (built in 1914) and the tin-sided Todd Mercantile (built in 1910)—host traditional music events. The General Store hosts a bluegrass jam on Friday nights from 6:30 to 9:15 P.M. The Todd Mercantile, now a bakery and café, has square or contra dances one Friday evening a month, January to April. The dancing happens on an old wooden floor in a room that otherwise functions as a gallery for local artisans whose work is also for sale.

During the summer, the Todd Community Preservation Organization holds free concerts every other Saturday from the end of June through the beginning of August in Cook Park. The concerts often feature quality traditional music from the region and beyond. Past performers there even included a well-known neighbor from Deep Gap, Doc Watson.

In October, the town of Todd celebrates the natural and cultural heritage of the New River, which runs along the edge of town. The Todd New River Festival, staged at Cook Park, offers an old-fashioned gospel sing, a checkers playoff, a horseshoe toss, craft displays, storytelling, and a fishing tournament. There is also a full day of bluegrass and old-time music, and craft and food vendors.

EVENT: Todd New River Festival
WHEN: Second Saturday in October, 9 A.M. to 6 P.M.
WHERE: Cook Park, Railroad Grade Road, Todd, 28684. Todd is located about 11 miles north of Boone on NC 194, across the Ashe County line. Look for Railroad Grade Road on your right and Three Top Road on your left.
ADMISSION: Free
CONTACT: Todd Ruritan Club, 828-964-1362
WEBSITE: http://www.toddruritan.com

EVENT: Jam Sessions at the Todd General Store
WHEN: Fridays, 6:30 to 9:15 P.M.
WHERE: The Todd General Store, 3866 Railroad Grade Road, Todd, 28684. See directions to Todd New River Festival, above.
ADMISSION: Free
CONTACT: 336-877-1067
WEBSITE: www.toddgeneralstore.com

EVENT: Todd Concert Series
WHEN: Some Saturdays, June–August. Check website for details.
WHERE: Cook Park on Railroad Grade Road, across from the Todd General Store. See directions to Todd New River Festival, above.
ADMISSION: Free
CONTACT: Todd Community Preservation Organization, 336-877-5401
WEBSITE: www.toddnc.org

EVENT: Dances at the Todd Mercantile
WHEN: One Friday evening a month, January–April. Check website for details.

O Dorothy Hess

Dorothy Hess lives in a beautifully manicured mountain cottage that's surrounded by a yard full of carefully maintained flower beds. She continues to sing and play the dozens of love songs she learned as a child from her mother.

I didn't take my first step until I was five years old. I'll always remember that day. I stood up, and I cried, "I can't do it!" But the doctor said, "Just take one step. If you fall, I'll catch you." I took one step and over I went. But he caught me! I got brave then and I started walking a little bit more each day.

I was born in Lebanon, Virginia, in 1929. I was born with a bone deformity, and I guess being able to sing and strum on my guitar kind of compensated for that. My legs were bent backwards against my bottom and my feet turned under 'til my toes touched my heels. I spent most of my first seventeen years in the crippled children's hospital in Richmond, Virginia. When I'd get to come home, Mother would sing for me. I loved to hear the music. She would sing all these folk songs, real sad things. I loved them. When I'd go back to the hospital, I would try all of those songs out. I knew them right down pat. I'd lay there and sing all the time. That was just my thing.

Mom and Dad always tried to get me to make a recording when I was just a youngster. They said I was really good. And I would just yodel as hard as I could. I'd have the nurses piled around my bed saying, "Do that again!" But getting out in front of the public was another story. I had been teased so much at school—the other children gave me a hard time. You would think that they would understand that I couldn't help how I was, but, you know, children can be cruel. They were cruel.

Mother played the banjo. My sister played guitar. They were on the radio in

Bristol, Virginia. They had a Saturday night jamboree there in a huge auditorium, and it was always packed full of people. My mom and my sister, they had these old, old outfits with black bonnets and black dresses, and they went as "Lizie and Kate." Sort of comedians, you know. They really took the shows! Mama played banjo, claw-hammer style. My younger sister took up the banjo. My older sister taught me to play the guitar. One day she said, "Do you want to learn to play?" And I said, "Yes, I do, but I don't think I can do it." But I did. I sang on the radio. I was just a little thing, and I was in my braces. The crowd loved it.

Sometimes I'd stay there at the hospital for a year and a half at a time without ever coming home. To a child, that's a long time. I'd be so homesick. While I was in the hospital, I cried every night. *Every* night. I'd lay in the bed and I'd hear a train way off somewhere, and I'd lay there and cry. It was probably just a freight train, but I didn't care, I'd wanted to be on it headed home. It was a hard life, but I think it has made me see things a lot different from other people. Things look a lot better to me than they might to somebody else, because of the things that I have endured. I'm a fighter. I'm really a fighter.

Now I've started going to the fiddlers' conventions, singing all of Mama's songs that she had taught me. I love to sing around in the background at the fiddlers' conventions after the stage part is over, and entertain people. You really meet a lot of people that way. And they love the songs. I want this music to be passed on to the younger generation. And I'm seeing more of it now than I ever have. It pleases me. I don't want it to be forgotten. I want what I knew in my younger days to be carried on. I want my songs to be passed on to someone who will pick up on them and carry them on.

WHERE: Todd Mercantile, 3899 Railroad Grade Road, Todd, 28684. See directions to Todd New River Festival, above.
ADMISSION: Fee
CONTACT: Todd Community Preservation Organization, 336-877-5401
WEBSITE: toddmercantile.blogspot.com or www.toddnc.org

WATAUGA COUNTY

MUSIC AT THE JONES HOUSE COMMUNITY CENTER
Boone

The town of Boone, at an elevation of more than 3,300 feet above sea level, might be best known as the home of Appalachian State University, which

The Doc Watson statue in downtown Boone was dedicated in 2011. Doc got his start busking on the streets of Boone and Lenoir in the 1940s and 1950s. Photograph by Fred C. Fussell.

has a student population of more than 17,000. Named for pioneer woodsman Daniel Boone, who supposedly camped where the town is now located, Boone is also a vacation destination for lowlanders trying to beat the summer heat. Boone has a thriving arts and music scene. Watauga County's most famous traditional musician, Arthel "Doc" Watson (1923–2012), lived nearby. In 2011, the town of Boone dedicated a life-sized bronze statue to Doc Watson, who got his start back in the 1930s "busking" on Boone's King Street.

A block east of the Doc Watson statue is the Jones House, a historic home built in 1908. Situated on a hill overlooking downtown Boone, the Jones House is owned by the town of Boone and hosts Concerts on the Lawn, where traditional music groups set up on the elevated front porch of the Jones House and present a free concert. Friends and visitors bring their chairs and blankets or sit right on the grassy lawn while enjoying some of the High Country's best traditional music, in addition to other genres like blues and country music.

Jones House is also the venue for old-time jam sessions on Thursday evenings. Musicians from all around the area gather in the many rooms on both floors of the two-story house and play fiddles, banjos, guitars, and other traditional instruments. They even spill out onto the front porch in warm weather. Since the Watauga County Junior Appalachian Musicians (JAM) program holds its classes in the Jones House, it is not uncommon to see musicians from three generations participating in a single session. The jam sessions are open to anyone who wants to play, and listeners are always welcomed.

WHEN: Concert on the lawn: Fridays, June–September, 5 P.M.; jam session: Thursdays, year-round, 7:30 P.M.

"THE FARMER IS THE ONE WHO FEEDS THEM ALL": A WORD ON FARMERS' MARKETS

Songs and tunes about life on the farm are a part of the repertoire of almost every Blue Ridge musician. Any fiddler worth his salt does a unique version of "Cacklin' Hen," with the bow and strings imitating the sounds of the chicken coop. There are songs about food and farming by the score, and fiddle tunes with names like "Tater Patch" and "Blackberry Blossom." In the past, the cycles of agriculture also afforded opportunities for musicians. Cornshuckings, tobacco markets, livestock auctions, and molasses boils were places where musicians could meet, play and sometimes pick up some extra cash.

Traditional music remains connected to agriculture and rural life for many of the people who live in western North Carolina, and many musicians raise gardens, farm, or are part of the farming community. At local farmers' markets across the region, you will often see the two traditions—agriculture and music—side by side. Occasionally, you may even see musician-farmers playing music between sales, or selling CDs alongside their fresh North Carolina produce, baked goods, and crafts. Some farmers' markets go a step further and hire musicians or host jam sessions as a way to attract customers to their wares. Examples of that practice are the Saturday morning sale at the Watauga

County Farmers' Market in Boone and the historic Haywood Farmers' Market in Waynesville. The North Carolina Department of Agriculture provides a list of farmers' markets at www.ncfarmfresh.com.

Roadside produce stands and farmers' markets are a common sight in the Blue Ridge Mountains.

WHERE: 604 West King Street, Boone, 28607
CONTACT: Jones House Community Center, 828-262-4576
ADMISSION: Free
WEBSITE: www.joneshousecommunitycenter.org

MUSIC FEST 'N SUGAR GROVE
Sugar Grove

During the Great Depression, the Works Progress Administration (WPA) funded the building of schools throughout Appalachia. Many school buildings were made from local stone fashioned and placed by local hands. In addition to serving as schools, the beautiful buildings provided a place for the local community to meet and enjoy social events. As school systems consolidated, many of the old stone schoolhouses were abandoned or demolished. Some of these historic structures are finding new life as community centers, among them the Cove Creek School, site of the Music Fest 'n Sugar Grove.

After the Cove Creek School was closed in 1995, alumni of the school, assisted by other local citizens, formed a nonprofit organization to turn the school into a multi-use space, one that would serve both small businesses in the area and also function as a local community center.

The Music Fest 'n Sugar Grove takes place on the second Friday and Saturday in July on the grounds of the Cove Creek School, which is now a National Register of Historic Places landmark. The festival is similar in some respects to MerleFest, presenting a line-up of local as well as nationally known bluegrass and roots musicians. The deeper focus, however, is on Appalachian music. Admission fees from the festival go toward building renovations and funding the Doc and Merle Watson Museum, located inside the old school. The museum depicts the lives and careers of various Watauga County musicians and folk artists, with a focus on the careers of Doc and Merle Watson. It houses a variety of the Watsons' musical instruments, some of the many awards and gold records they earned over the years, and stage apparel Doc has worn while performing.

A distance away from the stage, there are several rows of tents arranged for vendors to sell food and handmade crafts. Many of the musicians who perform there sell their own merchandise—CDs and such—providing a chance for them to interact with their fans. The music under the main performance tent lasts throughout the day and continues well into the night. Smaller concerts, along with programs for children, take place inside the museum.

The Music Fest 'n Sugar Grove is presented through a partnership be-

Region 2

Doc Watson at Sugar Grove in 2000. The building behind him has a small museum devoted to Watson and other traditional artists from Watauga County. Musicians can often be found at tables near the stage signing autographs and selling merchandise after their set.

tween the Cove Creek Preservation Association and the Sustainable Development program at Appalachian State University. The university provides equipment and material resources and volunteers and assists in funding the solar-powered side stage. Parking areas are available off-site. A shuttle service is provided.

WHEN: Friday, 4 P.M. until ?, and Saturday, 9 A.M. until ?, second weekend in July

WHERE: Cove Creek School, 207 Dale Adams Road, Sugar Grove, 28679. From Boone, take US 421 north toward Tennessee. Take a left on US 321. Take a slight right onto Old 421. Follow signs to parking.

ADMISSION: Fee

CONTACT: 828-297-2200

Website: http://musicfestnsugargrove.org or www.covecreek.net.

○ DOC WATSON: A TRIBUTE

Few musicians have had as great an influence on mountain music as Arthel "Doc" Watson. Doc Watson played and sang nearly every genre of mountain music—unaccompanied ballad and religious singing, old-time music, bluegrass, blues, gospel, country, even rockabilly and jazz. His influence on guitar styles, particularly flat-picking, is immeasurable. But he was also skilled on the banjo, the autoharp, the harmonica, and the mandolin, and he had a rich, soulful singing voice. Doc interpreted the older styles through his own personality, producing something that was simultaneously gritty and clean and combined authentic tradition with innovation. For many lifelong devotees, his recordings were the gateway to their love of traditional music.

Doc Watson's musical life had its roots in family and in community. He was born in the Stoney Fork community near Deep Gap, North Carolina, on March 3, 1923, one of nine children. From his earliest days of childhood, the Watson home was always filled with homemade music. The family all sang at church. His father, General Dixon Watson, was a banjo and harmonica player. His mother, Annie Greene Watson, sang old-time ballads and hymns. The family owned a windup Victrola that enabled young Doc Watson to hear and learn from such early rural southern recording artists as the Carter Family, Grayson and Whitter, and the Carolina Tar Heels. But they also had blues and popular music recordings. From his earliest days, he listened to everything.

Doc Watson suffered an eye infection while still an infant and lost his sight before the age of one. Despite this handicap, his father instilled in him a fierce belief in self-reliance. Even though he was unable to see, Doc Watson learned to saw lumber using a crosscut saw and to help out in many other ways around the farm. His father also encouraged him musically, thinking it might be away for his son to make a living. He was just five years old when he picked up his first instrument—a harmonica. Later, at age eleven, his father built him a banjo with a catskin head, and he quickly mastered both the two-finger and the clawhammer styles. But the guitar had always fascinated him on records. He spent a few adolescent years at the Governor Morehead School for the Blind in Raleigh. There he met a fellow student, a young jazz musician named Paul Montgomery. Montgomery gave Doc guitar lessons in exchange for some pointers on the banjo. On a visit back to the mountains, Doc knew he had to get one. According to Doc's friend David Holt: "General Watson heard Doc noodling on his older brother's guitar. General said, 'If you can learn to play a song by the time I get home from work, we'll put our money together and buy you a guitar of your own.' Doc didn't tell him that Paul Montgomery had been teaching him and that evening played 'When the Roses Bloom in Dixieland' for General. The next day they bought a little Stella guitar."*

He started out with the "Carter scratch," the style made famous by Maybelle Carter. But he soon learned flat-picking and the alternating thumb-finger style of Merle Travis.

In the 1940s, he began performing at land sales, on the radio, and on the streets of Boone and Lenoir, wherever he could make some money. He got his nickname during a radio performance in Lenoir. The announcer proclaimed that Arthel was just too long a name for the airwaves. A woman in the audience called out, "Name him Doc!"

Doc met Rosa Lee, his wife of over sixty-five years, while visiting her father, the great old-time fiddle and banjo player Gaither Carlton. Doc and Rosa Lee were married in 1947. The marriage produced two children—Eddy "Merle" Watson and Nancy Ellen Watson. During his early years of marriage, Doc supported himself and his family by tuning pianos and playing electric guitar in a local country band. It was then that he began developing his own flat-picking style of lead guitar. When the crowd wanted a square dance tune, he would use a flat pick to play traditional mountain fiddle tunes like "Blackberry Blossom" and "Black Mountain Rag" note for note. The dances could last for twenty minutes, giving him plenty of time to hone what would become one of his trademark original sounds.

When folklorists Eugene Earl and Ralph Rinzler were in North Carolina in 1960 looking for old-time musicians, they found Doc Watson through musician Clarence Ashley. Ashley was one of the original Carolina Tar Heels, a popular string band from the 1920s and 1930s, and his music had earlier been featured on the *Harry Smith Anthology of American Folk Music*. Ralph Rinzler didn't want anything to do with the young rock and roller, until he heard him play Tom Dooley on the banjo and realized that despite the Les Paul and the amplifier, Doc knew traditional music. The folk music revival movement was in full swing at the time, and new young audiences were hungry for authentic folk music from the southern mountains. With Rinzler's encouragement, Doc Watson headed north and performed at various urban folk clubs and the Newport Folk Festival, all to great acclaim. He released several record albums on the Folkways Label, first with Clarence Ashley, Fred Price, and Clint Howard, and then on several subsequent albums that featured duets with Bill Monroe and Jean Ritchie. Later he recorded seminal albums that included the entire

*David Holt, "Music Is Such a Wonderful Sound," from David Holt's website, www.davidholt.com, May 29, 2012.

Watson family, introducing the listening public to Doc's fiddling father-in-law Gaither Carlton, to his wife Rosa Lee, his mother Annie Watson, and his grandmother Dolly Greer, all singers; and to his brother Arnold Watson, a great banjo player, and his cousin Willard, who also played banjo.

Throughout the 1960s and 1970s, Doc Watson enjoyed ever growing successes as a musician. He was joined, both on recordings and on the road, by his son Merle, who had himself become a fine guitarist. The pair released several now-legendary records and collaborated with the Nitty Gritty Dirt Band, Chet Atkins, and several other popular recording artists. They toured widely, all the while bringing dozens of traditional songs of the Blue Ridge into worldwide circulation.

In 1985, Merle Watson was tragically killed in a tractor accident when he was only thirty-six years old. Recalling that horrific incident, Doc Watson later told *Acoustic Magazine*:

> The night before the funeral I had decided to quit, just give up playing. Well that night I had this dream. Now, usually I do have some light perception, but in this dream it was so dark I could hardly stand it. It was like I was in quicksand up to my waist and I felt I wasn't gonna make it out alive. Then suddenly this big old strong hand reached back and grabbed me by the hand and I heard this voice saying, "Come on dad, you can make it. Keep going." Then I woke up. I think the good Lord was telling me it was all right to continue with my music. It's been a struggle, but I still have the love for the music.*

Three years later, in 1988, the first MerleFest, staged in memory of Merle Watson, took place on the campus of Wilkes Community College in Wilkesboro. That same year, Doc Watson won a National Heritage Fellowship, the nation's highest honor for a traditional artist. In its first quarter-century, MerleFest has grown from a small festival to a four-day event to which audiences numbering 75,000 or more come from all over the world.

In his later years, Doc Watson typically performed close to his home community of Deep Gap often to the accompaniment of his grandson, Richard. He lived his whole life in western North Carolina, in a home that he maintained himself, despite not being able to see. Though he loved to play music, he often said he would have rather made a living as a carpenter or an electrician. He always considered himself "one of the people." Doc passed away on Memorial Day, May 29, 2012.

* Dan Miller, *Flatpicking Guitar Magazine* 2, no. 6 (September/October 1998).

THE MOUNTAIN BANJO

The area around Beech Mountain, which straddles the border of Watauga and Avery Counties, is renowned for its storytelling tradition. A native of the area, Ray Hicks (1922–2003), was a world famous teller of Jack tales, folktales centered around a clever character nicknamed "Jack." Today his son Ted and relative Orville Hicks are still telling the old tales. Where there is good storytelling to be heard, good musicians are also often close at hand. Many fine ballad singers and banjo and dulcimer players have made their homes on Beech Mountain.

In past generations when cash was scarce for many families, mountain musicians made musical instruments by hand rather than ordering a manufactured instrument from a catalog or purchasing one from a music store in town. However, factory-made banjos, with their complicated machined parts and metal brackets, were difficult to replicate. Instrument makers in the southern mountains innovated an instrument that is now referred to as the "mountain banjo." On Beech Mountain, this was the type of banjo that was

Rick Ward, a third-generation banjo maker and fifth-generation musician, plays outside his shop in Sugar Grove. Note the lack of frets and metal brackets and the inset head, characteristic of the mountain banjo. Courtesy of the photographer, Mark Freed.

most commonly used by the old-time musicians. On the homemade, hand-crafted mountain banjos, the metal parts found on fancier instruments were replaced with wooden frames and dowels. The hooped rims of the instruments were made from split and smoothed strips of local mountain hardwood. In addition, the small, inset animal-skin heads on mountain banjos were made from the hides of squirrels, groundhogs, or even cats. An old-school mountain banjo maker named Clifford Glenn claimed that you had to be a good enough shot to hit a squirrel exactly through the right eye in order to have a hide that was big enough to make a mountain banjo. Mountain banjos are fretless, devoid of any "speed bumps," an adaptation that allows musicians to easily slide their fingers up and down the fret-board between notes. The tuning pegs are made of wood, like fiddle pegs.

The folk boom of the 1960s led to an increased interest in the mountain banjo and in another traditional handmade instrument, the mountain dulcimer. Mountain instrument builders and musicians Frank Proffitt, National Heritage Fellow Stanley Hicks, Ed Presnell, and Leonard and Clifford Glenn sold mountain banjos and dulcimers to clients across the United States and as far away as Europe and Japan. The mountain banjo continues to be played today by members of the same families that have made them for generations. If you should be fortunate enough to hear a maker like Rick Ward or Charlie Glenn play one of his beautiful creations of native cherry, maple, or walnut, not only are you hearing the expression and ingenuity of the maker, but you're hearing a musical tradition that goes back to the nineteenth century.

It Strikes with Terror in My Heart

Many of the old ballads sung in the Blue Ridge tell the stories of real people, people who once lived, loved, and died in the communities travelers may pass on their way to a fiddlers' convention or a dance hall. Their stories live on in the memories of those who grew up nearby, and those memories are still present in the landscape, for those who know where to look. Not all landscapes in the Blue Ridge have the racing waters of a mountain river, the wet dark shadows of a temperate rainforest, the lofty heights of a dizzying overlook, or the shimmering skylight of a dramatic vista. Some places are special for the mysterious quality that comes when one has an understanding of the human conflicts and interactions that have occurred there.

The tranquil community of Kona, in Mitchell County, is such a place. The century-old Kona Baptist Church, at the center of the community, is a small, neatly painted, white wood-frame chapel poised just above the curving paved surface of Highway 80. It sits beside the summit of a round sod-covered peak. Its front overlooks the broad lush valley of the Toe River and peeks westward beyond the treetops toward the lofty blue hills of Yancey County. The dual tracks of the Clinchfield and Yancey Railroads run parallel along the margin of the riverbank below. For several miles, the twin railroad tracks hug the low river bluff, traveling from northwest to southeast. They then split apart, each to follow its own chosen branch of the river—the Yancey sticking with the westerly flow, and the Clinchfield hanging with the more southeasterly branch.

On a grassy knoll immediately behind and uphill from the Kona Baptist Church, a small graveyard overlooks the ancestral mountain homeplace of the Silver family. An old log dogtrot house, the Silver family pioneer homestead, sits several hundred yards away from the graveyard, down the hill and under a slope, almost hidden from view. The final resting places of several generations of the Silver family and their kin are entombed here in this isolated High Country burial ground. Among them, side by side and close together, are three marked graves—three graves for one man named Charles Silver.

The Kona Baptist Church and Silver Family Museum in Mitchell County.

To the north of the cemetery, down a steep hill, through a quarter mile or more of nearly impenetrable forested slope, lie a number of flat stones scattered about, hidden among the trees and the bushes. Those stones are the only remaining vestiges of a now infamous hewn-log mountain cabin that was once the pioneer home of the young Charles Silver and his wife, Frankie.

Charles Silver, or Charlie, as he was often called, was murdered by Frankie, who chopped off his head with an ax as he napped on a pallet on the cabin floor on December 22, 1831. Their little child, a toddler named Nancy, was asleep in his arms, apparently the only witness to the murder— or so the story sometimes goes, a story that has sustained both popular and academic interest among North Carolinians for nearly two centuries. English and journalism professor Lana Whited writes on her website (http://www2.ferrum.edu/lwhited/frankiesilver/):

Region 3

On Dec. 22, 1831, Charles Silver was murdered at his cabin in Burke County, N.C. His body was dismembered and parts subsequently found at various locations in and around the cabin. On Jan. 10, 1832, his wife, Frances ("Frankie") Stewart Silver, her mother Barbara Stewart, and brother Blackstone Stewart were taken to Morganton, N.C., and charged with the crime. Barbara and Blackstone Stewart were released on Jan. 17 due to insufficient evidence, but Frankie was indicted by the grand jury in March 1832 and tried later that month. She was convicted on April 2, and sentenced to be hanged on July 27 of the same year. Documents were sent to the N.C. Supreme Court for appeal, but oral arguments were not made on her behalf. The verdict was upheld, and Frankie Stewart Silver was hanged in Morganton on July 12, 1833. Charlie Silver is buried behind the Kona Baptist Church in Mitchell County, N.C., in three separate graves. Frankie Silver is buried about nine miles west of Morganton.

At the time of the murder, Frankie Silver was only eighteen years old. Her husband, Charlie, was nineteen.

Nobody knows why this young mountain wife and mother slayed the young man, but it's been said by some that Charlie was a popular dancer, a fanciful fellow who may have been more than just a sociable companion to some of the other young ladies around the isolated community; he had a roving eye, and jealousy was the motivation for the killing. Others think that he was abusive and mean to Frankie, and she acted to defend herself. Another notion still is that Frankie wanted to leave the remote Blue Ridge hilltops and Toe River backwoods and move westward to Kentucky to search for greener pastures. But such a move would have necessitated

THE BALLAD OF FRANKIE SILVER (AS SUNG BY BOBBY MCMILLON, DECEMBER 1, 1999)

This dreadful, dark and dismal day
Has swept my glories all away;
My sun goes down, my days are past,
And I must leave this world at last.
Oh! Lord, what will become of me?
I am condemned, you all now see;
To heaven or hell my soul must fly,
All in a moment when I die.
Judge Daniels has my sentence passed;
These prison walls I leave at last;
Nothing to cheer my drooping head,
Until I'm numbered with the dead.
But, Oh, that zealous judge I fear;
Shall I that awful sentence hear?
"Depart, ye cursed, down to hell,
And forever there to dwell."
There shall I meet that mournful face,
Whose blood I spilled upon this place;
With flaming eyes to me he'll say,
"Why did you take my life away?"
I know that frightful ghost I see,
Gnawing flesh in misery,
And then and there attended be,
For murder in the first degree.
The jealous thought that first gave strife,
To make me take my husband's life;
For days and months I spent my time,
Thinking how to commit this crime.
And on a dark and doleful night;
I put his body out of sight;
To see his soul and body part,
It strikes with terror in my heart.
I took his blooming days away,
Left him no time to God to pray;
And if sins fall on his head,

Must I not bear them in his stead?
My mind on solemn subjects roll,
My little child, God bless its soul,
All ye that are of Adam's race,
Let not my faults this child disgrace.
You all see me and on me gaze,
Be careful how you spend your days;
And ne'er commit this awful crime,
But try and serve your God in time.
Awful indeed to think of death,
In perfect health to lose my breath;
Farewell my friends, I bid adieu,
Vengeance on me, you must now pursue.
Great God! How shall I be forgiven?
Not fit for earth, not fit for Heaven;
But little time to pray to God,
For now I try that awful road.

Here's a final verse of the ballad that, according to Bobby McMillon, could only have been sung by those who took Charlie's side, because, in it, Frankie admits a reason for her actions.

In my deep sleep I see him now,
A beautiful peace on his handsome brow,
Our winsome babe on his heaving chest;
The crimson blade of greed must rest.

Charlie's selling his house and land, which he refused to do. But, if he were dead, then Frankie would inherit the place and be free to sell it. Then she could head west. Among certain related mountain families and in certain mountain communities, all these possibilities and many more are tossed around, discussed back and forth, and argued over, just as they have been since 1832, as though the murder took place only last year.

Frankie Silver was accused and charged with violently murdering her husband. When she was brought to trial, according to the custom of the times, Frankie was not allowed to speak up in her own defense in court. She was found guilty and was condemned to die. Somehow she escaped while she awaited her death, was recaptured, and then was finally executed by hanging—an execution that caused a great controversy at the time, especially since she was female.

Even now, after more than one hundred and seventy-five years of supposition, investigation, gossip, and scholarly research, there is little agreement regarding the actual facts and circumstances of this unlikely murder. Not so long ago, a contingency of North Carolina students petitioned the governor to pardon Frankie Silver for the crime on the basis that she was abused by Charlie and therefore acted in self-defense.

The truth behind the deadly dispute that occurred so far back in time between those two young mountain people may never be fully known. Maybe that's how it should be. In fact, that's probably how it must be if the story is to continue to live on as it has lived for so very long. If every fact were known and every question answered, what would be the fun in that? Where would be the intrigue then? There's nothing better than a good unresolved, blood-curdling murder to keep folks up at night, no matter where they're from, and no matter which particular version of a song they sing.

Wayne Silver (1940–2001), a descendent of Charlie Silver, and singer Bobby McMillon discuss motives for the murder inside the Kona Baptist Church. Photograph by Sally Council. Courtesy of the North Carolina Arts Council.

To this day, the causes and consequences of the hostility that occurred so many years ago between two mountain teenagers continue to be a powerful source of controversy in North Carolina and beyond. The murder of Charlie Silver and the subsequent condemnation and execution of Frankie Silver has been the subject of long-standing family and community disputes, numerous articles and television stories, a pair of full-length books, and a long-lived North Carolina ballad. The mystery continues into the twenty-first century.

REGION 3 AT A GLANCE

MITCHELL COUNTY

YOUNG'S MOUNTAIN MUSIC
Spruce Pine

As soon as visitors arrive at Young's Mountain Music, they are greeted with the sounds of live mountain music. Along the driveway that leads to Young's Mountain Music and in the parking areas behind the building, musicians gather to jam and to form bands for the evening's shows. Inside, additional groups of players get together in the hallways, in the practice rooms, and in the designated smoking areas to rehearse. Every Saturday night, Young's Mountain Music, located between Burnsville and Spruce Pine, welcomes a crowd of two hundred or more mountain music and dance lovers to its warm, hand-hewn interior to enjoy stage performances by regional musicians who play country, bluegrass, and gospel music. Visitors to the place enter a spacious lobby and concession area where volunteers sell freshly made popcorn and homemade desserts. The performance hall, with its raised stage, hardwood dance floor, and theater-style seating is adjacent to the lobby. Inside, the bands play and dancers enjoy clogging, buckdancing, and the mountain two-step. There's another room nearby that's reserved

THE PLACE

Traveling around this region will lead visitors past some of the most famous peaks in the Blue Ridge. Beginning in the north is the weathered rocky summit of Grandfather Mountain and the ski mountains of Avery County, which has the highest county seat—Newland at 3,600 feet—and highest town—Beech Mountain at 5,500 feet—east of the Rocky Mountains. While driving along the Blue Ridge Parkway in Avery County, visitors will pass near Linville Gorge, one of the deepest canyons in the southeastern United States and the site of the legendary, yet-unexplained Brown Mountain Lights. Following a short break for some good mountain music and chilled apple cider at the Orchard at Altapass in McDowell County, you can wind your way up and up and up, all the way up to the crest of the Black Mountains. This fifteen-mile-long range contains six of the ten highest peaks east of the Mississippi River. Mount Mitchell is the loftiest, with a summit that reaches 6,684 feet above sea level. Mitchell County was formed in 1861 from parts of Burke, Caldwell, Yancey, Watauga, and McDowell Counties to honor Elisha Mitchell, president of the University of North Carolina, who fell to his death while exploring the mountain. Standing on the peak of Mount Mitchell, one can look downward to the base of the eastern foothills of McDowell County, nearly a mile below. To the west are the famous "balds," the treeless meadow summits of the Roan Mountain Highlands. Between those two high ranges lies the Toe River valley.

U.S. Highway 19 is the main artery that passes through Avery, Mitchell, and Yancey Counties. Just as in Watauga and Ashe Counties, this is Christmas tree country. It is also known for the many gemstones and veins of mica that are still taken from the ground. Near the Mitchell County seat of Spruce

Pine is the Penland School of Crafts, a world renowned institution dedicated to the teaching of fine and traditional crafts. Route 19 continues on in the shadow of the Black Mountains to the scenic town Burnsville, the largest municipality in Yancey County.

Linville Falls, near the Blue Ridge Parkway and the Linville Gorge.

O Bobby McMillon

As a child, Bobby McMillon developed an avid interest in the traditional songs that had been handed down in his family. He is one of the foremost living authorities on the subject of traditional mountain music. He lives in Yancey County.

My father, Gordon McMillon, was born in eastern Tennessee, in the McMillon settlement, near Cosby. My grandfather was called to preach in Caldwell County, so he brought the members of his family and they settled here. About three years later, my mother's mom and dad moved from Mitchell County to run a grocery store in Caldwell County. It was at that little store where my mother met my father.

I was born in Lenoir in December of 1951. As a child, I listened to the stories that the family told. I grew up listening to the scary stories and the witch tales and things that our family knew about. I just loved to listen to 'em. My grandfather had a Victrola talking machine, and he had a lot of old records. About the time I was twelve, I began to realize that some of the songs that my granddaddy had on records were similar to the songs that were being sung out and about in the community. When I was between twelve and fourteen, I started learning the songs that people I knew were singing. I was thirteen or fourteen when I became aware of the recorded and written folklore collections, and I began to read everything I could about them. I slowly began to learn what all this was about.

Toward the end of the 1960s my father went up to an electronic store and bought me a tape recorder. That summer I began to record everything that was being said or sung. It was about that time, also, that I met a man from Watauga County named Rolf Ellison. Rolf, he had a banjo and he got to playin' a few songs. He started out with one called "Down Yonder," and then he took the picks off his finger and started playing in a different style. He kept the picks off his fingers and just hooked his forefinger up on the second string and went to playing in a modal key.
He started out:

> Oh, the first came down was dressed in red,
> And the next come down in green;
> And the next come down was Daniel's wife,
> Dressed fine as any Queen, Queen;
> Dressed fine as any Queen

and he proceeded to sing "Lord Daniel." I knew I had hit the jackpot then! That was just exactly what I was looking for. The hair was standing up on my arms 'cause he played the banjo real well and it was in a minor key. Then he did,

> Well met, well met my own true love,
> Well met, well met said he;

I've just returned from the salt, salt sea
And it's all for the love of thee.
I've just returned from the salt, salt sea,
And it's all for the love of thee.

We began a friendship that night that lasted the rest of his life.

One of my best friends in school had an uncle who was a doctor in North Wilkesboro who just loved old-time music. We had become close friends, so I called him up and asked him was he going to the Fiddlers' Convention at Union Grove. He said, yeah, come on down. So we went down to Union Grove. There was this couple from Tennessee that were there singing named Jean and Lee Schilling. Lee Schilling played the recorder and Jean played the autoharp. The songs they were singing were familiar to me, so I went and introduced myself to them after one of their performances. They told me that if I would come to their festival, which was called the Folk Festival of the Smokies, that they would introduce me to Jeannette Carter. Jeanette is the daugh-

ter of A. P. and Sara Carter, and Maybelle Carter's first cousin. They had composed the original Carter Family, and Jeannette was singing their music and carrying on the tradition. One night during the festival the Schillings asked me to perform. So they set me up a time to sing, and I did a couple of songs. The last one I did, I did a Carter Family song. I didn't know that Jeannette Carter was in the crowd. After it was over, she came backstage there and introduced herself to me, and we became fast friends after that. That was my first real public performance.

My friend in Lenoir named Cody Lowe was a student at UNC in Chapel Hill. During the years that he was in college, I used to go down there every so often and spend a few days with him. He'd take me to the library, because I was an avid fan of books. It was just like putting Alice in Wonderland for me to go to Chapel Hill. I mean, that was just like being in the Treasure House of Captain Kangaroo!

From the perspective of having visited the United Kingdom, I've found a great resurgence of interest in all kinds of old songs and singing. It's revivalist in nature, but still, it's keeping it on. If it wasn't for the revivalists, and if it wasn't for the Yankees [laughs], I think we would have lost four-fifths of all this music. I have to put that on the record.

I'm not sure about the future of folk music. There's probably very few people left now that have it strictly from the traditional culture which they grew up in. But there's some people today whose families, in an unbroken tradition, have had a song like "Barbara Allen" for three or four centuries. Maybe, someday, when people become enlightened to the point that they can accept something besides their own narrow view of what the world should be like, they'll reaccept the traditions that they have left behind.

for socializing, jamming, and smoking. This room leads backstage to a series of rooms in which the bands warm up before going onstage.

Meanwhile, owners Bill and Shirley Young and local musician Alice Wyatt Powers emcee the stage. They present eight to ten bands every Saturday evening, and each band plays a twenty- to thirty-minute set, much to the delight of an appreciative audience of listeners and dancers. The musicians all perform without payment. Many of them from the area had their first experience playing in front of an audience at Young's, and some have kept coming back for years to repay the favor.

The tradition at Young's Mountain Music is for the audience to stand during the performance of a gospel selection or other religious number.

This venue draws a crowd of Saturday-night regulars who come from as far as seventy-five miles away. Visitors to Young's Mountain Music come from all around the globe.

Stage performance at Young's Mountain Music.

Visitors choose from a wide assortment of cakes and pies at Young's Mountain Music.

WHEN: Saturdays, 7 P.M.

WHERE: 26 Mountain Music Drive, Spruce Pine, 28777. Located on NC 19 east, between Spruce Pine and Burnsville, on the Yancey-Mitchell County line.

ADMISSION: Free, but donations are welcome

CONTACT: Alice Powers, 828-675-4790, or Bill and Shirley Young, 828-675-4365

WEBSITE: www.youngsmountainmusic.org

AVERY COUNTY

SINGING ON THE MOUNTAIN AT MACRAE MEADOWS
Grandfather Mountain

For the better part of a century, since 1924, there's been an annual gospel singing at MacRae Meadows, near Linville in Avery County, not far from the western base of Grandfather Mountain. The event, called Singing on the Mountain, is the oldest ongoing gospel convention in the Southern Appalachians. The event's motto has remained the same from the beginning: "Whoever will may come." Founded by Joe Hartley Sr. as a family reunion, it features a dozen or more of the most popular southern gospel groups.

The singing starts in the early morning and continues more or less without stopping until midafternoon, breaking only for a midday sermon. The large outdoor stage where the singing groups perform is positioned near the base of a natural amphitheater-like grassy hillside that covers approximately one hundred acres, and by midmorning that hillside is filled to nearly overflowing with an enthusiastic and appreciative audience of sev-

A preacher at Singing on the Mountain in the 1940s. Courtesy of the North Carolina
Collection, University of North Carolina at Chapel Library.

eral thousand listeners and worshipers. No permanent seating is provided,
so most folks bring along their own folding chairs. And since this is an outdoor summertime event, many attendees also bring along their umbrella
for shade, along with sunscreen and bottled water. Casual dress is the order
of the day at this gathering, so many of the worshipers wear shorts, loose-
fitting, lightweight shirts or blouses, and straw hats.

Food vendors scattered along a dirt roadway that runs alongside and behind the stage area offer snacks, soft drinks, and fast food. There's a large
parking area in an adjacent field, and additional parking is available all
along the roadside that leads to the festival site. Camping (no hookups) is
available on the grounds on a first-come, first-served basis. It's a good idea
to call ahead for details if you plan to camp.

WHEN: Fourth Saturday in June, 8:30 A.M. to 3:00 P.M.
WHERE: Grandfather Mountain, US 221, Linville, 28646. Located
    2 miles north of Linville and 1 mile south of the Blue Ridge Parkway,
    Milepost 305.
ADMISSION: Free

GRANDFATHER MOUNTAIN AND THE BLUE RIDGE PARKWAY

The Blue Ridge Parkway winds across 469 scenic miles of the crest of the Blue Ridge Mountains of North Carolina and Virginia. In the spring the road is lined with blooming azaleas, rhododendron, and mountain magnolias. In the fall the ridges burst with autumn color. In winter icicles hang from the springs that are the source of the state's mightiest rivers, and in all seasons the views are spectacular. The parkway had its birth in the lean years of the Great Depression. People needed jobs, and policymakers saw the economic potential of a new breed of tourists traveling by car. The road connected two newly created national parks, Shenandoah in Virginia, and Great Smoky Mountains in North Carolina. The work begun by the Civilian Conservation Corps wasn't entirely finished until 1983, when the Linn Cove Viaduct was built over Grandfather Mountain. The viaduct is a segmented concrete

Musician Floyd Gragg and his produce stand on Grandfather Mountain, which he has run since the 1950s. Photograph by Steve Kruger.

bridge curving gracefully off the mountainside for nearly a quarter mile, at an elevation of over 5,000 feet. This remarkable feat of engineering enabled Grandfather Mountain's unique cliffside ecosystems to be preserved.

Grandfather Mountain soars to nearly 6,000 feet, a craggy, rocky contrast to the rolling, tree-covered mountains to the west and the steep descent of more than 2,000 feet to the eastern foothills. The high peaks nurture sixteen distinct ecological communities, and the mountain is home to seventy-three rare and endangered species. The United Nations designated Grandfather Mountain as an International Biosphere Reserve. For decades the mountain was owned and kept in its natural state by the Morton family, but in 2009 most of the mountain became Grandfather Mountain State Park. The family still operates a visitor center at the top of the mountain, with an enclosed wildlife habitat, hiking trails, and the famous "mile-high swinging bridge."

MacRae Meadows at the top of Grandfather also hosts the Singing on the Mountain and the Grandfather Mountain Highland Games.

Traveling the Blue Ridge Parkway, you can see some of North Carolina's iconic natural landmarks: the Linville Gorge, the deepest canyon east of the Mississippi; the legendary and mysterious Brown Mountain Lights; Mount Mitchell, the highest point in the eastern United States; and Looking Glass, a huge granite dome near Brevard; and the high peaks of Great Smoky Mountains. Riding down the parkway also can shed light on the human story of the region. Roadside exhibits describe farmhouses, mills, and churches, some of which have been preserved by the National Park Service. Travelers on the parkway will also encounter music and mountain culture. The Blue Ridge Music Center straddles the Virginia–North Carolina border and features exhibits on mountain music and daily performances. Two of the venues detailed here, the Orchard at Altapass and the Cradle of Forestry are a short distance from the road. The Folk Art Center at Milepost 383 outside Asheville is home to the Southern Highlands Craft Guild with its galleries of contemporary and traditional mountain crafts, including handmade instruments. Driving on the parkway in bad weather can be hazardous, and sections are closed during the winter. Be sure to check the website for road closures at www.nps.gov/blri /index.htm before you make your trip.

CONTACT: Grandfather Mountain, 1-800-468-7325 or 828-733-4337
WEBSITE: www.grandfather.com

MCDOWELL COUNTY

LIVE MUSIC AT THE ORCHARD AT ALTAPASS
Altapass, on the Blue Ridge Parkway
The historic apple orchard at Altapass stretches for over a mile along the Blue Ridge Parkway. Most of the trees are at least eighty years old. The apples from the orchard are picked and sorted by hand, an operation that is open for visitors to view. The packinghouse is also a gift shop, snack bar, exhibit space, and music hall.

The gift shop at the Orchard at Altapass offers an amazing array of irresistible edible goodies: homemade fudge, ice cream, hot sandwiches, and

nearly every imaginable kind of culinary concoction that can be made using apples. Apple preserves, apple jelly, apple butter, apple jam, apple barbecue sauce, apple and pepper relish, and apple cider line the shelves. But the Orchard's products feature more than just apples. Various kinds of syrups, honey, pickles, fruit and berry preserves, several varieties of jelly, and a selection of relishes, sauces, and marinades tempt visitors as well. And then, of course, there are the apples all by themselves, picked fresh right from the trees of the surrounding orchard. Fresh apple season at Altapass begins in mid-July and lasts through the end of October.

Inside the packinghouse is a large stage area that takes up one end of the room. That's where mountain music is presented. Every weekend throughout the open months, the Orchard hosts a variety of authentic Appalachian musicians who play gospel, blues, folk, show tunes, classical, country, and bluegrass. In front of the bandstand is a floor space reserved for dancing. Beyond that, rows of chairs are provided for the music lovers who gather there to listen. There's seating for around a hundred people. At Altapass, the music is lively, the mood is festive, the chairs are comfortable, the food is tasty, and the mountain air is fresh. There are worse ways to spend an afternoon.

Bill and Judy Carson, the friendly operators of the Orchard, are well versed in its history. The orchard celebrated its 100th birthday in 2008. It was originally built by the Clinchfield Railroad. The Clinchfield crossed the Blue Ridge at Altapass along nearly the same route used by the Overmountain Men during the Revolutionary War. Thousands of immigrants helped build the steep grade and eighteen tunnels known as the "Loops" that climb the thirteen miles up and over the gap at Altapass. After many productive years, the orchard gradually fell into decline when construction of the Parkway cut it in half. Today it is one of the iconic stops along the scenic roadway, and the view from the big, red packinghouse alone is worth a trip. Bill Carson's sister, Kit Trubey, bought the property in 1994 to save the area from being developed. The Altapass Foundation, Inc., which manages the orchard and the activities that happen there, was established in 2002. Its mission is to preserve the history, heritage, and culture of the Blue Ridge Mountains; to protect the underlying orchard land with its apples, wetlands, butterflies, and other natural features; and to provide educational programming to the public about the Appalachian experience. In addition to the mountain music and dancing, storytelling sessions, hayrides, a monarch butterfly preservation project, a honeybee exhibit, and herb walks entertain visitors. On Wednesdays, Thursdays, and Fridays, visitors are welcome to bring along an instrument and join in with the resident musicians. Each Saturday and Sunday afternoon, the Orchard features two guest bands.

WHEN: Wednesday–Sunday, May–November. Check website or call for detailed schedule.

WHERE: 1025 Orchard Road, at Milepost 328.3 on the Blue Ridge Parkway. Take NC 225 north from Marion or south from Spruce Pine. Enter the Blue Ridge Parkway directly across from the North Carolina Minerals Museum, then travel *north* on the parkway for approximately 3 miles to Orchard Road. Turn onto Orchard Road and follow the dirt trail through the apple trees and down the hill. Park near the big red building—that's the packinghouse.

ADMISSION: Free

CONTACT: 1-888-765-9531

WEBSITE: altapassorchard.com

YANCEY COUNTY

MUSIC IN THE MOUNTAINS FOLK FESTIVAL
Burnsville

The small town of Burnsville is nestled in the Black Mountains, the highest mountain range east of the Mississippi River. The centerpiece of Burnsville is the town's historic square, a grassy and shady park within walking distance of restaurants and other local businesses. Historic buildings ring the square, including the old Yancey County courthouse, the library, and the historic Nu Wray Inn. Elvis Presley once spent the night at the Nu Wray, and North Carolina author Thomas Wolfe stayed there while serving as a witness in a murder trial.

Bob Aldridge dances to the music of the East Tennessee State University Old-Time String Band at the Music in the Mountains Folk Festival in Burnsville. Photograph by Steve Kruger.

The annual Music in the Mountains Folk Festival takes place at the Town Center, right off of the square on South Main. Though it is a newer building, the Town Center harmonizes with the older architecture, and the bricked portico calls to mind train depots and arcades of the early twentieth century. The festival is a sit-down evening concert, held in an auditorium that can accommodate up to four hundred people. Old-time, bluegrass, and gospel music are presented, and the festival usually features traditional flatfooting demonstrations and storytelling. The festival has a tradition of presenting musical elders from the region, although some local and up-and-coming groups also perform. The Town Center also hosts the annual RiddleFest celebration devoted to Yancey County native Lesley Riddle and a seasonal farmers' market on Saturday mornings from 8 A.M. to 12:30 P.M. Since 2012, the festival has coincided with the Yancey Old Timey Fall Festival, an all-day event in the town square. This free festival is put on by the Yancey History Association and features a full day of bluegrass and old-time music, as well as clogging demonstrations, children's events, and a parade of classic cars and trucks.

WHEN: Last Saturday in September, 5 to 10 P.M.
WHERE: Burnsville Town Center, 6 South Main Street, Burnsville, 28714
ADMISSION: Fee
CONTACT: Toe River Arts, 828-682-7215
WEBSITE: www.toeriverarts.org

RIDDLEFEST
Burnsville

A young African American blues musician and the "first family" of country music may seem strange bedfellows, but the partnership between Lesley Riddle (1905–80) and the Carter Family had an extraordinary impact on American music. Lesley Riddle was born in the Silvers Gap community of Yancey County. The young Riddle, known locally as "Esley," split his time

Lesley Riddle (right) and Brownie McGhee, c. 1937. Courtesy of the Blue Ridge Institute and Museum of Ferrum College/Leslie Riddle.

between Burnsville and Kingsport, Tennessee, where his mother moved when he was young. As a teenager, Riddle lost his lower leg in an accident that occurred while he was visiting a friend at a cement plant. Shortly afterward, two fingers on his right hand were destroyed from a shotgun discharge. Incapacitated, Riddle took up the guitar, learning blues and gospel songs from his uncle Ed Martin and other musicians in East Tennessee.

A. P. Carter, who was often on the lookout for new material that the Carter Family could perform, heard Riddle play when he passed through the area. Impressed, Carter invited him home to Maces Spring, Virginia, where Riddle made music with A. P., wife Sara, and Sara's cousin, Maybelle. Riddle himself was the source for several of the Carter Family's best-known songs, including "The Cannonball Blues," which he taught to Maybelle Carter. Maybelle, who would become the best-known country guitarist of her generation, later claimed that Riddle's guitar playing had a strong influence on her own style, especially on her runs and finger picking.

In addition to sharing his own music, Riddle teamed up with A. P. to document and learn traditional songs from musicians in the mountains of Tennessee and Virginia. Together they made a series of song-collecting trips to remote hollows, bustling mill towns, and coal camps. When they heard a new song they liked, A. P. would write down the words and Lesley Riddle would commit the tune to memory. Many of these songs became hits for the Carter Family and are still part of the southern canon played today, not just by traditional musicians but also in the genres of rock and roll, gospel, and country music.

The collaboration and friendship between Riddle and the Carters in a time of stark racial segregation and prejudice is emblematic of the complicated cross-cultural nature of music in the Blue Ridge. While the Carters credited Riddle for his influence, he never made a living playing music, and his contributions remained largely unknown. In 1937, Riddle married and moved to Rochester, New York, where he worked shining shoes and as a school crossing guard. Mike Seeger heard about Lesley Riddle from Maybelle Carter and visited him in the 1960s. By that time, Riddle had almost given up music. However, Seeger encouraged him to pick his guitar back up and eventually helped Riddle release an album of his own material, titled *Step by Step*. Through this recording and several appearances at folk festivals around the country, Riddle's voice was at last heard, but sadly only a few years before his death.

A portrait of Lesley Riddle hangs on the wall of the auditorium at the Burnsville Town Center. The Town Center hosts an annual event to honor the memory of Riddle and his musical contributions. During the day, a seminar, lecture, or presentation takes place, each year with a different theme. In the evening, special guests from afar join local musicians of all types to work up their own version of the songs that Lesley Riddle played or helped arrange for the Carter Family. Sometimes descendants of Lesley Riddle and other relatives attend and perform.

WHEN: Third Saturday in February, seminar during the day; concert,
    7 to 9 P.M.
WHERE: Burnsville Town Center, 6 South Main Street, Burnsville, 28714
ADMISSION: Fee
CONTACT: Traditional Voices Group, 828-682-9654
WEBSITE: www.tvgnc.org

Asheville Junction

Many people consider mountain music to be a purely rural form of music. In fact, a lot of traditional mountain music originated and was sustained in the towns and small cities of the Blue Ridge. This is certainly true in Asheville—the largest city in the southern mountains, located in a valley that's formed by the north-flowing French Broad River. Visitors to the Blue Ridge often use Asheville as a jumping-off point from which to explore the surrounding area, including numerous places of musical, natural, and historical significance.

Asheville's contributions to sustaining old-time and bluegrass music go a long way back. The Mountain Music and Dance Festival, organized in 1928 by Bascom Lamar Lunsford, is the longest-running folk festival in the nation. In 1925, the Okeh Recording Company brought recording equipment and sound engineers from New York to Asheville, seeking to record mountain musicians and hoping to cash in on the growing national market for old-time country music. In Asheville, at a historic recording session conducted at the Vanderbilt Hotel, Kelly Harrell, Henry Whitter, Wade Ward, Ernest Stoneman, and several other musicians now familiar to fans of old-time music were all recorded, including local musicians like Bascom Lamar Lunsford, Ernest Helton, and Dedrick Harris. At the helm of the search for new talent was a man named Ralph Peer, who, in 1928, would preside over a recording trip to Bristol, Tennessee, where he would make the first recordings of the Carter Family and Jimmie Rodgers—an event that is considered by many to mark the beginning of modern country music.

An Asheville radio station, WWNC, played an equally pivotal role in the popularization of country music. As the region's flagship radio station, WWNC broadcast the music of regional musicians J. E. and Wade Mainer and, in 1938, had the distinction of introducing Bill Monroe and his new band, the Blue Grass Boys, to the wider world of country and popular music.

During and after the folk music revival of the 1960s and

1970s, Asheville once again became a center for Appalachian music. A number of rural mountain musicians looking for work moved to Asheville. Others, including the Grammy Award–winning artist and folklorist David Holt and musician and radio host Don Pedi, moved there to be close to the mountain music and the traditional mountain culture that they already admired. Still others, many of whom played traditional music, moved into the surrounding rural areas to become part of a back-to-the-land movement that had gained widespread national popularity.

The Mountain Dance and Folk Festival, after lagging a bit during the 1960s, soon gained renewed momentum. New music events, including Shindig on the Green, soon followed. By the 1990s, regional educational institutions like Warren Wilson College in Swannanoa and Mars Hill College developed camps at which to teach traditional music and dance. Today, Asheville remains the urban capital of old-time, bluegrass, and Americana music in the Appalachian Mountains. Aspiring musicians, aware of the availability of large audiences that appreciate and support traditional music and of the opportunities provided by the numerous music venues in the city, move to Asheville hoping to make a living playing music. On most Friday and Saturday evenings, buskers can be found playing for tips on downtown Asheville's street corners and around Pack Square. Jam sessions and traditional music concerts enliven numerous bars, nightclubs, and restaurants throughout the town.

Two exciting music shows are broadcast on Asheville's station WCQS, 88.1 FM. The first, called *Country Roots*, hosted by Wayne Erbsen on Sunday evenings from 7 to 9 P.M., focuses on bluegrass and old-time music. Don Pedi hosts a second radio show, called *Close to Home*, on Saturday nights from 8 to 10 P.M. It features old-time, blues, and all varieties of folk music.

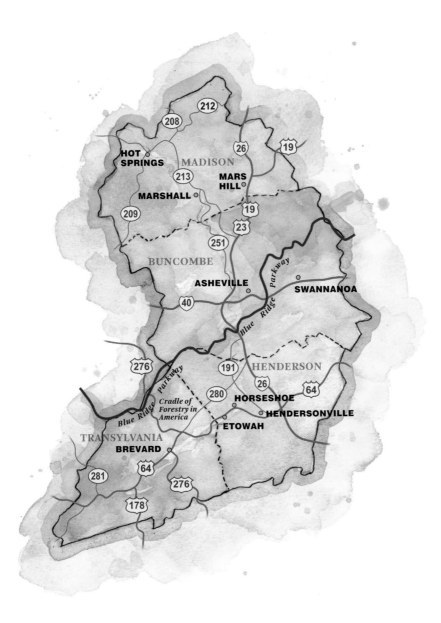

Buskers play for tips on the streets of downtown Asheville on most nights. On weekends in the summer, there may be a different group on every corner. Photograph by Steve Kruger.

Madison County, located on the west side of the region, is a few miles down the French Broad River from Asheville. Madison was formerly the home and the main stomping grounds of the great traditional singer, banjoist, and folk song collector Bascom Lamar Lunsford. The hollows of Madison County are also known for producing great fiddlers and families of ballad singers—the Norton, the Wallin, and the Chandler families. Their artful yet unrestrained way of singing unaccompanied ballads, or "love songs," as they call them, has influenced folk musicians all around the world. Some of their songs, which have been passed along orally from generation to generation, are now hundreds of years old. The three major towns in Madison County, the county seat at Marshall, Mars Hill, and the old resort town of Hot Springs, all host music events where visitors can enjoy hearing local singers who are carrying on the traditions today.

REGION 4 AT A GLANCE

THE PLACE

Region 4 stretches from the edge of the Blue Ridge mountains in eastern Buncombe County all the way to the Tennessee line in Madison County. South of Asheville, Interstate 26 runs through Henderson County, home to the communities of Hendersonville and Flat Rock. Etowah, located nearby, is known

for its century-old Christian Harmony shape-note singings, a tradition that remains strong in the region. Henderson County borders South Carolina to the south and Transylvania County to the west. The name Transylvania literally means "across the forest." This is an appropriate name since most of Transylvania County lies deep within the Pisgah National Forest. This area, which is also home

The French Broad River runs through the town of Marshall in Madison County.

to Brevard College, has a greater number of waterfalls than any other county in North Carolina. It was here, at a site now called the "Cradle of Forestry," that the first modern forestry school in the United States was established. Down the Blue Ridge Parkway from Cradle of Forestry is Looking Glass, a huge exposed Granite Dome that is completely surrounded by a forested wilderness. These sites are all within a day's drive from the city of Asheville, with its booming population and rich musical history.

Asheville is the largest city in western North Carolina, home to slightly under 100,000 people. Located at the confluence of the French Broad and Swannanoa Rivers, the place where Asheville was founded was also where two early Indian trading paths met. That spot is known today as Pack Square, and it's located right in the heart of the modern city. During the early to mid-1800s, Asheville became a major market on the Buncombe Turnpike, a road that crossed the mountains and connected the region's farms and plantations to the French Broad River and from there to the major market towns of the Southeast. Following the Civil War, the construction of railroads into the region allowed for the creation of industry in Asheville, which supported factories that produced textiles, furniture, and other goods and staples. These industries attracted thousands of mountaineers, both white and African American, who came there seeking jobs and wages. The rail system also enabled the development of tourism, which brought in waves of outsiders to Asheville and the surrounding mountains.

As a result of the increasing importance of tourism in the region, Asheville's origins as a market, railroad, and textile town were eventually eclipsed by its brand as a visitor destination and gateway to outdoor recreation and arts. It has become a place where green living and urban culture are served up with a distinctively Appalachian flavor, one that has attracted thousands of new residents to the city just in the past several decades. Asheville hosts a burgeoning music scene that boasts a strong connection to the region's traditional culture and its mountain music.

BUNCOMBE COUNTY

MOUNTAIN DANCE AND FOLK FESTIVAL
Asheville

Downtown Asheville is the scene of an annual celebration that features three days of festivities—the Mountain Dance and Folk Festival. This event is the oldest continuing festival of traditional mountain music and dance in the United States. It began in 1928 when the city of Asheville asked well-known musician and folk historian Bascom Lamar Lunsford to present a group of musicians and dancers from various Appalachian communities at the city's Rhododendron Festival. The presentation proved to be so popular that Lunsford presented the event on its own a few years later, calling it the Mountain Dance and Folk Festival. The festival soon became a model for other folk festivals around the country and inspired the beginnings of the National Folk Festival in 1935 and the Mountain Dance and Folk Festival's sister event, Shindig on the Green, in 1967.

Bascom Lamar Lunsford calling a big circle mountain dance during the Mountain Dance and Folk Festival. Courtesy of the Mountain Dance and Folk Festival and Shindig on the Green Collection, D. H. Ramsey Special Collections, University of North Carolina, Asheville.

Today, the Mountain Dance and Folk Festival occurs inside the Diana Wortham Theatre at Pack Place, in the heart of downtown Asheville. The event starts on the first Thursday evening in August with a series of presentations by individual musicians, bands, and mountain dance groups and continues on Friday and Saturday evenings with similar performances. Outside the theater auditorium in the lobby, before and following the shows, many of the featured musicians set up tables to talk to fans, sign autographs, and sell recordings.

WHEN: Thursday–Saturday, first week in August, 7 to 10 P.M.
WHERE: The Diana Wortham Theatre, Pack Square, Asheville, 28801
ADMISSION: Fee
CONTACT: The Folk Heritage Committee, 828-258-6101, ext. 345. For the
   Diana Wortham Theatre, call 828-257-4530 or visit www.dwtheatre.org
WEBSITE: www.folkheritage.org

SHINDIG ON THE GREEN
Asheville
This weekly concert in downtown Asheville spotlights bluegrass and old-time string bands, mountain dancers, ballad singers, and storytellers. It's staged on Pack Square Park's Bascom Lamar Lunsford Stage, right in front of the Buncombe County courthouse. Shindig on the Green is an extremely popular and well-attended public event. Hundreds of people of all ages converge for each week's performance to enjoy a summer evening of music outdoors. They show up early, find a spot somewhere on the grassy lawn

Asheville Junction

141

EXCERPT FROM "MOUNTAIN DANCE AND FOLK FESTIVAL: A LIVING TRADITION," BY LOYAL JONES

Western North Carolina native Bascom Lamar Lunsford developed, from an early age, a passion for the ballads, folk songs, and dances of the Southern Appalachian Mountains. As a young boy, he began playing the banjo and fiddle, learning many songs, tunes and dances from his neighbors. By the time Lunsford settled in Buncombe County, then an attorney and gentleman farmer, he had also established himself as a well known singer, musician and collector, the General Phonograph Corporation already having released two disks with four of his songs.

In 1928, the Asheville Chamber of Commerce planned to stage the Rhododendron Festival to call attention to the beauty and climate of what the promoters had taken to calling the "Land of the Sky." Chamber officials approached Lunsford to arrange a folk song and dance program as a part of the Festival, which also included handicraft displays, romantic pageants, and beautiful baby contests.

Lunsford recruited five square dance clubs to compete for prizes and invited ballad singers, fiddlers, banjo pickers and string bands to entertain on Pack Square. Five thousand people descended upon downtown Asheville and were backed up against office buildings, draped across Zeb Vance's statue and hanging out of the windows of local businesses. The *Asheville Citizen* described the music as a ". . . throwback from the modern jazz world . . ." and went on to say that it should be ". . . a permanent thing, something that might be continued from year to year as a festival of Western North Carolina—on the order of the great festivals of older nations which have been handed down from generation to generation."

Like any event, though, the Mountain Dance and Folk Festival has had its ups and downs. With the coming of television, social activities, the Civil Rights movement, and rock and roll, the audience dwindled in the early 1960s. However, the folk revival of the late 1960s rekindled interest in the Mountain Dance and Folk Festival, the oldest festival of its kind in the country. People from all over the United States had moved to Western North Carolina as part of the back-to-the-land movement, and many of these young people were drawn to the folk arts as an example of the simple and honest lives they were seeking. Also, many visitors loved to return to Asheville during the Festival to get an annual taste of Appalachian folk arts. Thus the 1960s stood for a time of rebirth for the Mountain Dance and Folk Festival, which continues to cater to sold out shows through its 75th year.

Loyal Jones is author of Minstrel of the Appalachians: The Story of Bascom Lamar Lunsford *(1984; reprint, Lexington: University Press of Kentucky, 2002). His essay appeared in the Folk Heritage Committee's publication* Along about Sundown . . . The Mountain Dance and Folk Festival Celebrates 75 Years *(2003).*

of the park to spread a quilt or a blanket or to set up folding chairs, and then sit back to enjoy the music and dance. When it's time to stretch a leg, they wander over to one of several onsite food vendors for a bite to eat, or they hang out near one of as many as a dozen impromptu jam sessions that form in open spaces behind the stage or beneath the nearby trees. If they've brought along a banjo or a harmonica, they might join in a jam session. The jams are open to all who enjoy listening and to anyone who wishes to join in and sing or play.

Shindig on the Green takes a break from its regular Saturday evening schedule twice during July and August. The first break happens on the last Saturday in July when the event closes for the city's Bele Chere festival, the largest free arts and music festival in the southeastern United States. It closes once again the following Saturday, the first Saturday in August, for the Mountain Dance and Folk Festival at the nearby Diana Wortham The-

The Indian Creek Music Company teaches students to play dulcimers made out of cardboard at Shindig on the Green.

Asheville Junction

143

STORY OF A SONG: THE SWANNANOA TUNNEL

The Swannanoa Tunnel is the largest of seven tunnels that were constructed during the nineteenth century to enable the Western North Carolina Railroad to climb the eastern edge of the Blue Ridge. These rail lines connected the city of Asheville to the eastern part of the state. The Swannanoa Tunnel is 1,800 feet long and was drilled through solid granite. Most of the work was done by African American inmates from the state penitentiary, who were contracted out to the railroad by the State of North Carolina. Construction began in 1877. It took two years before Governor Zebulon Vance was notified that "daylight entered Buncombe County through the Swannanoa Tunnel." The work was extremely hazardous, and construction cost at least 125 lives and possibly as many as 300. Twenty-three workers were lost in a single incident in 1877 when part of the tunnel collapsed. A work song that may allude to that deadly incident was allegedly sung by tunnel workers before making its way into the surrounding communities under the title "Swannanoa Tunnel," or, alternately, "Asheville Junction." The song was collected by Cecil Sharp in 1916 and also performed by the great musician and folk song collector Bascom Lamar Lunsford. The verses to Lunsford's version follow a standard work-song call-and-response pattern, a form meant to be sung to the rhythm of hard manual labor.

The Swannanoa Tunnel, still in use, was built at the cost of hundreds of lives and inspired a song that is still sung today. Courtesy of the North Carolina Collection, University of North Carolina at Chapel Hill Library.

> I'm going back to that Swannanoa Tunnel,
> That's my home, baby, that's my home.
> Asheville Junction, Swannanoa Tunnel,
> All caved in, baby, all caved in.
> Last December, I remember,

The wind blowed cold, baby, the wind blowed cold.
When you hear my watchdog howling,
Somebody around, Somebody around.
When you hear that hoot owl squalling,
Somebody dying, Somebody dying.
Hammer falling from my shoulder
All day long, all day long
Ain't no hammer in this mountain
Outrings mine, outrings mine.
This old hammer, it killed John Henry,
It didn't kill me, it didn't kill me.
This old hammer rings like silver,
Shines like gold, shines like gold
Take this hammer, throw it in the river,
It rings right on, baby, it shines right on.
Some of these days I'll see that woman,
Well that's no dream, that's no dream.

The Swannanoa Tunnel is still in use, just as the song is still sung by musicians from western North Carolina. A state historical marker can be seen near the tunnel's entrance, on the corner of Yates Avenue and Old US Route 70 in Ridgecrest.

atre. Both the Mountain Dance and Folk Festival and Shindig on the Green are produced by the same organization, the Folk Heritage Committee.

Parking for the festivities is available in marked and metered spaces throughout downtown Asheville (free after 6 P.M.) and at the city's municipal decks (evening rates vary). The new College Street Parking Deck is located directly across College Street from Pack Square Park and the Buncombe County Courthouse.

WHEN: Saturdays, July 4th–Labor Day weekend, about 7 P.M. (except the last Saturday in July and first Saturday in August)
WHERE: Pack Square Park, Downtown Asheville, 28801
ADMISSION: Free
CONTACT: Folk Heritage Committee, 828-258-6101, ext. 345
WEBSITE: www.folkheritage.org

● Donna Ray Norton: I'm Proud of Where I Came From

Donna Ray Norton is part of a younger generation of North Carolina ballad singers. She was born and spent her formative years in Sodom in Madison County, a community that has produced many traditional ballad singers. She now lives in Weaverville in Buncombe County.

When I started singing I was already seventeen years old, but [ballad singing] has been around me my whole life. My mom would go over to my cousin Sheila Kay Adam's house. She had kids that were my age. We would play and do our thing, but we could always hear them singing. The adults would go in the kitchen, and we'd hide outside the door and listen. I knew the songs in my head, but I never actually learned to sing them until I was a senior in high school. I really never wanted to sing when I was younger. It was something I wasn't really proud of.

I lived in Sodom until I was in the fifth grade. Then we moved to Asheville. I didn't go to a high school where everybody knew about ballad singing and bluegrass. It was time for my senior exit project, and as my teacher was going through the classroom asking everybody what we were going to do, I thought of something that I knew a lot about that nobody else did. I said "Ballads?" My teacher really encouraged me. It helped me understand who I am and where I come from. This is my heritage, and I don't want it to die out.

I've got the music coming from both sides of my family. I'm fifth generation on my dad's side and eighth generation on my mom's side. Her father was Byard Ray. I remember him coming to the house and playing music. He always had his fiddle with him. He would open up his fiddle case, and he had rattlesnake rattles and rosin for the bow in there. He would tell me that the rosin was this magical jewel that he found, and he kept it for good luck.

My other grandfather was Morris Norton. He played the tune-bow and the banjo and sang. I felt like I was doing all this stuff with my Mom's side of the family and not embracing the Nortons. So I went to see my uncle Emmett. He told me, "I know some words to some songs that Pap used to sing if you want them." So I learned "Dickie and Johnny," something that my grandfather sang. Then I learned "Little Mathey Groves," a song my Dad used to sing before he died. I'm trying to respect both sides of the family. I feel like I owe it to them.

The first ballad I actually sat down and learned was "Young Emily." Back in the old days everybody lived around one another, and that's how people learned. They did "knee to knee." If you were sitting in front of me and I was trying to teach you a ballad, I would sing a verse and then you would sing it back to me. Then I would sing the next verse and you would sing the first verse and the second verse and so on. Now it's hard, because my next-door neighbor is not my cousin or my aunt. You have to resort to a new way in order to learn something that's old. Now it's just play, pause, and rewind.

I like singing the love songs. Sometimes you can *feel* how old they are, and I think that they're special. They don't hold anything back. It's like a drama in song, but very short. People love that. They love a good story. Sometimes you'll sing a love song where somebody's head is getting cut off and kicked against the wall, and people will laugh. *What the heck are these people thinking?* But then I joke with them about it. "You guys are really morbid!" They think it's super funny when I pick at them like that. My favorite songs are the real funny ones. Like the "Farmer's Curst Wife," about the woman that goes down to hell and the devil brings her back. I swear, those are the women from Sodom that they are talking about in some of those songs. That reminds me of my grandma so much, really, it's hilarious.

It's really neat to know how much this music touches people. A lot of times I have had someone come up to me and say they heard someone sing the same song when they were little, or their grandfather used to sing that and he passed away and they haven't heard it since then. That means a lot to me. I got to go to California to sing in 2007. I was thinking, I'm going out there and those people are going to hear me and think, "What is this girl doing with no music!" But that was one of the best shows I have ever done. They were so welcoming. They wanted to hear what I had to say. They invited me to their houses to sing. It made me realize the appreciation for ballad singing is not just in the mountains.

I am really proud of who I am and where I come from. I really hope that my kids will carry on the same tradition. A lot of times it's hard to make it work because of your work schedule or your life schedule, you know, when you've got two kids running around. But if it's something that you love, you've got to do it. You can't just give up.

Former Blue Grass Boy and Grammy Award–winner Bobby Hicks
hosts the Bluegrass Jam at Zuma Coffee in Marshall.

MADISON COUNTY

BLUEGRASS JAM AT ZUMA COFFEE
Marshall

Driving down NC 213 from the college town of Mars Hill to the town of
Marshall is just plain fun. The last several miles are a twisty, curvy, trail of
a mountain road that brings you slowly down to the flood plain of the historic French Broad River and, right before you get to town, to an intersection with Highway 25. It's a beautiful drive. As you turn right onto Main
Street, the wide, shallow river is revealed on your left and a mountainside
shoots nearly straight up beside you on the right. In between the river and
the bluff, on a narrow spit of flat land, lies Marshall, the seat of Madison
County. Bordered on the south by the French Broad River and on the north
by the sheer stone face of a mountain, the town of Marshall is only one

block wide. In fact, when a school was built there in 1925, it was constructed on an island that's right out in the middle of the French Broad River. There wasn't anywhere else to put it. Today, the school houses Marshall High Studios, a collection of twenty-eight artist studios, mostly in classrooms.

An old railroad depot sits directly beside the river in Marshall, its front door facing the narrow lane that is Marshall's main business street and, for several blocks, the only street that's not perpendicular to the channel of the French Broad River. Near the depot, attached to a wire fence that separates a row of streetside parking spaces from the river bank, is a sign that reads, "WARNING — WATER MAY RISE WITHOUT WARNING."

In fact, during the years since the old Norfolk-Southern Railroad depot was first constructed in the late 1800s, rising floodwaters of the French Broad River have washed it off its foundations at least twice. And now, after more than one hundred years as a center of activity, the depot has gone out of use as a train station and now serves as a community center. On Friday evenings the depot has mountain music and dancing starting at 7 P.M.

A block or so down the street from the depot, at 7 North Main Street, is a corner storefront called Zuma Coffee. During most of the week, the place is a coffee shop and health food bar and café, but on Thursday evenings it becomes a crowded bluegrass and old-time music venue. A North Carolina fiddling legend and local resident named Bobby Hicks often hosts the weekly bluegrass jam sessions that happen there. Over the years, Hicks, a Grammy winner and a veteran mountain musician, has played with Bill Monroe, Jesse McReynolds, Porter Wagoner, Ricky Skaggs, and many other noted country musicians.

Even though the music at Zuma Coffee is advertised as starting at 7 P.M., those who want to get a seat inside the place should arrive a good bit earlier.

More often than not, the eager-to-play musicians who assemble there each week get going before seven, and the gathering crowd of appreciative listeners soon grows large as a result. This jam session is actually part jam and part stage show. The musicians are situated inside the coffee shop in an area that backs up to the front windows of the store. They face the audience and not each other, as is the customary arrangement at a mountain jam session, and most stand to play, rather than sitting. Nevertheless, all musicians who want to join in and play are welcomed, regulars or not, and a place in the line is made available to them. The jam session is open to everyone and focuses on old-time and bluegrass music. Listeners are welcome and the coffee is tasty.

WHEN: Thursdays, 7 to 9 P.M.
WHERE: Zuma Coffee, 7 North Main Street, Downtown Marshall, 28753
ADMISSION: Free
CONTACT: 828-649-1617
WEBSITE: http://zumacoffee.blogspot.com

BASCOM LAMAR LUNSFORD "MINSTREL OF APPALACHIA" FESTIVAL
Mars Hill

On the first Saturday in October, a two-tiered celebration of mountain culture is held on the streets of Mars Hill and on the adjacent Mars Hill College campus. At the Madison County Heritage Festival, craft and food vendors line Mars Hill's Main Street, which is closed off for the event. Attendees can stroll over to a small stage on the college's grassy quad for the daytime portion of the concurrent Bascom Lamar Lunsford "Minstrel of Appalachia" Festival. This festival was founded by a group of local music lovers, including Lunsford himself, who was born in Mars Hill. The original vision was to showcase the unique musical heritage of the surrounding area and the college. More than forty years later, the lineup is a who's who of the county's prolific ballad singing, dancing and fiddling traditions.

In addition to the outdoor performances, the Lunsford Festival features a ballad swap held indoors on campus. At these small, intimate, and casual performances, audience members get a chance to get to know the singers and hear the stories behind the songs. A square dance in the grass in the afternoon closes out the daytime performances. For those who prefer to watch, clogging teams, including Mars Hill's own champions, the Bailey Mountain Cloggers, dance in a nearby amphitheater. After sundown, the second part of the festival is staged in the 1,500-seat Moore Auditorium on the college campus.

WHEN: First Saturday in October, 10 A.M. to 4 P.M.; concert, 7 to 11 P.M.
WHERE: Mars Hill College campus (Upper Quad and Moore Auditorium),
    Mars Hill, 28754
ADMISSION: Free, but fee charged for evening concert
CONTACT: Liston B. Ramsey Center for Regional Studies, 828-689-1571
WEBSITE: http://www.mhc.edu/ramsey-center/lunsford-festival

BLUFF MOUNTAIN MUSIC FESTIVAL

Hot Springs

The Bluff Mountain Music Festival is a daylong outdoor festival that features traditional, old-time, and bluegrass musicians and dancers from in and around Madison County. The festival is always held on the second

Stranger Malone (1909–2005), made records in the 1920s with members of the famous North Georgia string band the Skillet Lickers. He accompanied six-year-old Clay Sutton at the Bluff Mountain Music Festival in 2000.

HOT SPRINGS

Hot Springs can lay claim to being the only place in western North Carolina where you can bathe in hot mineral water piped up from underground thermal springs. Native Americans used the water of the spring for medicinal purposes before Europeans settled the area in the eighteenth century. Over the next two centuries, elegant hotels were built and a beautiful town arose on the banks of the nearby French Broad River. Most of the hotels succumbed eventually to fire, flood, or bankruptcy, and in 1917 the federal government leased the area around the springs for the internment of German sailors captured in U.S. ports at the outbreak of World War I. Today you can soak outdoors along the river, or rent hotel rooms or cabins with thermal tubs.

The Appalachian Trail passes through downtown Hot Springs, the only town in North Carolina where that happens. Look for the white blazes and the "A" symbol painted on the sidewalks. Many trail hikers stay overnight at the historic Gentry House in Hot Springs, but it was nearly a century ago when another visitor to the Gentry House made an immeasurable impact on American folk music. The English folklorist Cecil Sharp came to the Appalachian Mountains searching for singers who knew British ballads that had been passed down through the generations. In western North Carolina, he was excited to hear some ballads that were no longer sung in the British Isles. Sharp visited Hot Springs in 1916 and visited singers there and in the nearby region. Jane Hicks Gentry of Hot Springs sang seventy ballads for Sharp, more than any other singer sang for him during his visit to the southern mountains. Sharp included forty of her songs in his book *English*

The Appalachian Trail runs through downtown Hot Springs. This trail marker is a few blocks from the home of Jane Gentry, one of the main sources for the ballads collected by Cecil Sharp. Photograph by Steve Kruger.

Saturday in June and is located on the grounds of the Hot Springs Resort and Spa in Hot Springs. The Hot Springs resort was one of many that were built at the turn of the twentieth century in response to visitors seeking the healing powers of mountain mineral waters. Over time, the attraction of hot springs faded, and the resort was beset by fires and floods. The number of people who visited dwindled, and the facility fell into disuse. In 1990, the hot springs of Madison County came into new ownership, and the facility was revived. The mineral waters of the Hot Springs Spa maintain a 100-degree temperature all year round. Jacuzzis filled with curative waters are available at the spa, and the campground features full hookups and hot showers.

The Bluff Mountain Music Festival features many of the best traditional music performers and dancers in the region. Madison County has one of the oldest continuous ballad singing traditions in the United States, and local ballad singers are often part of the program. Clogging teams continue the mountain dance tradition. Bring your folding chair or blanket for a full day of music under the trees beside the French Broad River. The festival was originally started to help prevent logging on Bluff Mountain, and the proceeds from the festival now benefit the Madison County Arts Council.

WHEN: Second Saturday in June, 10 A.M. to 8 P.M.
WHERE: Hot Springs Spa and Resort, Hot Springs, 28743. If you're heading into town from the east, the resort is located immediately after you cross the French Broad River, on the right.

Sheila Kay Adams: She Appointed Me

Sheila Kay Adams is the inheritor of a family ballad tradition that goes back to the days of early settlement in North Carolina.

I was child of the sixties—the whole nine yards. I listened to Steppenwolf and Led Zeppelin and the Rolling Stones and the Beatles. But when I was at college I started to realize how important tradition is. I also realized that nobody else was learning it.

I was born in Madison County. Born and raised there. My parents were also from there—from a community called Sodom. I'm the great-niece of Dellie Norton, who was one of the renowned ballad singers. When I was growing up, there were eight traditional ballad singers around our home still singing the old love songs. Cass Wallin was one of 'em. So was Inez Chandler. They were all family members. As I got older and started to appreciate my heritage, I got really serious about learning from all of 'em.

I spent a lot of time at my granny's house, and there was music there all the time. Granny was also a really neat storyteller, but it was the singing that was the most important. They called the way they did it "round robins." They would sing an old love song and then they would turn around and sing a song like "Angel Band" or "We'll Camp a Little While in the Wilderness." They'd sing those right along with the old love songs. If you listen real close to the singing of the sacred songs, especially those old camp meeting songs, you'll see that they've got the same quality as the love songs. Their voices break in the same places. They kinda "feather" the end of a line. Granny would lift her voice at the end of a line when she sang a sacred song, just like she'd do when she sang "Young Emily." She said the purpose of it was to get you back into the pitch that you had started in. There's only a few little pockets left where the ballad singers do it that way.

I remember one time Granny and I went to a round robin. I was seventeen, and I had driven all the older ladies to the singing. After they got into this big circle, it was announced that one of the singers had recently passed away. I was out in the lobby smoking cigarettes, and Granny sent for me. Ceelie was her pet name for me—it's the Gaelic pronunciation for Sheila. She said, "Tell Ceelie to come in here." So I went in there and she said for me to sit down. So I sat down next to her, and she leaned over and put her hand on my knee. She told me that she had been looking around at all the people in the circle, and she had realized how old they were, and she had thought, "If we don't get some young folks to singing these old love songs, it's all gonna all be gone! When these folks here are gone, every song they know will be gone too, unless somebody young learns them." She appointed me.

I remember the first love song I ever learned. I was five years old. It was a ridiculously suggestive thing that goes like this:

There was an old farmer who lived by the sea,
A merry old farmer was he.

He had a fair maiden who laid on the grass,
Ever' time she turned over, she'd show her fair . . . ruffles and tucks

. . . and so on and on.

I learned that one quickly! Granny said, "As easy as she learned that one, she can probably learn the bigger ones." Not too long after that I learned "Lord Bateman," which has ninety-six verses. So I fell in love with the old stories. All that violence! All kinds of *nasty* stories. I loved the stories.

He took her by the lily-white hand,
And he led her across the hall.
He pulled out his sword and cut off her head,
And kicked it against the wall!

There were verses like that all the time. And anytime I heard something like

How do you like my snow-white pillow?
How do you like my sheet?
How do you like my pretty little woman,
Who lays in your arms asleep?

Then I immediately wanted to learn it, because I knew that it was one of those kinda risqué, off-color love songs. Granny just called them all "love songs."

Here in Madison County music is so wrapped up in family that it's really hard to separate the two. For instance, Jerry Adams is my first cousin. And Josh Goforth

and I are related. The list just goes on. Now my daughter, Melanie, is taking it up. She's twenty-eight. For a time she strayed away from it and I wasn't sure if she was ever going to come back to it. But Granny kept saying, "She'll come back, she'll come back." She was very fortunate in that she learned from the same people that I did. She learned from Granny and the others.

I have always said that mountain people are actually an unrecognized minority in this country. Some of our speech patterns are now being studied by language scholars. They're hunting for pockets here in the mountains where the people are still using some middle English and Chaucerian styles of speech. Sometimes I tell outside people about that. I say, "Your English has become homogenized. If you think I talk funny, it's simply because my English is a lot older than yours."

People see that what I do is a part of a long tradition, and they really crave it for themselves. A music scholar once told me, "Sheila, are you aware that the tradition that you carry on was ancient by the time of Mozart?" Isn't that amazing? My family has been singing those old love songs, as best we can figure, for seven generations. I'm the eighth generation, and my daughter is the ninth. I can't think of any other family tradition that can beat it, unless it might be a recipe. I think that makes those old folks pretty special. They just loved to sing.

ADMISSION: Free
CONTACT: Madison County Arts Council, 828-649-1301
WEBSITE: www.madisoncountyarts.com; or www.nchotsprings.com for the Hot Springs Resort

HENDERSON COUNTY

ETOWAH CHRISTIAN HARMONY SINGING
Etowah

While a hymnal titled *The Sacred Harp* is probably the best-known songbook in the southern shape-note pantheon, *Christian Harmony*, published by William Walker in 1867, was more widely used in the North Carolina mountains. Walker became known for pairing religious poetry with melodies already familiar to people in the South. His earlier *Southern Harmony* was the first hymnbook to include the song "Amazing Grace." Many other canonical southern hymns, including "Angel Band," made their debut in the Walker books. *Christian Harmony* was also one of the first hymnbooks to use seven shapes (do, re, me, fa, so, la, ti, do) for the scale, as opposed to older systems that used three or four shapes.

Shape-note singing is unaccompanied by instrumentation of any kind. The music is created entirely by the human voice—the "sacred harp." Often the notes of the hymn's melody are sung by name before the actual words of the first verse are sung. At a typical shape-note singing, singers separate into different groups based on their approximate vocal range. Each group will sing a different line of notes in the hymnbook. They face each other, across an empty space, known as the hollow square. An individual stands

The *Christian Harmony* hymnbook is popular among shape-note singers in southwestern North Carolina. Photograph by Mary Anne McDonald. Courtesy of the North Carolina Arts Council.

in the middle to lead the song by setting the key and tempo. The result is powerful: poetry, set to four-part harmony, in stereo.

The second-longest-running Christian Harmony Singing event in the North Carolina mountains takes place twice a year in the Etowah community in Henderson County. It began in 1907 at a private home but soon grew so popular that it was moved to a nearby church. Then, in 1952, the singing was relocated to the Etowah Elementary School. Since 2010, it has shifted between the Etowah United Methodist Church and the Cummings Memorial Methodist Church, located in the nearby community of Horseshoe. The singing lasts for several hours, with a break for a potluck "dinner on the grounds." Visitors are encouraged to bring a dish of food to share, but it is not required. Everyone from beginners to old hands is welcome to sit in the hollow square and sing along. Regulars bring along their own hymnbooks, but they are provided for visitors and newcomers. You can find a listing of Christian Harmony singings across the Southeast at www .christianharmony.org, and a list of shape-note singings in western North Carolina at BlueRidgeMusicNC.com.

WHEN: The Saturday before the first Sunday in May, and the Saturday before the first Sunday in September, 10 A.M. to 3 P.M.
WHERE: Cummings Memorial Methodist Church, 1 Banner Farm Road, Horseshoe, 28742. Turn onto Banner Farm Road from US 64 in

Asheville Junction

RELIGIOUS FOLK SONG TRADITIONS IN THE BLUE RIDGE

Many different styles of religious songs and congregational singing developed in Blue Ridge churches throughout the 1800s, and many of them continue in use today. One of the older styles—practiced by whites, blacks, and Cherokees—involved unaccompanied congregational singing of hymn texts to traditional ballad melodies. Where congregations had few hymnbooks or could not read, a song leader would "line out" or chant a line or two of the text, then pause while the congregation repeated that text, singing the familiar hymn tune, sometimes in a highly ornamented version. Such singing is practiced still by Primitive Baptists and German Baptist Brethren.

Early Methodists developed another style of unaccompanied song that could be caught easily by ear. Their camp meeting and revival spirituals featured repeated lines and choruses and often used melodies derived from traditional dance tunes. Shape-note hymnbooks, which used a special shape for each note of the scale to facilitate sight-reading, picked up both of these repertories but arranged them in three- or four-part unaccompanied choral performance. Singing masters taught rural people how to read this musical notation, and the song settings came into use both in church worship and in periodic sing-

Singing accompanies a full-immersion baptism in Ashe County.

ing conventions. The most popular shape-note books in the Blue Ridge were William Walker's *Southern Harmony and Musical Companion* (1835) and *Christian Harmony* (1867); the latter is still used in singings today. Among the oldest Christian Harmony sings in the Blue Ridge region are the ones at Morning Star Church in Canton and the singing at Etowah.

Musical instruments were not allowed at Methodist and other churches for many years, and they're still not permitted at Primitive Baptist churches. The churches either did not find them authorized by the New Testament or associated them with dissolute behavior, so church singing was unaccompanied and stood in contrast to much of the music in the secular world outside. By the twentieth century, yet another style of singing entered both black and white churches in the Blue Ridge: up-tempo gospel songs performed with pianos, guitars, and other instruments, together with solo performances by featured groups.

The more mainstream congregations, rural and urban, have shifted from local Blue Ridge traditions to singing from hymnals issued by the national or regional printing houses of their denominations. The indigenous music has been little noticed by outsiders and overshadowed by national trends, but the older religious songs and traditional singing styles have been pervasive nevertheless. Well known to many longtime residents, they continue to enrich the musical landscape of the region.

—Daniel W. Patterson and Beverly Patterson

Horseshoe. The church is located down the hill, between the stoplight and the railroad tracks.

CONTACT: Scott Swanton, 828-577-1889
WEBSITE: www.christianharmony.org

TRANSYLVANIA COUNTY

THURSDAY NIGHT JAM AT THE SILVERMONT MANSION
Brevard

At the southern end of the Blue Ridge region of North Carolina, in Brevard, there's an unusual and entertaining jam session every Thursday night at the Silvermont Mansion, a community center that's owned by Transylvania County and co-operated by the Friends of Silvermont, a volunteer group. The Silvermont Mansion, built in 1917, is a massive, three-level brick house with an impressive colonnaded front portico and spacious front and side porches. A set of broad front steps and a massive front entry lead into a central hallway that is flanked on either side by a pair of elegantly appointed formal parlors. Silvermont Mansion is about as unlikely a place for a mountain music jam session as you can imagine.

The Silvermont jam began back in 1981 when a trio of local traditional musicians was asked to play on a regular basis out on the front porch of the

mansion, sponsored by the Transylvania County Recreation Department. News of the session quickly spread by word of mouth throughout the community, and the number of participating musicians who showed up to play in the following weeks eventually grew to the point where the session was moved inside to one of the front parlors. And there it remains, every Thursday evening, year-round.

The Silvermont jam session is unusual not only because of its elegant setting but also for its interesting form. The musicians—typically there are around fifteen, and eighteen is the limit—set up folding chairs in a large circle inside the left front parlor of the house. Within the circle is a single microphone on a stand. As each musician takes a turn leading a song, the microphone is passed along, person to person, in a clockwise manner. Each player is expected to choose and announce a tune, start the song, and lead the group as the tune is played and sung. And so the evening goes, song after song. Meanwhile, nonplayers who are there to enjoy listening sit in folding chairs out in the hallway or in an adjacent connecting dining room area. Some in the adjoining audience areas flatfoot or clog a little whenever a particularly bright tune is played. The music played at Silvermont ranges from bluegrass and old-time to country and gospel. Since this session is truly open to all who want to participate, there's even an occasional jazz or classical player in the mix. Generally, when their turn comes to lead, most of the other players just sit quietly back and enjoy the nonconformer's solo performance.

On Tuesday nights there's another good jam in Brevard, an old-time music session at Celestial Mountain Music, a restored 1892 storefront on West Main Street. Celestial Mountain Music is a great resource in the area

JAM PROTOCOL

The majority of jam sessions in the Blue Ridge are friendly affairs where people gather to play and listen to traditional music in an informal setting. The seating, or standing arrangement, of the participants varies from place to place and from time to time. However, there seems to be a general custom that the most experienced musicians will occupy the most central positions of the group. Generally, but not always, the assembled players at mountain jam sessions form a circle, and the veteran musicians sit or stand right in the middle of the circle.

The other musicians often place themselves closer to or more distant from the center in accordance with their particular skill levels. Beginners will occa-

sionally select a spot entirely removed from the main group, a few chairs or steps away, sometimes even to the point of retreating into an adjacent room, if one is available. But as with many aspects of mountain music, there are no hard-and-fast rules. But there are certain parameters to be considered before unpacking a banjo or guitar. Visitors are almost always welcome to join in, but every jam is different, so musicians who have an interest in joining in should be observant and respectful of local protocol, which can include what style of music is played, and whether solos are taken.

Laura Pharis, a professor of studio art at Sweet Briar College and a fiddle player, came up with the following tongue-in-cheek guidelines for participating in jam sessions:

The Ten Commandments of Jamming
  1. Thou shalt not forsake the beat.
  2. Thou shalt always play in tune.
  3. Thou shalt arrange thyselves in a circle so thou mayest hear and see the other musicians and thou shalt play in accord with the group.

4. Thou shalt commence and cease playing in unison.
5. Thou shalt stick out thine own foot or lift up thine own voice and cry, "This is it!" if thou hast been the one to begin the song, this in order to endeth the tune, which otherwise wilt go on and on forever and forevermore.
6. Thou shalt concentrate and not confound the music by mixing up the A part and the B part. If thou should sinneth in this, or make any mistake that is unclean, thou mayest atone for thy transgression by reentering the tune in the proper place and playing thereafter in time.
7. Thou shalt be mindful of the key of the banjo, and play many tunes in that key, for the banjo is but a lowly instrument which must be retuned each time there is a key change.
8. Thou shalt not speed up nor slow down when playing a tune, for such is an abomination.
9. Thou shalt not noodle by thine ownself on a tune which the other musicians know not, unless thou art asked or unless thou art teaching that tune, for it is an abomination and the other musicians will not hold thee guiltless, and shall take thee off their computer lists, yea, even unto the third and fourth generations. Thou shalt not come to impress others with thine own amazing talents, but will adhere to the song, which shall be the center around which all musicians play.
10. Thou shalt play well and have fun.

for acoustic music, particularly old-time. The sessions are free and start at 7 P.M.

WHEN: Silvermont: Thursdays, 7:30 to 10:00 P.M.; Celestial Mountain Music: Tuesdays, 7 P.M.

WHERE: Silvermont Mansion, 364 East Main Street (US 276 south), Brevard, 28712; Celestial Mountain Music: 16 West Main Street, Brevard, 28712

ADMISSION: Free

CONTACT: Silvermont: 828-884-3166; Celestial Mountain Music: 828-884-3575

Students at the Cradle of Forestry, circa 1906. Courtesy of the USDA Forest Service.

SONGCATCHERS MUSIC SERIES AT THE CRADLE OF FORESTRY
Pisgah Forest

The Cradle of Forestry is itself cradled in a beautiful high valley crisscrossed by streams. Historic buildings from the school of forestry's early days and an antique logging locomotive are main attractions, along with the new Forest Discovery Center, an interpretive museum that tells the history of the school and of forestry in the United States. Craftspeople give demonstrations at indoor and outdoor exhibit areas on most weekends. On Sunday afternoons in July, music takes center stage at the Cradle's Songcatchers Music Series. Old-time and bluegrass musicians perform in the shaded outdoor amphitheater, and there is sometimes jamming before and after the concert. The series focuses on the older mountain music traditions, and the featured artists often take a historic or educational approach to performing. Visitors get a chance to learn about the history of the music and the people who made it, many of whom lived in communities affected by the logging industry. The site is operated by the USDA Forest Service.

WHEN: Sundays afternoons in July. Check website for schedule. The site is
    open from mid-April to early November.
WHERE: 11250 Pisgah Highway (US 276), Pisgah Forest, 28768. Located
    south of the Blue Ridge Parkway and 11 miles north of Brevard.
ADMISSION: Fee
CONTACT: 828-877-3130
WEBSITE: www.cradleofforestry.com

Asheville Junction

NATIONAL FORESTS IN THE NORTH CAROLINA BLUE RIDGE

Pisgah and Nantahala National Forests spread over more than a million acres in western North Carolina and contain six wilderness areas. When visitors take in the view of undulating ridges covered in bluish-looking deciduous forests, they are seeing a different landscape than if they had stood at the same spot in the early 1900s. At that time, many of the mountains were clear-cut, with bare hillsides pocked by erosion and catastrophic flooding. The need to protect watersheds and manage timber resources in the Southeast led to the passage of the Weeks Act in 1911, which authorized Congress to purchase land for national forests. Pisgah became the first eastern national forest. The science of managing American forests had its birth in North Carolina decades earlier. That history is on display at the Cradle of Forestry in America, a 6,000-acre historic site in Transylvania County that was the home of the nation's first forestry school. In 1889, tycoon George Vanderbilt purchased thousands of acres in western North Carolina for an estate, which he named Biltmore.

Frederick Law Olmsted, the designer of Central Park in New York City, was hired to design the grounds of the estate. Olmsted recommended finding a forester who could restore the natural landscape and also harvest timber without endangering the health of the forest. The forester hired was the young Gifford Pinchot, a Connecticut Yankee. Pinchot had trained in Europe since forest management was not taught in America at the time. He would later go on to be the first chief of the national forest system. Vanderbilt's second head forester, Dr. Carl A. Schenk, managed the forest for fourteen years and set standards for the emerging field of American forestry

The Wasilik poplar was too big to cut when the area around it was logged in the 1930s. Though the tree has died, it remains standing in the Nantahala National Forest in Macon County, the second-largest yellow poplar tree in the nation. Photograph by Steve Kruger.

science. Schenk trained many of the first generation of American foresters at the Biltmore Forest School.

Though its origins are in managing timber resources, today the national forests of North Carolina hold some of the state's most popular hiking trails, swimming holes, and recreation areas. Be sure to pick up information on Transylvania County's many famous waterfalls at www.visitnc.com and visit nearby Looking Glass Rock, which can be viewed from the Blue Ridge Parkway.

The Flint Hill Special

The cradle of bluegrass banjo playing lies in the southeastern foothills of the Blue Ridge Mountains of North Carolina. In the 1920s and 1930s, the region was a hotspot for two- and three-finger-style banjo playing. And Shelby, the county seat of Cleveland County, produced a famous son, Earl Scruggs, whose musical skills changed the way that most people play—and hear—the banjo.

Earl Scruggs was born on January 6, 1924, in the Flint Hill community near Boiling Springs in a family of traditional musicians. His father, George, played the banjo, and his grandfather, George Elam Scruggs, was a fiddler. From infancy onward, Scruggs lived in a household where there were always a variety of musical instruments and a number of family members who played them. His brothers were all musicians, and they encouraged the younger Earl to pitch in and learn to play music with them. He did. By the time he was ten years old, Earl Scruggs had mastered the banjo using the locally prevalent three-finger picking style. As a teenager, Scruggs often played in local bands for community dances; he also worked at the Lily Cotton Mill in the nearby town of Shelby. In 1945, he left Shelby and joined a band playing radio shows in Knoxville, Nashville, and other towns where radio stations featured live country music. In December 1945, Scruggs joined a group called the Blue Grass Boys. That group included Chubby Wise on fiddle, Bill Monroe on mandolin, and Lester Flatt on guitar. Scruggs made his first recording with the Blue Grass Boys in 1946 and stayed with them for two more years. That lineup helped set the standard for the genre that would soon bear the band's name. Later, Scruggs and Lester Flatt formed their own band, called Flatt and Scruggs and the Foggy Mountain Boys. The Foggy Mountain Boys played together very successfully for more than twenty years and in the process became one of the most influential bluegrass groups of all time. Earl Scruggs was an innovator—a man with a deep sense of tradition who took that tradition, sped up the tempo and made something creative, something all his own.

Though their style may be rooted in the old-time three-

Earl Scruggs with his brother Horace, circa 1940. Courtesy of the Horace Scruggs Family.

Earl & Horace Scruggs

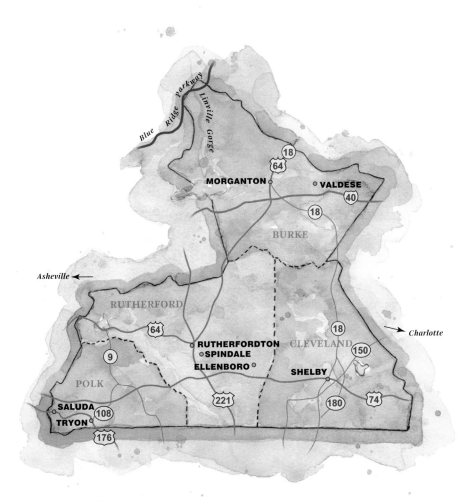

Blue Ridge Parkway

Linville Gorge

18
64
MORGANTON ○   ○ VALDESE
40
18

BURKE

Asheville ←

RUTHERFORD

64   RUTHERFORDTON ○   18   → Charlotte
9   ○SPINDALE   CLEVELAND   150
                      ELLENBORO ○   SHELBY
POLK
SALUDA
108   221   180   74
TRYON ○
176

Region 5

THE PLACE

This region begins along the edge of the mountains and follows a southwestern arc through Burke, Cleveland, Rutherford, and Polk Counties, ending at the South Carolina border. Like other regions in the foothills, these counties tend to drop significantly in elevation from west to east. Along the edge of the Blue Ridge there are some places of intense beauty—the rugged Linville Gorge Wilderness in northwestern Burke County and Chimney Rock and Lake Lure in Rutherford County. Towns such as Saluda and Tryon in western Polk County are identified with the mountains and have an economy that is based principally on tourism.

With the exception of the isolated South Mountains in Burke and Rutherford Counties, the landscape of the region falls away to the east into a beautiful landscape of hilly farmland and small towns. Columbus in Polk County and Forest City and Spindale in Rutherford County grew around the furniture and textile industries. Spindale is the home of WNCW, one of the most important mountain music radio stations in the state.

This area has a long and interesting history. The Spanish conquistador Hernando de Soto passed through this region on his way to the mountains and to a place that he had been led to believe would yield untold riches, treasures similar to those that Francisco Pizarro had discovered earlier during explorations in Peru. A later Spanish expedition, led by Juan Pardo, built a fort near the Native American town of Joara in 1567 in what is now Burke County. More than 200 years later, a ragtag band of Revolutionary soldiers from the interior of the mountains traveled the same path as de Soto, going in the other direction. These Overmountain Men fighting another colonial power,

A vintage postcard of the Linville Gorge. Courtesy of the North Carolina Collection, University of North Carolina at Chapel Hill Library.

England, helped to turn the tide of the Revolutionary War at the Battle of Kings Mountain. In the early 1830s, a gold rush briefly swelled the population of the region, and a mint was established at the town of Rutherfordton, which was founded in 1787. Rutherfordton is said to be the home of the first post office, the first newspaper, and the earliest school in the Blue Ridge region, and it boasts many other historic homes and buildings.

finger styles that were popular in the 1920s and 1930s, nearly all bluegrass banjo players performing today play what is often called "Scruggs-style" banjo. Scruggs's individual playing style helped make bluegrass a distinctive musical genre, one that, for many, has become synonymous with Appalachian music.

Earl Scruggs died on March 28, 2012, but the music he helped shape is alive and well in the southeastern foothills of North Carolina. Some of the best bluegrass in the state can be heard at such places as the Old Rock School in Valdese and the Red, White and Bluegrass Festival, held every Fourth of July in Morganton. Some say bluegrass wouldn't be what it is today if it weren't for a man from a little place called Flint Hill in Cleveland County—Earl Scruggs.

REGION 5 AT A GLANCE

CLEVELAND COUNTY

EARL SCRUGGS CENTER
Shelby

In the center square in the town of Shelby is the former Cleveland County Courthouse, a striking neoclassical revival building that was built in 1907. Today, the old courthouse is the new Earl Scruggs Center. It features an exciting exhibit titled *Music & Stories of the Carolina Foothills.* Several of Earl Scruggs and the Scruggs family's most personally prized musical instruments are showcased—a Gibson J-45 guitar, a 1945 Martin guitar, and the banjo and fiddle of Earl's grandfather, George Elam Scruggs. Moving through the rotunda of the courthouse, visitors enter an orientation space where a short film welcomes them to the exhibit and provides some general information about Shelby, Cleveland County, and the history of Earl Scruggs and his family. Radiating from the central rotunda on the main

Earl Scruggs performing in his hometown of Shelby in 2009. Scruggs continued to tour until shortly before he passed away in 2012. Photograph by Brittany Randolph. Courtesy of the *Shelby Star.*

floor of the Center are three additional major exhibit components: In These Hills Gallery, Out of Carolina Gallery, and Turning Road Gallery. Each of these galleries interpret various aspects of local history and local culture, with emphasis on the life of Earl Scruggs and his career as a nationally prominent and widely influential performing artist and the story of his family. Exhibits feature a section on the local cotton mill industry and related agricultural and transportation topics, a section on the saga of early radio broadcasting in the region and its role in the development of country music as a popular art form, a section on the importance of the banjo in the story of the music of the region, and a section on Earl Scruggs as a musician and his impact on the banjo. Finally, there's a section on the contemporary music scene in Shelby as expressed through the music of local African American soul and R & B performers. A unique interactive exhibit explains and demonstrates the several distinctive styles of banjo finger picking, including the method that Earl Scruggs made famous and for which he became canonized in the development of bluegrass music and banjo playing as a national phenomenon.

The upstairs floor of the Earl Scruggs Center will feature a "Great Hall" space (inside the refurbished courtroom) for live performances, meetings, and lectures. Plans also call for a resource and archival facility, a studio space for teaching music lessons, and a small gallery space that's reserved for special and changing exhibits.

WHEN: Check website for details.
WHERE: Old Cleveland County Courthouse, 103 South Lafayette Street, Shelby, 28150
ADMISSION: Fee
CONTACT: Destination Cleveland County, 704-487-6233
WEBSITE: www.earlscruggscenter.org

LIVERMUSH EXPO AND THE ART OF SOUND MUSIC FESTIVAL
Shelby

In the Piedmont town of Shelby, in Cleveland County, there's an annual festival known as the Livermush Expo. It's always been one of the big events of the year in the North Carolina foothills. Then, in 2008, the Travel Channel's *Bizarre Foods* host Andrew Zimmern attended the expo and featured livermush on his television show. The festival, which was already a popular event and more than two decades old, jumped several additional notches in popularity as a result.

Livermush is an inexpensive loaf meat product with pork as the main ingredient—principally the liver and head parts. Cornmeal is also a major ingredient. Certain spices and seasonings, usually salt and sage, but some-times red pepper, are added to enhance the already flavorful concoction. When purchased in its customary square loaf form, livermush is a fully cooked product, ready to be eaten as is. But it's typically cooked a second time—deep-fried, broiled, or microwaved—before being served. Liver-mush can be eaten at any meal—breakfast, lunch, or dinner. However, like bacon, ham, or sausage, it's most often eaten for breakfast—with bis-cuits, eggs, pancakes, hash browns, grits, and so on. It's also used in sand-wiches, in which case it's often combined with onions, slaw, mustard, and mayonnaise.

On Livermush Expo day, the action begins early. Although its official starting time is advertised as 10 A.M. on Saturday, long before that pet lovers have assembled to register their dogs for a pet parade and costume contest; the mothers of dozens of girls of all ages, from preschoolers to teens, who have signed up to compete in the annual Miss Livermush com-petition, are applying final adjustments to the costumes and hairdos of their fancifully dressed daughters (Miss Livermush competition categories include Baby Miss, Tiny Miss, Miniature Miss, Little Miss, Young Miss, Teen Miss, Junior Miss, and Miss Overall Grand Majestic); elementary and middle school choral groups stand assembled near the outdoor stage, itch-ing to sing their long-rehearsed musical numbers; and the line of fans who wait patiently for their chance to have a taste of hot livermush for break-fast has grown to a city block long. That line, which moves steadily along as patrons purchase their livermush biscuits and bottles of Cheerwine or Sun Drop sodas (two favorite regional soft drinks), will not diminish in its length until nearly noon. Livermush is a very popular early-morning, early-autumn culinary treat in Shelby.

Meanwhile, over on the courthouse lawn, children paint Halloween pumpkins, and, nearby, shaded by canvas canopied street stalls, local ven-dors offer a variety of handicrafts, folk carvings, homegrown and organic fruits and vegetables, fresh-baked goods, jams, syrups, preserves and jel-lies, freshly butchered meats, and neatly packaged, three-pound loaves of—what else?—livermush.

The expo overlaps with another major weekend event in Shelby, the Art of Sound Music Festival, which begins on Thursday and presents a pot-pourri of music at four downtown venues, including the Don Gibson The-atre. For three days, more than twenty-five acts perform in a diverse range of musical styles, from old-time and bluegrass to country, jazz, blues, rock, and Americana. Local acts are heavily represented in the lineup, but the festival also brings in artists from the thriving music scene in Asheville, and there are always a few well-known touring acts on the bill. The Heritage Bridge Award ceremony is a highlight of the festival. The award honors those who have made lifelong contributions to Cleveland County's diverse musical heritage. Like the festival, the award celebrates all of the region's homegrown music. Winners have played bluegrass and gospel but also local incarnations of popular genres, like big-band jazz, country, and soul music.

The Livermush Expo and Art of Sound Festival are very well attended events that fully occupy the yard and streets around the beautifully groomed Shelby town square.

WHEN: Thursday–Saturday, third weekend in October
WHERE: Old Cleveland County Courthouse, 103 South Lafayette Street, Shelby, 28150
ADMISSION: Outdoor events are free, but fee charged for some concerts
CONTACT: For the Livermush Expo, call Cleveland County Travel and Tourism, 704-482-7882; for the Art of Sound Music Festival, call the Cleveland County Arts Council, 704-484-2787.
WEBSITE: www.ccartscouncil.org/artofsound/ and www.tourclevelandcounty.com/

DON GIBSON THEATRE
Shelby

Before becoming a best-selling recording artist and country music star, Donald Eugene Gibson, born April 3, 1928, in Shelby, had been a textile mill worker, a delivery man, a dishwasher, a soda jerk, and a truck driver. Don Gibson's career as a performer began in 1948 when his band, Sons of the Soil, played frequent live gigs on radio station WOHS in Shelby. In 1949, he cut his first song for Mercury Records, and the following year, in 1950, he left Mercury and signed a contract with RCA. Don Gibson appeared on the Grand Ole Opry for the first time in 1958 when he was thirty years old.

During the 1950s and 1960s, Don Gibson became one of the most popular and influential artists in country music. He created numerous highly successful records as a performer and as a songwriter. His first hit single, "Sweet Dreams," was released in 1956. During the next several years, from 1958 to 1961, he wrote and recorded an amazing array of top-ten singles, including "Blue Blue Day," "Who Cares," "Don't Tell Me Your Troubles," "Just One Time," "Sea of Heartbreak," "Lonesome Number One," and "I Can't Stop Lovin' You."

Don Gibson's songs have been recorded many times by many musicians, and some have made big hits of them. To date, "I Can't Stop Loving You"

People line up outside the Don Gibson Theatre in Shelby. Courtesy of Destination Cleveland County.

alone has been recorded by more than seven hundred other artists, including Elvis Presley, Roy Orbison, Count Basie, and, notably, Ray Charles, for whom it was a smash hit.

Don Gibson died in Nashville on November 17, 2003, and is buried in the Sunset Cemetery in his hometown of Shelby.

In downtown Shelby, the old State Theater, a movie house that first opened in 1939 and was described then by the local newspaper as "one of the most strikingly beautiful building fronts of the modern day," has, after three decades of being closed, been recently restored to its former glory and renamed The Don Gibson Theatre in honor of the town's famous musical native son.

Today, this 400-seat performance venue, operating under the auspices of a nonprofit support group, offers a slate of live shows and concerts that fill the house several times every month. The theater also operates again as a movie house, where both new and classic films are screened periodically throughout the year.

WHEN: Concerts are scheduled throughout the week, 8 P.M.
WHERE: 318 South Washington Street, Shelby, 28150
ADMISSION: Fee
CONTACT: Don Gibson Theatre, 704-487-8114
WEBSITE: www.destinationclevelandcounty.org or www.dgshelby.com

BURKE COUNTY

BLUEGRASS AT THE OLD ROCK SCHOOL
Valdese

The Old Rock School in downtown Valdese is a renovated 1920s school building constructed of local rock in the distinctive Waldensian style. The Waldenses are descendants of a group of French religious dissenters who settled in Italy. In 1893, a group of Waldenses immigrated to Burke County and created the community of Valdese. They brought their language, distinctive cultural traditions, and occupational skills, including masonry, with them. Waldensian masons use a technique in which roughly cut stones are carefully fitted together into thick, solid walls using little or no mortar.

Valdese's Italian ancestry remains evident today. Traditional Italian foods are available at several local eating establishments, including Myra's Little Italy and Giovanni's Restaurant. Both places serve good pizza. And since 1976, Valdese has hosted an annual Waldensian Festival to celebrate the "Glorious Return" in 1689 of the Old World Waldenses from their place of exile in Switzerland to their native valleys in the Cottian Alps of Italy, an

Waldensian masons built the Old Rock School in the 1920s.

● GEORGE SHUFFLER: BLUEGRASS PIONEER

As a young boy, George Shuffler attended shape-note singing schools held in local schools. The teacher quickly noticed George's ear for harmony. Any student who had trouble with a part was admonished to "listen to Shuffler there, he'll keep you right." At home, George would hear his father "thump around" on the banjo. When George expressed an interest in music, his father traded an old car for a guitar. One of his father's coworkers in a Valdese textile mill taught George three basic chords, and he soon began improvising "homemade" accompaniment inspired by musicians he heard on the radio. In 1941, at the age of sixteen, George joined a local band that performed live radio shows. When George played with the Bailey Brothers, an established professional band, as a substitute for their missing bass player on a show date in Granite Falls, they offered him a full-time job. He packed his bags and left for Nashville, Tennessee.

Eventually tiring of life on the road, George returned to North Carolina and performed with his brother, John, and a local fiddler, Lester Woodie. In 1950, he began a twenty-year association with the Stanley Brothers, helping set the standard for bluegrass guitar picking and bass playing. To complement Ralph and Carter Stanley's singing on slow songs, George developed a unique cross-

picking style that transformed the guitar into a lead as well as a rhythm instrument. His "walking" bass technique, which energized breakdowns and fast songs, has been emulated by successive generations of bluegrass musicians.

His teenage daughters inspired George to make the transition from bluegrass to southern gospel. After hearing them sing in a small church choir, George remembers thinking, "My goodness gracious, what have I been missing here! And so I asked them, 'If y'all will sing with me, I'll do all the

George Shuffler.

legwork and we'll go from there. And I'll never put you in an embarrassing position.'" The Shuffler Family started out singing traditional songs but soon began performing George's compositions. His best-known song, "When I Receive My Robe and Crown," stayed on the national gospel music charts for eleven months.

George is retired from music, but his influence remains strong. On any weekend you might find some of the finest musicians in the business dropping in to see him and his wife, Sue. He tells visitors he remains loyal to the musical styles he heard growing up in rural Burke County. A lot of modern country and bluegrass music has "turned to hairspray and rhinestones," he says. "If the music hasn't got a good cornfield sound to it, it just don't interest me."

event celebrated by other Waldensian communities around the world. The Waldensian Heritage Museum, located beside the beautiful Waldensian Presbyterian Church, has 12,000 square feet of interpretive displays of vintage photographs, clothing, home and church furnishings, farm implements, carpentry tools, wine-making tools, toys, and other items related to Waldensian culture and history in Valdese.

The refurbished Old Rock School at Valdese serves as a community cultural center for the area and features a 473-seat auditorium, an art gallery, the Piedmont and Western Railway Museum, a town meeting space, and offices. Once a month, from September through April, there's a bluegrass concert there that features both locally and nationally known musicians.

WHEN: One Friday or Saturday each month, September–April; shows start at 7:00 or 7:30 P.M.; check the website or call for details.
WHERE: 400 West Main Street, Valdese, 28690
ADMISSION: Fee
CONTACT: 828-879-2129
WEBSITE: www.visitvaldese.com

RED, WHITE AND BLUEGRASS FESTIVAL
Morganton
Annually, from June 30 to July 4, thousands of bluegrass fans converge on the Catawba Meadows Park in Morganton for one of North Carolina's

Etta Baker: A Wonderful Life

Etta Baker (1913–2006) was taught to play guitar by her father at the age of three. Baker is admired by thousands for her finger-picked style of blues guitar playing.

I was born in Caldwell County, west of Lenoir. That was in nineteen and thirteen. My daddy was Madison Boone Reid. He was Indian and Irish. Cherokee. My mother was Sarah Sally Wilson. I've had people ask me, "What nationality are you?" I say, "I'm so mixed up, if I ever find out, I'll let you know."

When I was almost three, my daddy decided he'd move to east Virginia. So we went down there. Then when I was fourteen my dad moved back to his father's place on John's River in Caldwell County. And there is where I spent the most of my time, until I was twenty-three years old. It was a community that seemed like one big family. Back then they'd dance, play music, have a good time. They'd break long enough for dinner and then they'd go right back into playing again. It would be at my daddy's house one night, and then the next night it would be at one of his friends. It was a wonderful, wonderful life.

I got married to Lee H. Baker at the age of twenty-three, and we raised a family, a family of nine children. I lost one son in the Vietnam War. But the good Lord blessed me with the raising of eight of my children. Now they're scattered all about. But they all remember me, and they all come home as often as they can. They still find time to come visit with me. The good Lord has blessed me with a lot of merry chatter.

When I was three, coming onto three years old, I would hear my dad tuning up the guitar or the banjo. That tuning got me out of the bed! I would get up and go over to

my dad, go through under his knee, and stand up between him and the guitar so I could peep over and see what he was doing. I learned where he was putting his fingers. He'd set me up in the middle of the bed, and I'd lay the guitar across and put my fingers where I had seen him put his. Finally he bought me a little Stella guitar, a little tiny one, and I began to make chords. I could do my three basic chords when I was three.

Daddy and his brothers, they all learned guitar. My mother played the harmonica. They played mostly what they call country music, but when we moved to Virginia, Dad started hearing those blues musicians down there. They taught blues to my daddy, then my daddy taught me. That's the way blues got into my family. A lot of people nowadays hear records and different music and learn from that, but my family had their own way of playing and their own sounds. I think the kind of music I play has a lot do with the race that we are.

I worked at the Buster Brown plant here in Morganton when I was raising my family. I stayed there for twenty-five years. When I was working, I would play my guitar at home. I'd sleep a little while and then I'd get up and play a little while. You know, when you working at night, daytime sleep don't do you no good no way, so I just stayed up and played.

While I was working there at Buster Brown, a man came through here from Portland, Oregon. He heard me play my music and he said, "Etta, why do you punch the clock and work a hard eight hours?" I said, "That's all I *can* do." And he said, "No, pick up a guitar and make it that way, that'll be so much easier." I'd gotten disgusted with my job. Everybody was nice to me and all, but I had stayed there 'til I was just tired of it. Well, that was on a Wednesday, and I went to the office and told them, "I'm quitting on Friday." They were all *so* surprised. They said, "You're what?" I said, "I'm quitting on Friday!" But I went on and quit on Friday. I never *did* go back. I was seventy-three years old when I quit. I think it was high time.

The first little music trip I made was to Winston-Salem, down at the Reynolda Building. And from there I went to Wolf Trap, and I played there. Different people, you know, would come by and they would hear me play. Then it wouldn't be long before I'd hear from somebody else. Mr. Joe Wilson was one. And I've loved doing it ever since the first day. I have really been blessed.

I made some good records that turned out real good, I think. It's just mostly the type of music that was in my father's family. I love other people's music, but I don't think it's fair to take other people's music. Let their way be theirs and I'll do mine. Mine is fully homemade! The first pieces I played were "Goodbye Booze," "Railroad Bill," "Looking for the Bully of the Town," and "Never Let Your Deal Go Down." I love that one. In fact, I played it yesterday.

I have to say it—I have really enjoyed my life. I've tried to make the very best of it that I could. It's been a very, very happy life.

BANJOS AND BLUES

Fans of two-finger guitar picking recognize Etta Baker as a virtuoso instrumentalist in the Piedmont blues style. However, few know that the banjo, not the guitar, has deeper roots within her family history. This tradition sheds light on possible origins of "mountain music" as well as the connections between string band music and the blues.

Etta often said that her earliest musical memories were of waking up to the sound of her father, Boone Reid, playing banjo or guitar. Etta categorized many of his guitar pieces during this period—tunes such as "Railroad Bill," "Bully of the Town," and "John Henry"—as "folk songs." She asserted that it was only after the family moved to Virginia's eastern piedmont in 1916 that Reid begin to play blues. When they returned to Caldwell County ten years later, blues songs and instrumental styles had become popular there as well and could be heard on guitar and banjo, and even in string bands.

Etta described Boone Reid's banjo repertory, including "Sourwood Mountain" and "Johnson Boys," as "mountain songs." Boone played banjo in a style likely influenced by his father, Alexander Reid, who Etta remembered could make a banjo "smoke." Born in 1845 in Mecklenburg County, North Carolina, to Washington and Eliza Reid, Alexander was a baby when the Reid family, as free persons of color, moved to the foothills of the Blue Ridge and settled on the John's River. What is not known is whether the family brought a banjo tradition with them or whether they encountered this tradition once they arrived in western North Carolina.

Boone Reid encouraged his children to play music. Etta took up the fiddle and Etta's older sister, Cora, added the guitar to their father's banjo playing. Although she spoke most often of Boone's influence, Etta heard other banjo players in Caldwell County. Her family often gathered at the home of white neighbors Jasper and Ota Crisp to make music with the Crisps' sons, who played "Peace Behind the Bridge" on banjo and fiddle. Etta's cousin, Babe Reid, lived nearby and played songs such as "Corinna" and "John Henry" on the banjo. Cora married Theopolis Phillips from Lenoir, who was proficient on banjo and employed a three-finger picking style on a tune called "Marching Jaybird."

When Etta's musicianship became widely known much later in her life, a young musician visiting from Maine gave her a banjo. Etta reconstructed the pieces she had heard her father play, though she adopted a two-finger guitar-playing style rather than using the clawhammer brush stroke employed by her father. Once she took up the banjo, she played it throughout the remainder of her life and recorded an album of banjo music at the age of ninety-two.
—Wayne Martin

largest music events. Red, White and Bluegrass grew out of the city's municipal Fourth of July celebration. What had been a one-day event now boasts a lineup of more than thirty of the biggest names in bluegrass. In 2010, it was nominated for an International Bluegrass Music Association award for "Bluegrass Festival of the Year." Visitors to the festival can enjoy a fantastic fireworks display on the night of the Fourth. Over fifty vendors set up near the stage, selling food, CDs, and other bluegrass-related items.

RV and tent camping is available in the park. After the show stops on the main stage, musicians jam in the campground under the light of Coleman lanterns. Nowadays you see license plates from all over the country in the parking lot, but for its size, tickets are very reasonably priced.

WHEN: June 30–July 4; music starts at 12:30 P.M. each day
WHERE: Catawba Meadows Park, 220 Catawba Meadows Drive,
    Morganton, 28655. Located off of the US 64 bypass between NC 181
    and NC 18/US 64.
ADMISSION: Fee
CONTACT: Gary W. Leonhardt, 828-439-1866 or 828-438-5350
WEBSITE: www.redwhiteandbluegrassfestival.com

JAM SESSIONS AT THE BARBER SHOP
Drexel

One of the more quaint musical venues in the Blue Ridge region is the tiny Barber Shop in the little town of Drexel. Around noontime, the "regular pickers" start strolling into the Barber Shop. On Saturdays they favor old-time bluegrass. If you prefer country and western or gospel music, you may want to visit on a Thursday or Friday.

Lawrence Anthony, a veteran of General Patton's Third Army and the driving force behind the jam, owned and operated the Barber Shop in its present location from 1964 until shortly before he passed away, in December 2009. He began his career in 1949 in his first little shop, just across from the railroad tracks, and enjoyed "pickin' with the guys" for almost sixty-one years. Visitors can see the guitar he took with him through World War II hanging on the wall. Anthony's son Carroll learned to play on that very instrument. He's continuing the tradition of music at the Barber Shop today by setting up the Barber Shop Preservation Fund, a nonprofit fund to keep the shop open as a memorial to his father—and to keep the music alive.

The jam sessions occur year-round on most weekends, but visitors should call ahead to check the schedule. The jam sessions are informal, but

The inner sanctum at Drexel Barber Shop.

the music is high quality, provided by some of the finest pickers in the area. In 2012, the Barber Shop was the subject of an Emmy-nominated documentary film, called *Pickin' and Trimmin'*, for obvious reasons.

WHEN: Saturdays, 11 A.M.
WHERE: 100 South Main Street, Drexel, 28619. Take I-40 to Exit 107 (Drexel Road/NC 114); go north 2.5 miles to downtown Drexel.
ADMISSION: Free
CONTACT: Carroll Anthony, 704-907-8863
WEBSITE: Follow on Facebook

RUTHERFORD COUNTY

CHRISTIAN HARMONY SINGING AT SAINT JOHN'S CHURCH
Rutherfordton

A Christian Harmony singing takes place on the Saturday before the second Sunday in December in a picturesque white church in downtown Rutherfordton. For those interested in historic architecture, Saint John's Church (built in 1849) is both the oldest church building in Rutherford County and one of the best examples of Greek Revival architecture in western North Carolina.

DEWITT "SNUFFY" JENKINS

Before Scruggs, there was Snuffy. Most people think that Earl Scruggs was the first banjo player to perfect a three-finger banjo style. While he did develop the "Scruggs style," which dominates bluegrass today, other banjo players were using the three-finger technique in the 1920s and 1930s. Charlie Poole, one of the earliest country recording artists, played in the style. North Carolina produced many three-finger players, but the region around Scruggs's home in the southern foothills was especially fertile ground. Many of those musicians, though not as well known today, have an important role in the history of bluegrass, and banjo playing in general.

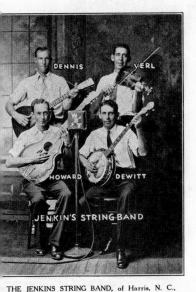

THE JENKINS STRING BAND, of Harris, N. C., The Farmer Musicians," comprise one of the finest string bands in the country playing the old time mountain tunes like very few can, and in that "peppy" style that is peculiarly their own. Thousands of listeners are always delighted when the "Jenkins String Band" is announced on the Crazy Barn Dance program. The group is composed of C. V. Jenkins, Dewitt Jenkins, Dennis Jenkins and Howard Cole. If you want to hear the genuine, old time music at its best, don't miss the "Jenkins String Band."

Dewitt Jenkins was born in 1908 in the Harris community in Rutherford County. Jenkins's style of music, born of the medicine show and schoolhouse circuits and fine-tuned for radio and public performance, was known for its showmanship. It was meant to be entertaining and always included clever lyrics and comedy routines interspersed with high-energy instrumentals. One of those comedy routines resulted in his nickname, "Snuffy."

He picked up the fiddle at age five and later moved on to guitar and two-finger banjo. In the late 1920s he met Cleveland County musicians Rex Brooks and Smith Hammett, who utilized the three-finger style. Snuffy developed his own manner of smooth, continuous three-finger playing and was also possibly the first widely heard three-finger banjo player to use metal fingerpicks.

His professional career began on the influential *Crazy Water Barn Dance*, a pro-

Promotional materials for wbt in Charlotte, circa 1935. Snuffy got his start on the *Crazy Water Barn Dance*, a radio program that jump-started the career of many other influential artists. Courtesy of Marshall Wyatt.

gram on Charlotte's WBT. That was where he would meet Homer Lee "Pappy" Sherrill, a lifelong friend and collaborator. Jenkins joined J. E. Mainer's Mountaineers in 1936. His three-finger banjo style, combined with that group's fast-paced breakdowns and harmonized singing would heavily influence the bluegrass bands that emerged a decade later. Jenkins later played in a group that included legendary radio announcer Byron Parker (also known as "The Old Hired Hand") and Pappy Sherrill. After Parker's death, Sherrill and Jenkins kept going as the Hired Hands, playing on radio and television into the 1950s. It was a musical partnership that would last until the end of Jenkins's life.

A new generation discovered Jenkins and Sherrill's music in the 1960s and 1970s. They cut several new records and played at bluegrass and folk festivals around the country. Snuffy's last performance was just a month before he passed away, on April 29, 1990. The great bluegrass banjo player Don Reno, who grew up just across the South Carolina line, said that Jenkins "was the first one who ever put it together. He had a perfected, as far as I'm concerned, the three-finger roll."

In the 1970s and 1980s, music festivals were held in Snuffy's honor every year in Rutherford County. In 2008, the event was staged again for the first time in twenty years, this time at Isothermal Community College in Spindale. There were remembrances of Snuffy and a lineup of big names and local favorites. In 2012, it moved to Globe Park in Forest City, where festival planners hope it may find a permanent home. For more information, visit www.snuffyjenkinsfestival.com or contact the Rutherford County Arts Council.

The Saint John's singing is known for the great acoustics provided by the wooden interior of the church building. Fifty to sixty singers often show up, making it one of the largest Christian Harmony singings in North Carolina. Like other shape-note singings, there is a potluck dinner on the grounds.

In 2011, a fire nearly destroyed the church, but the community, including the singers, worked to raise money to restore it. A benefit album of songs recorded at the singing was produced. Today, the building has been restored to its original beauty and serves as the headquarters of the Rutherford Historical Society, which keeps it open for visitors.

WHEN: Saturday before the second Sunday in December, 10 A.M. to 3 P.M.
WHERE: 702 North Main Street, Rutherford, 28139. Take US 221 into Rutherfordton. US 221 becomes Main Street; look for Saint John's at the intersection of Main and 6th Street.

ADMISSION: Free
CONTACT: Jane Spencer, 706-410-0982
WEBSITE: www.christianharmony.org

POLK COUNTY

KING PUP RADIO SHOW

Polk, Rutherford, and Cleveland Counties

Phil and Gaye Johnson are frequent performers at festivals and music halls around the region. The couple, based out of Polk County, made a name for themselves in the 1980s with their close harmonies, instrumental virtuosity, and charismatic stage presence. They began turning out a series of radio programs reminiscent of the *Grand Ole Opry*, the *Crazy Crystals Radio Show*, and the WLS *Barn Dance*. Twenty years later, the *King Pup Radio Hour* is a syndicated radio show, heard on over fifty stations across the country. In the Blue Ridge, you can listen in on WNCW on Sunday mornings or at the King Pup website.

The Johnsons tape their down-home program at parks, music shops, and town squares across Polk, Rutherford, and Cleveland Counties. The shows feature performances by the Johnsons, who are joined by guest bluegrass and old-time musicians.

The Flint Hill Special

Phil and Gaye Johnson of the *King Pup Radio Show* warm up before a show.

WHEN: Check website for times
WHERE: Different locations around Region 5
ADMISSION: Depends on location
CONTACT: Phil Johnson, 828-863-2860
WEBSITE: www.radioyur.com

COON DOG DAY IN SALUDA
Saluda

In 1963, a local hunting group started Coon Dog Day in Saluda as a "celebration of dogs and their people" and to present this old mountain tradition to the public. A large part of the festivities take place on the baseball field of the Saluda School, where hunters with their walkers, plotts, black and tans, redbones, and bluetick hounds share the art of coon hunting with curious visitors. Under a tent in the field, there is a bench show and a tree-

WNCW: CONTINUING CAROLINA'S RADIO LEGACY

Two stations dominated western North Carolina's airwaves during the Depression, WWNC (Wonderful Western North Carolina) in Asheville and WBT based out of Charlotte. Beginning around the same time that the *Grand Ole Opry* broke onto the scene, WBT and WWNC broadcast vernacular music to country audiences and to displaced rural residents who moved in droves to burgeoning mill towns. The Monroe Brothers and, later, the first incarnation of Bill Monroe and his Blue Grass Boys played regular fifteen-minute slots on WWNC, as did Jimmie Rodgers, "the Singing Brakeman," and a host of other musicians from the golden age of hillbilly music. In the 1930s, WBT's *Barn Dance*, sponsored by the laxative company Crazy Water Crystals based out of Texas, was particularly popular. The company credited its high sales to the popularity of its music programs. In an era when recording royalties were nonexistent, radio provided a way for musicians to increase personal appearances and thereby earn a steady income. Nationally known touring acts from outside North Carolina, including the Monroe Brothers and the Carter Family, played under contract for WBT. Some musicians from western North Carolina launched their careers with the help of radio and became professional entertainers. The Blue Sky Boys, from Catawba County, gained wide acclaim for their duet singing, J. E. and Wade Mainer, from Buncombe County, brought to radio a high-energy string band sound that featured close-harmony singing.

Sadly, neither WBT nor WWNC broadcast music today. But you can tune into the next generation of mountain radio on WNCW, which is based at Isothermal Community College in Spindale in Rutherford County. WNCW plays an eclectic mix with a heavy emphasis on traditional music of the South. During the week it is not uncommon to hear old-time, bluegrass, Americana, blues, rock, reggae, and soul music all in the same program. On Saturdays, bluegrass rules the airwaves from 11 A.M. to 7 P.M. with the popular *Going Across the Mountain* program. On Sunday mornings, you can hear gospel in the early morning, the *King Pup Radio Show* at 9 A.M., and *This Old Porch*, a program of old-time and bluegrass music from 3 to 6 P.M.

From its beginnings in 1989, WNCW has had a strong commitment to broadcasting local music. It's also a good place to hear underground or alternative Americana from around the country. The show *Local Color* on Sunday nights features groups from the listening area, and periodically bands stop by "Studio B" for interviews and performances. WNCW can be heard throughout

ing contest, where a master of ceremonies takes bids auctioneer-style on the amount of time a dog will bay at a stuffed raccoon raised in the air. A night hunt takes place on Friday evening before the festival for those who want the whole experience.

There is more to the event than the presentation of dogs and hunting lore, though. The day begins with a 5K run followed by a parade at 10 A.M. down the historic main street of Saluda. In addition to the standard marching bands, civic organizations, and boy scouts, there are coon-hunting floats and jalopies with possums tied to the fender, the drivers dressed in patched overhauls and with their teeth blacked out. To some this hillbilly pageantry is offensive, to others it's simply comic, and to many locals it is

Coon Dog Day showcases the traditions carried on by hunters such as Brent Dula of Caldwell County.

a way of co-opting Appalachian stereotypes and thereby stripping them of their power. The music starts up on the Main Street stage after the parade and lasts all day. Most of the acts are local, and most play bluegrass, though there may be some blues or country as well. The festival ends with a bluegrass street dance in the evening.

Coon Dog Day attendees have a choice of craft vendors, food booths, and children's games and rides, and all of the town's stores and restaurants are open for business, including the historic M. A. Pace's General Store, which dates back to Saluda's days as a railroad boom town at the turn of the twentieth century. The town is perched at the top of the Saluda Grade, the steepest standard-gauge stretch of railroad in the United States.

WHEN: First Saturday in July, 9 A.M. to 11 P.M.
WHERE: Downtown Saluda, 28773
ADMISSION: Free
CONTACT: City of Saluda, 828-749-2581
WEBSITE: http://www.cityofsaludanc.com/public/events.php

NINA SIMONE'S POLK COUNTY ROOTS

Nina Simone doesn't fit very neatly into any single musical category. Her music weaves pop, jazz, and classical music together with blues, gospel, and commercial folk music. During the tumultuous decade of the sixties, Simone gave an eloquent and unfaltering voice to the civil rights movement as an activist and by writing and popularizing such songs as "To Be Young Gifted and Black," "Four Women," and "Mississippi Goddam." Even though Nina Simone became an international musical sensation, most of her fans know little about her roots in the foothills and in the musical traditions of North Carolina's Blue Ridge Mountains.

Nina Simone was born Eunice Waymon in the town of Tryon in Polk County in 1933. Her father, John Davan (J. D.) Waymon was an entrepreneur and a jack-of-all-trades. He was also a skilled musician who played guitar, banjo, and harmonica. Her mother, Mary Kate, was a domestic worker and a minister in the Colored Methodist Episcopal (CME) Church. Kate and all her children sang or played music. Eunice's uncanny musical talents made themselves known when she was just a little girl. She had a strong voice, a steady sense of rhythm, and the ability to pick out tunes by ear on the family's upright piano.

She sang publicly for the first time at a church in Tryon. Later, she accompanied her mother on her circuit, visiting different churches and playing hymns on the organ or piano, her feet swinging high above the pedals. Despite her mother's disapproval, her father and her brother John taught the young Eunice blues and other secular music.

One of the women her mother worked for in Tryon was a wealthy widow named Katherine Miller. Mrs. Miller heard Eunice playing with her sister Dorothy at a recital and immediately recognized her potential

Eunice Waymon (Nina Simone) at age eight sitting on the wall of the Tryon Cemetery. In 2010 a statue of Waymon was erected in Tryon. Courtesy of Frances Fox and the Nina Simone Project.

and paid for Eunice to take piano lessons with Muriel Mazzanovich, a native of Great Britain who lived nearby. Not yet ten years old, Eunice Waymon fell in love with classical music.

A good student, the teenage Eunice left Tryon to attend one of the only private high schools for African American girls in the southern mountains. It was there, at the Allen School in Asheville, that she honed her musical abilities. She also joined the local chapter of the NAACP. After finishing high school, Eunice went to New York City, where she studied briefly at the Julliard Institute.

In 1954, while performing at a club in Atlantic City, she took the name Nina Simone, marking the beginning of a long, illustrious, but often rocky career. By the time of her death in 2003, Simone was considered one of the twentieth century's most influential musical artists—and an innovator in soul, jazz, pop, and classical music.

Simone's feelings about the South, and her home in North Carolina, were understandably complicated. The South was where she had come from, where she discovered her love for music, but it was also the place where she had first experienced poverty, segregation, and racism. Yet her roots in the living vernacular tradition of African American gospel music and in the musical landscape of her native North Carolina had helped establish her place in the development of modern popular music.

In 2010, on what would have been Waymon/Simone's seventy-seventh birthday, a bronze sculpture of her was unveiled in downtown Tryon, down the street from her childhood home. Today, visitors can see that statue in the Nina Simone Plaza, located just off of Tryon's Trade Street.

Walking the King's Highway

In Haywood County, people dance. They dance at the Stompin' Ground in Maggie Valley, they dance at the annual Smoky Mountain Festival at Lake Junaluska, they dance on Main Street in Waynesville, and they dance in the park at Canton. They dance at Hazelwood and at Fines Creek. Haywood County people are serious about dancing. They clog, they two-step, they flatfoot, they buckdance, they square dance. In Haywood County, they cut loose!

Dancing is an integral part of the lives of many people in Southern Appalachia. Social group dancing is a vital part of the region's long and complex cultural history. Dancing to the sounds of traditional music is a community pastime that runs back to the very beginning of European settlement and even earlier with the Cherokees. Mountain dance is also a wonderful way to express creativity and individuality.

For those reasons, dancing, both social and individual, is a much loved, much appreciated, and much practiced diversion among many people who live in the Blue Ridge. Just as certain as "where there's smoke, there's fire," in the Blue Ridge, "where there's music, there's dancing." And even though precision team clogging, western-style square dancing, and choreographed line dancing have become extremely popular group dances all across America, in the Blue Ridge, you're as likely to see single individuals flatfooting, buckdancing, and clogging as you are to see group dancing.

In the introduction to his book on solo mountain dance, folklorist and musician Mike Seeger wrote,

> Mountain dancing had many things in common with traditional ballad singing, solo fiddling and banjo picking. They were all part of the same everyday life, and existed side by side in the same time and place. They are usually subtle and style is always personal. Dancers, singers and musicians all learned from, entertained and danced with family and nearby community members. Although some dancers may speak a similar body language, each has

Demonstration dance teams in southwestern North Carolina often perform "smooth-style" square dancing.

their own brogue, that is, their own style, with moves that differ in varying degrees from those of other dancers.*

Dancing in the Blue Ridge, as in most places, is done only to the accompaniment of secular music. Listen carefully before you get up and dance to
a fast-paced fiddle or banjo tune, especially if the group playing the music
is a bluegrass band. Some bluegrass gospel tunes are difficult to distinguish
from secular ones, even for experienced listeners. Often the lyrics of the
song are the only real clue that the song is a religious one. If you should
happen to start dancing to a gospel tune, you may be gently admonished
by some old-timer or other who's there in the audience. But if that happens
to you, don't be offended or feel embarrassed, it occurs fairly often.

Customarily, the manager of a Blue Ridge music festival or concert, especially if it's outdoors, will furnish a specially prepared surface for dancing. Several sheets of plywood—sometimes three or four—will be nailed
together and laid down side by side on the ground, close to the music stage.
This creates a low platform that's large enough to accommodate five or six
dancers at a time. If more people than that want to dance, they generally
just spill off onto the surrounding grass. Many will simply stand up and
dance right where they've been sitting. There's no set protocol. If you're at a
place where there's mountain music and you feel like dancing, then dance!
Chances are you won't be the only one.

Many music venues are configured specifically for group dancing—square
dancing or clogging—and for couples who want to dance together. Traditional square dancing, unlike contemporary square-dance-club dancing, is

*Mike Seeger, *Talking Feet: Buck, Flatfoot, and Tap: Solo Southern Dance of the Appalachian,
Piedmont, and Blue Ridge Mountain Regions* (Berkeley, Calif.: North Atlantic Books, 1992).

Jingle taps worn on their shoes enable cloggers to create a more percussive sound during performances.

relatively simple. Traditional square dancing is almost always performed to the sound of live music—either an old-time or a bluegrass band—unlike contemporary square-dance clubs, which often as not will use recorded music for the dance. Many traditional mountain dancers in the Blue Ridge believe that dancing to recorded music is a serious affront to local musicians who play live dance music. And, by the same token, the music of a mountain dance band is considered by many traditional musicians to be incomplete unless it's accompanied by the rhythmic sounds of dancing feet.

The mountain square dance is open to anyone who wants to try. Since there are seldom more than a dozen calls or movements in the traditional dance, lessons are not required, although some callers will provide a brief "walk through" just before the dance begins, for the benefit of newcomers to the circle.

REGION 6 AT A GLANCE

THE PLACE

The southwestern corner of North Carolina is among the most remote sections of the Blue Ridge. Murphy, the county seat of Cherokee County, is closer to the capitals of five other states than it is to Raleigh, the capital of North Carolina. Some of the state's wildest, and most scenic, countryside is in this region. The Nantahala National Forest is here, and the Nantahala Gorge is a prime area for whitewater rafting. At the terminus of the Blue Ridge Parkway is the Great Smoky Mountains, home of the nation's most visited national park. To the south lie the less-traveled Slickrock Wilderness, Cherohala Skyway, and Joyce Kilmer Memorial Forest, home to one of the most impressive groves of old-growth forest in the southeastern United States. During the Great Depression, the Tennessee Valley Authority built dams on many of the tributaries of the Tennessee River, creating the capacity to bring electricity to the homes and businesses of Appalachian Mountains. Today, the resulting lakes—Fontana, Chatuge, and Hiawassee—are popular summer destinations for visitors who come there for recreation from Georgia, Tennessee, eastern North Carolina, and beyond.

This region is the home of the Eastern Band of Cherokee Indians, most of whom live within the Qualla Boundary in Swain County. Until their forced removal in the 1830s and 1840s, this was the heartland of the Cherokee Nation. However, many of the Cherokee people hid in the high valleys of the region and never left their ancient homeland. Others who made the removal's arduous trek to Oklahoma turned around and made the long journey back to the mountain country that they loved, and many of their descendants remain there today. Some of the present-day towns in this region, including Franklin, the county seat of Macon County, were originally Cherokee towns. Many Cherokee place-names remain in use today.

Jackson County is home of Western Carolina University, where the annual Heritage Day and Mountain Heritage Center draw thousands of visitors each year. Haywood County, with its rich dance tradition, is the "Gateway to the Smokies," reaching from the fringes of Asheville to the heavily visited towns of Maggie Valley and Lake Junaluska.

The Stecoah Valley in Graham County. Photograph by Steve Kruger.

HAYWOOD COUNTY

THE WAYNESVILLE STREET DANCE
Waynesville

An unsuspecting traveler driving into the Haywood County town of Waynesville late on a summer afternoon might be puzzled to discover that Main Street in front of the Haywood County courthouse has been closed to vehicular traffic. Instead of the usual clutter of automobiles and pickup trucks, the traveler finds the street filled with people and hears the sounds of a live fiddle band. On alternate Friday evenings beginning on the first

Young and old are delighted as a snowfall of cornmeal transforms the street in front of the Haywood County Courthouse for the Waynesville Street Dance.

The caller at the Waynesville Street Dance leads the participants through the figures.

Friday after the Fourth of July and continuing through the end of August, people dance on the street in Waynesville. They've done so now, off and on, for the better part of a century.

In the 1930s, Haywood County resident Sam Queen, who was known as "the dancing-est man in the land," organized the legendary Soco Gap Dance Team, which was among the very first practiced mountain square dance and clogging demonstration teams in the country. In 1939, Sam Queen and the Soco Gap Dance Team performed at the White House for President Franklin Roosevelt, First Lady Eleanor Roosevelt, King George VI, and Queen Elizabeth of England. That legendary performance and the publicity that followed it confirmed what local people believe and hold dear—that their ancestors created a distinctive form of American dance that is an important part of our nation's heritage.

A little while before 6 P.M. volunteers, led by Joe Sam Queen, the architect grandson of the famous dance team leader, pull sawhorse road blocks into the intersections at either end of the street in front of the Haywood County Courthouse. They drag metal bleachers from permanent resting places onto the pavement of Main Street and form an elongated open rectangle that is defined by the bleachers on two sides, the folding chairs of dancers and spectators on a third, and an elevated bandstand on the fourth. Then they carefully sprinkle the resulting square with a thick dusting of dry cornmeal, laid down to facilitate the shuffling movement of dancing feet. Once these preparations are completed, the fun begins.

Through the evening, Main Street in Waynesville is alive with the rhythmic movements of mountain dance. The surrounding bleachers, the grassy courthouse lawn, the concrete sidewalks, and the courthouse front steps are all crowded with hundreds of spectators—people who have come from far and near to dance, to hear lively mountain music, to watch the dancers, and to watch and greet each other.

The caller first yells out for the dancers to "circle up," and the cornmeal-blanketed asphalt immediately becomes crowded with the feet and bodies of scores of dancers. Everyone present is encouraged to join in and, in fact, so many dancers respond that obeying the caller's command to form a simple circle is nearly impossible in the space provided, big though it is. The requested circle becomes something that more generally resembles a badly distorted egg. But soon, after a short welcoming statement from the caller and some simple instructions regarding the form and the symbolism of the dance, the music begins and the dance gets under way.

Probably most Americans have had at least brief encounters with square dance, typically in a physical education class. Even in North Carolina, most square dancing is done in elementary school gym classes. When it comes to skills and knowledge of square dance movements, dance participants in Waynesville range from veteran expert to novice. And the dancers range in age from toddlers and babes-in-arms to octogenarians. Tall folks, short folks, fat and skinny folks, young and old, athletes and limp-alongs—they all get out there on the street together. It's a sight to behold!

Apparently there is a strangely mysterious force in mountain dance circles that causes beginners to mistake their left hands for their right. The traditional starting command from the caller, who's the boss of the dance, of "all join hands and circle right" nearly always creates momentary grief among some of the more unpracticed participants who, without fail, confidently take off going in exactly the wrong direction. But, after a moment of embarrassed laughter, they quickly recover and fall into step with the majority.

Next, the caller orders the circled dancers to execute the "Grand Right and Left." In this simple circular movement, the male dancers circle to the right while the female dancers simultaneously circle to the left. But there's a catch. The dancers must also weave in and out and touch hands as they travel the circle. So, in going around from start to finish, every man and boy and every woman and girl makes direct hand-to-hand contact with every member of the opposite sex who's there in the circle with them. Again, confusion reigns. But after some hesitation and a few times of weaving in when out is the way to go, the novices catch on and the action proceeds to the next level—making "squares."

Initially, it's another mess. But it's a lighthearted mess, and the skilled and experienced dancers patiently assist those who get lost in the fray. Most of the lost are gently led back into place by the hand while others are more firmly directed home by hands placed from behind on confused shoulders.

Joe Sam Queen

Joe Sam Queen is an architect who lives and works in his native Haywood County. He is also a flatfoot and buck dancer, a clogger, and a square dance caller.

The street dances here in Waynesville are a traditional thing. They've happened here ever since the time when we first got a good paved road in town, and they danced on the dirt road before that. These little venues really started with the centennial of the town of Waynesville. That was the year my grandfather died. They asked me to bring back some of the old street dances, which we hadn't had in fifteen years or so. We had such a great success of it that we've had them ever since. That was thirty years ago. I've been helping out with street dances here for thirty years. I'm in the third generation in my family to do so.

The dance always starts in a big circle. The circle of joining hands is a symbol of the community. The first movement of the Appalachian American big round dance is the Grand Right and Left. That's where you turn and greet your partner, and then you go right and left all the way around the circle. If you're a country-bumpkin, you have eye-to-eye and hand-to-hand contact with all the young ladies of the community—along, of course, with your grandmother, your aunts, your sisters, and everybody else. After the dance gets started, the figures break down into various shapes. All these shapes are little play parties—little parables and stories. Like the one that you usually open a dance with—it teaches people manners:

"How do you do?"

"Fine, thank you."

It teaches you how to embrace your partner and also your opposite-in-the-circles' partner. You swing your opposite and then you come back to your own. Then you move along, with your own. My grandfather would say. "You're dancing to the music, with your partner, in the circle." If you can understand those kinds of things in life, then you'll know a lot about yourself as an individual. You learn how to relate to a young lady in a polite way. And you learn how to let her go and to let her dance with another gentleman without jealousy or rage. The symbolism is great.

There is a sense of personal expression in the Appalachian square dance—in the foot work and in some of the moves. We don't have the drum in the Appalachian venue, but we do have the foot, and the rhythm that the foot lends to the set is a part of the music. It's individualistic, but it's also a part of the music. In Europe, the traditions were set—the ways were set, the communities were set, and the traditions were so long and consistent that everybody knew just what they were doing. In America, that was not the case. The American square dance always has a caller. The call itself can be innovative, just like America. The American dance is something of a patchwork gathered from a lot of traditions.

They would have a square dance on special occasions in the Appalachia of the past. At harvest time, at any community gathering or reunion, you'd have musicians and you would gather in the dance. The American dance—the great Appalachian circle dance—has several expressions. The most traditional one is the smooth dance—the large circle with smooth steps, where you don't clog all the time. You only clog when you're doing special things like Walk the King's Highway. Walk the King's Highway—that's a part of the dance that allows you to buckdance, to cut up a little, to show your stuff—to show your individuality. It's very American.

Now we have clog teams. My grandfather was very instrumental in developing the very first organized clog teams. The mountain dance is really a participatory form, and that's the heart of it—it's a social dance. These square dance teams became very popular with the advent of radio, and during the folk revival in the twenties and thirties. They didn't dress up in any fancy costumes; they just wore

 what they considered to be their social best. My grandfather once brought a dance team out of Appalachia—a very famous dance team. They all went to the White House in the 1930s to dance for the king and queen of England. That was a real threshold for this community that, at the time, was in the throes of the Great Depression. They were all high-energy cloggers and dancers out of Maggie Valley and Waynesville—and they danced for the king and queen, who for the first time were visiting America. It was stuff of newsreel importance. It made *Life* magazine, the *Saturday Evening Post*, and everything. It really put my grandfather and his little dance team on the map.

These days you see a lot of dance teams with petticoats, western wear, and so on. That's the influence of the square dance going west and then ricocheting back this way. Whatever Nashville has done to music, it's done to dance as well. There are no Appalachian folks now who haven't heard western fiddling and seen a certain amount of western dance. I see things now, like line dancing, which excludes those who are not a part of the club. It teaches no social skills. Sociability is the whole point of the Appalachian dance. Appalachian big round dance includes everybody in the community. Everyone joins in, rich or poor.

One of my grandfather's dance teachers was a black man. In that generation, the blacks didn't get to enter the circle. It was a segregated community. There weren't a whole lot of blacks here, but they were often the musicians for the dance. They were themselves great buckdancers. But they could only dance on the side. The banjo was really their instrument—and it has really added to the Appalachian musical forms. Nowadays, blacks join the circle—all over the South. That's quite refreshing. We've evolved in America to include everyone. I like to tell my children that if you know who you are and where you're from, then you can go any place, meet anybody, and feel at home and a part of it. You're not an outsider to the world if you know where you're from. Instead you're a part of the world.

My belief is that if we can keep our sense of self and place, we will thrive. Appalachia is a bastion of individualism and of community. The people who settled here liked this place—they liked the isolation of it, they liked the peace of it, they liked the magnificence of it. I feel that it's very important for a community to have a sense of place. And for a person to have a sense of place: to belong to somewhere and to come from somewhere. What you learn from that is so critical to being a world citizen—that you come from someplace and that everybody else does too. That gives you a sense of tolerance, of openness, and of hospitality. I don't come from the best of everything. I come from where I come from. You can start from anywhere and go anywhere.

There are not a lot of places left that have such a strong sense of place, but Appalachia's one of them that does. It's a wonderful place to visit, and to learn to feel that sense. Maybe visitors who come here can take a part of that back home with them, and establish it where they came from—and learn to appreciate their own place in the circle.

Very soon, though, sooner than one might predict based on the level of the initial confusion, the dancers find their way and the dance smoothes out. Once again the dance, the world, and the streets of Waynesville are placed into order.

WHEN: First Fridays of each month, from the Friday after July 4th to the
    end of August, 6:30 to 9:00 P.M.
WHERE: Haywood County Courthouse, Downtown Waynesville, 28786
ADMISSION: Free
CONTACT: Downtown Waynesville Association, 828-456-3517
WEBSITE: http://www.downtownwaynesville.com

MUSIC AND DANCE AT THE STOMPIN' GROUND
Maggie Valley
Every Friday and Saturday night, April through October, there's lots of dance action at a remarkable Maggie Valley establishment called the Stompin' Ground. If you want to see a variety of Appalachian and other American

group dance styles performed all in one place and all at the same time, the Stompin' Ground is the place to go.

Built and operated by Kyle Edwards, whose mother was a member of the noted Soco Gap Dance Team that danced for the King and Queen of England, the Stompin' Ground is a highly popular commercial dance arena. It's located on Soco Road, the main drag of the tourist section in Maggie Valley.

The place is huge. At the entrance is a glassed-in booth where admission tickets are sold. A spacious lobby is furnished with exhibits telling the history of mountain dance and showcases displaying the many clogging trophies that have been won over the years by Edwards's son and daughter. There's also a concession stand where soft drinks, popcorn, candy, hot dogs, and gifts can be purchased.

The dance floor itself is enormous—sixty by eighty feet. There's seating on two levels to accommodate nearly a thousand people. The lofty, well-lit stage, furnished with a professional sound system, is where the house band holds forth. The band plays a variety of mountain and popular music, ranging from old-time fiddle and bluegrass tunes to contemporary country hits.

As soon as the first lick of music of the evening is played, the assembled dancers hit the floor with great gusto. Many of the dancers at the Stompin' Ground come dressed in fanciful mountain or western regalia. Couples wearing matching outfits—shirts, boots, scarves, and hats—enjoy dancing the mountain two-step, while the members of organized and practiced dance groups, ranging in size from twelve to twenty dancers each, perform square dance, clogging, and line dancing with exact precision. And while the audience members are frequently encouraged by the emcee to join in on the dance action, most are quite satisfied to simply watch the remarkable show that's happening there before them.

Dancers backstage at the America's Clogging Hall of Fame Competition at the Stompin' Ground.

Perhaps the biggest dance show of them all occurs each year on the last weekend of October. That's when the Stompin' Ground hosts an enormous clogging competition. At this event, as many as a thousand mountain cloggers spend the night dancing and standing in line waiting for their turn to dance.

Appalachian dance has unfolded over a period of many years from a variety of dance traditions brought in or borrowed from Ireland, Scotland, France, England, Germany, Africa, and Native America. Over the years, a little bit of this and a little bit of that got all mixed up together to create the wonderful Appalachian dances that are performed today. And since the dances are derived from the traditions of nearly everyone in the community, nearly everyone—regardless of ethnic, social, economic, or political position—is likely to celebrate life through participation in dance. By the same token, newcomers and visitors are invited—in fact are vigorously encouraged—to join in, have fun, and give themselves to the dance. It's a gesture of sincere community hospitality.

WHEN: Fridays and Saturdays, April–November, 8 to 11 P.M.
WHERE: The Stompin' Ground, 3116 Soco Road (Route 19), Maggie Valley, 28751
ADMISSION: Fee
CONTACT: Kyle Edwards, 828-926-1288

THE MAGGIE VALLEY OPRY HOUSE

Maggie Valley

In Maggie Valley there's a nightly stage show at the Maggie Valley Opry House, a place that's owned and operated by Raymond Fairchild and his wife, Shirley. The Maggie Valley Opry House show is centered around Raymond Fairchild's lightning-fast bluegrass banjo-playing style, a slew of other talented musicians, and even an occasional comedian.

Nestled between the Blue Mountain Inn and the Country Vittles Restaurant on Soco Road (the main tourist drag in Maggie Valley), the Opry House is a modest building that's set back behind a gift shop, almost hidden from view of the main road. The front section of the building is an open-air porch that serves both as an entryway and as a smoking area. It's also a place for tour groups to count heads and issue admission tickets. Inside are a ticket stall, a concession stand, and a performance stage. The rest of the Opry House is one big room furnished for audience seating. Walls are decorated with posters from events and concerts in which Raymond Fairchild has been featured, and there are numerous autographed photos on the walls of country music celebrities who have performed there in the past.

Raymond Fairchild is a celebrity in Maggie Valley—and beyond. For many years, there was a large sign posted near the edge of town that read:

Banjo player Raymond Fairchild performs with his band.
Courtesy of the photographer, Roger Haile.

● Travis and Trevor Stuart

Trevor and Travis Stuart are twin brothers and string band musicians from Haywood County. They began learning from local artists such as Quay Smathers and the Dutch Cove String Band. Later they played with Red Wilson, Ralph Blizard, and other notable old-time musicians from the region. They both teach in the Haywood County JAM program and tour regularly around the country and beyond.

Travis: We grew up in Bethel in Haywood County. Our dad worked at the paper mill in Canton and had a store, a little Exxon station. My mom worked at the store and cut hair and took care of us. They both sang, at home and in the choir at church, but they didn't play any stringed instruments.

Trevor: Our great-grandfather's name was Henry King. My grandmother always talked about him playing the fiddle. He'd play all night, then he'd go preach the next morning. She said before they had a funeral he'd cut the people's hair. He'd preach the service and cut their hair and get them dressed. She said he cut every dead man's hair in Sandymush. I spent a lot of time visiting, just sitting up and playing my fiddle for her. Talking about him made me want to play and find out more about the old music. Later I named a tune I wrote after him.

When we were coming up there was a band around here called the Dutch Cove Old Time String Band. They were playing in Canton at the farmers' market one morning. My dad brought home their album.

Travis: It was Quay Smathers and his daughters. One daughter played banjo and one daughter played fiddle. A daughter played bass too. They had a music store, plus they gave lessons right in town in Canton. We got our instruments and went there and took lessons from them. At first I wanted the fiddle and Trevor wanted the banjo, but for Christmas Dad got me a banjo and Trevor a fiddle. [Laughs.] I'm left-handed, so I was playing left-handed for a week or two, and then I turned it back over and just played right-handed. We are about ten or eleven then, I guess.

Trevor: They had people that came from all over that played in there. They played a lot of old-time, but bluegrass too, and even some Irish music.

Travis: I think that older generation didn't divide it as much as it is now. A singer would sing an old-time song and then turn around and sing a Bill Monroe song. I never really talked to them about it that way, like, is it old-time? Is it bluegrass? It was just music. I still feel that way, although even as a kid, the older fiddle tunes and stuff really stood out to me.

Trevor: We had our first band in high school. We used to play at picnics and rest homes. One time we played at a prison. I think altogether we got twenty-five dollars for that. We've been going strong, when we have the time, ever since.

Travis: In our shows we try to tell stories about the people we learned from. There are a lot of people coming up playing, but it's not just about hearing the recording. Those guys were real characters. They had a whole different approach to the music, and their lives were different too. We try to mention that when we play.

I met Red Wilson when I was working in a sawmill up in Burnsville. I saw an ad in the paper that said, "Fiddles and Banjos for Sale." And right below it was another ad looking for someone to play old fiddle music with the same number. [Laughs.] I called that ad and we went to his house and we played music all night. When I lived there, I'd visit him a lot, and when I moved back over here, I'd still go back whenever I could until he died. He was one of those guys, you'd go to his house you'd go over at eight o'clock and you might leave at two or three the next morning.

I used to play bass with Ralph Blizard. Sometime we'd play weddings, and he'd call me, then he'd send me a letter. It would be written out perfectly: "Could you please attend . . ." We learned a lot about improvisation from Ralph, and he was very inquisitive about all different kinds of music. He was so helpful and nice to us when we were starting out—always ready to play with young musicians. He had his own sound, same as Red, and they both encouraged us to find our own sound. Ralph and Red had played a lot when they were younger, and were friends. It was a hoot to be around them at the same time.

Trevor: We've been teaching in the JAM program in Haywood for about eleven years. We have around thirty students now. We have a banjo, fiddle, guitar class and we've got a band class, so if the students have taken it before, they can come and play together.

Travis: You've got to have somebody to play with. Anytime you grow up playing with somebody like we did, it makes it easier to learn. There's power in numbers. [Laughs.] We try to teach by ear. I show them a little bit of tablature so if someone's having trouble, they can actually get it, but I'd like to get them to be able to try and hear it, to try and pick out the notes and hear different sounds and get them really listening to the music.

Some of the kids have kept going outside the program. I have one girl, I guess she's sixteen now. She was in the school band playing horns, but she plays real good clawhammer and bluegrass banjo, and she sings too. She's starting to play out some.

Trevor: We've got one kid now, he's supposed to be out, he's about seventeen or eighteen. He comes in anyway every week and just helps out with the other kids. He volunteers, just because he likes it. It's really amazing how many young people are playing now. When we were teenagers we would go to the Mount Airy Fiddlers' Convention, and as far as kids our age go, there weren't many. There was me and Travis, maybe a few from Virginia: Brian Grim, his sister, and Riley Baugus and Kirk Sutphin. That's about all. Now there are multitudes of kids out there playing this music.

Travis: I remember walking down the street in Asheville when we were kids and seeing everything boarded up. There wasn't anything going on down there. They had one place called Stone Soup. They would have people like the New Lost City Ramblers come through. We were too young to drink, so we would help them set up chairs and they would let us stand at the window and listen. Things have changed a lot. Now there's music in town about every night.

"Welcome to Maggie Valley—Home of Raymond Fairchild." Raymond Fairchild was born on the nearby Qualla Boundary, the homeland of the Eastern Band of Cherokee Indians. He's been playing banjo since he was eighteen years old.

The show at the Maggie Valley Opry House typically opens with a medley of bluegrass and old-time tunes performed by members of the house band. Then—to enthusiastic applause from the audience—Raymond Fairchild himself comes onstage and joins the group. His extraordinary bluegrass banjo style becomes the focus of the evening's performance from that moment forward.

Between sets and during intermission, Fairchild moves to the rear of the 300-seat auditorium. He positions himself behind a table that's stacked with a huge assortment of tapes and CDs and proceeds to greet old friends and new acquaintances, autographing photos and CDs that he has produced or that were produced by other Opry performers.

Meanwhile, Shirley Fairchild sells soft drinks and bags of popcorn at the concession stand. The nightly routine at the Maggie Valley Opry House runs very smoothly. The performers are professional, the music is well played, and the jokes are corny. It's not a bad show.

WHEN: Most nights, May–October. Check website or call for details.

WHERE: 3605 Soco Road (Route 19), Maggie Valley, 28751. Look for a very small sign near the roadside and a very large sign on the front of the Opry House.

ADMISSION: Fee

CONTACT: Raymond and Shirley Fairchild, 828-929-9336

WEBSITE: www.raymondfairchild.com

THE SMOKY MOUNTAIN FOLK FESTIVAL
Lake Junaluska

The Smoky Mountain Folk Festival, directed by Joe Sam Queen, is held on the grounds of the Lake Junaluska Conference and Retreat Center, near Maggie Valley. The festival, which features regional old-time and bluegrass music, and clogging demonstrations, is staged outdoors and in the 3,200-

The Smoky Mountain Folk Festival on Lake Junaluska. Photograph by Amy Davis. Courtesy of the North Carolina Arts Council.

seat Stuart Auditorium. The seats in the 1913 auditorium are arranged in semicircular rows on the floor that slopes gently upward from the stage. The hall has wonderful acoustics. Large glass windows on both sides of the auditorium offer vistas of nearby Lake Junaluska. Many festival-goers watch the stage from the outside, leaning their heads and shoulders through the open windows.

In addition to the auditorium, there are tent-covered performance stages, adjacent to the auditorium. Throughout the day and evening, the free outdoor portion of the festival has performances, jam sessions, and a children's show. Refreshments are also available.

WHEN: Friday and Saturday, Labor Day weekend, 5 P.M.
WHERE: 91 North Lakeshore Drive, Lake Junaluska, 28745
ADMISSION: Fee; outdoor events are free
CONTACT: Lake Junaluska Conference Center, 828-452-2881
WEBSITE: www.smokymountainfolkfestival.com

SWAIN COUNTY

MUSIC IN THE MOUNTAINS AT THE BRYSON CITY DEPOT
Bryson City

Bryson City is the county seat of Swain County and is located a few miles away from Fontana Lake, the Great Smoky Mountains National Park, and the Nantahala Gorge. The town dates back to the 1870s and 1880s, when it was a stop on the rail line that linked Asheville with the far southwestern corner of the state. The historic railroad depot in Bryson City now hosts a weekly concert series. The Bryson City Depot is a charming historic building that's the embarkation point for daily excursion trains on the Great Smoky Mountain Railway. For the past ten years, crowds have gathered at the depot on Saturday evenings in the summer and early fall, finding a place in the refurbished church pews in front of the stage, or spreading out on the lawn to enjoy traditional country, bluegrass, and old-time music.

WHEN: Saturdays, June–October, 6:30 to 8:00 P.M.
WHERE: Bryson City Depot of the Great Smoky Mountain Railroad,
    226 Everett Street, Bryson City, 28713
ADMISSION: Free
CONTACT: Bryson City Chamber of Commerce, 1-800-867-9246
WEBSITE: www.greatsmokies.com/music.html

GREAT SMOKY MOUNTAINS NATIONAL PARK

Dedicated as a national park by President Franklin Delano Roosevelt in 1940, Great Smoky Mountains National Park spans more than 800 square miles. The park includes the greatest concentration of peaks above 6,000 feet anywhere in the eastern United States. Within the boundaries of this park, visitors can access some of the largest tracts of old-growth forest, some of the most beautiful waterfalls, and some of the richest diversity of native plant life and animal species in the Southeast.

Sadly, as happened with the construction and opening of the Blue Ridge Parkway and with a number of federal dam projects, some mountain families who lived on lands designated for the Great Smoky Mountains National Park were forced to leave their homes and their farms. Still, the presence of people on the park landscape remains evident today. Many of the buildings that were abandoned are still standing, and the family cemeteries that were left behind are lovingly cleaned and decorated each spring by mountain families who return annually to visit their old ancestral homeplaces. Although there have been controversies over access to these places, the park has preserved several historical sites and hosts a variety of cultural events. Many of these include traditional mountain music. For details, visit the park's website: www.nps.gov/grsm/.

When the Great Smoky Mountains National Park was established in 1934, many people still lived within the park's boundaries. Joe Quilliams plays the fife his father made during the Civil War outside his home in Cades Cove, circa 1927.

GRAHAM COUNTY

STECOAH VALLEY CULTURAL ARTS CENTER
Stecoah

The Stecoah Valley Cultural Arts Center, located in a picturesque valley about ten miles northeast of Robbinsville, was founded to preserve the old

Visitors view a 1926 photograph of Dedication Day at the Stecoah School.
Courtesy of the Stecoah Valley Cultural Arts Center.

Stecoah Union School building and to revitalize it as a center of community life. The auditoriums of small schoolhouses were once used as venues to attract some of the biggest names in country music—*Grand Ole Opry* stars like Roy Acuff, Bill Monroe, Lester Flatt, Earl Scruggs, and Uncle Dave Macon—to mountain communities. Continuing a tradition of schoolhouse concerts that dates back to the days before the Great Depression, the Stecoah Valley Cultural Arts Center hosts concerts in its historic auditorium. The acoustics in the hall are excellent, and the audiences are attentive. The auditorium has been fully renovated using the original Stecoah Union School colors, blue and gold, and over three hundred fully restored, original school auditorium seats. A panoramic photograph covers one entire interior wall. It shows proud citizens from the community standing outside the stone building on the day it opened in 1926.

The Cultural Arts Center now presents a variety of programs and events throughout the year, many with musical components. These include the summer concert and dinner series, "An Appalachian Evening," presenting bluegrass and old-time mountain music. Acts that play the concert series are generally well known and come from all across the Southern Appalachian region. A traditional Appalachian dinner is served in the school's old cafeteria before all of the shows. Be sure to make reservations if you want to eat dinner. Seating is limited. Season tickets are available. The Center also hosts an annual ramp dinner and concert, which celebrates the local love for a strong-tasting leek that grows wild in the Blue Ridge; and the annual Harvest Festival, featuring mountain music, clogging, an old-time tractor exhibit, and a Civil War encampment. In addition, the Center offers

traditional Appalachian craft classes, and a fine arts gallery of locally produced arts and crafts is onsite. The school is the home of a small tailgate
farmers' market and a local chapter of the Junior Appalachian Musicians
(JAM) program.

WHEN: Stecoah is open year-round. The Concert Series takes place
Saturdays from the end of June through August. Music starts at 7:30
P.M. (come early for dinner). Annual events take place in April and
October. Check website for details.

WHERE: 121 Schoolhouse Road, Robbinsville, 28771. Located off NC 28,
1 mile from US 143 and 11 miles from US 19/74. Follow the signs to the
Center.

ADMISSION: Fee

CONTACT: 828-479-3364

WEBSITE: www.stecoahvalleycenter.com

Traditional mountain
fare is served up at
Stecoah before each
concert.

Everyone is invited to participate in the Round Dance at the
Fading Voices Festival. Photograph by Steve Kruger.

FADING VOICES FESTIVAL AND THE SNOWBIRD MOUNTAIN SINGING
Snowbird Community near Robbinsville

The Cherokee presence in the Snowbird community in Graham County
dates back well before the time of the first contact with Europeans. During the forced removal of the Cherokee in 1838, a tragedy known as the
Trail of Tears, some Cherokees evaded federal troops by hiding in the remote mountainous wilderness of the Snowbird area. Today, approximately
three hundred tribal members live in or near the Snowbird community.
Even though Snowbird is located some fifty miles from the Qualla Boundary, where the largest number of Eastern Cherokees reside, the Snowbird
community serves as one of the state's major strongholds for the preservation of Cherokee traditions and the Cherokee language.

The Fading Voices Festival was originated and continues today as an
effort to teach the young people in the Snowbird community about their
Native American heritage. Interest in the event has increased over the
years, and now the festival is open to the general public. Visitors are openly
welcomed to the large grassy field where the festival is staged.

The Fading Voices Festival offers the visitor a rare opportunity to purchase traditional Cherokee crafts directly from the artists who made them,
and it affords an opportunity to taste authentic and traditional Cherokee
foods such as bean bread and hominy. There are demonstrations of traditional Cherokee crafts, displays of medicinal plants and teas, a blowgun

⦿ MANCO SNEED AND CHEROKEE FIDDLING

Evidence exists of a Cherokee fiddle tradition as early as the first decade of the nineteenth century, when a British army officer, Major John Norton, visited Cherokee towns and noted in his journal that young Cherokees were playing fiddles and dancing reels. Written records associated with Cherokee removal also reveal that some Cherokee in western North Carolina owned fiddles and purchased fiddle strings from local merchants.

Manco Sneed, a member of the Eastern Band of Cherokee Indians, is widely acknowledged as one of the finest tradi-

Cherokee fiddler Manco Sneed (left) and fiddler J. Laurel Johnson. Courtesy of the Blanton Owen Collection, Western Folklife Center Archives, Elko Nevada.

tional fiddlers documented during the twentieth century. He is remembered here by his daughter, Dakota Sneed Brewer, who lives in the town of Cherokee on the Qualla Boundary in western North Carolina.

> Manco Sneed was born in Graham County, February 18, 1885, the son of John Harrison and Sarah Lovin Sneed, but later moved to Cherokee and lived in the "Sneed Gap" section all of his life, where he and my mother, Rosebud Beck Sneed, raised their family of seven children. He was known among the "old-time fiddlers" of western N.C. as the "Indian fiddler" and was considered the best old time fiddler of them all, including Dedrick Harris from Cherokee County, Ozzie Helton and brother Ernest, and Bill Hensley, to name a few.
>
> These fiddlers and musicians came to our house many times to play music with dad because he could play by the hour without playing the same tune twice. He mainly played for pleasure but often played for square dance teams at the Cherokee Fair and on a few occasions played at the Mountain Dance and Folk Festival in Asheville, which was organized by

Bascom Lamar Lunsford, who was a friend of Dad's and came to our house many times.

Those who heard his music knew it was a sophisticated type of music because it was so pleasant to hear. The musicians who came to play music with him were always anxious to learn the tunes, which were many, such as "Polly Put the Kettle On," "Band Box," "Down Yonder," "Indian War Dance"; too many to name.

His sons, Lawrence and Russell Sneed, played guitars, and daughter Mary Russell also played the fiddle. Dad's brother Peco played the fiddle, and Uncle Osco would walk from his home in Birdtown to play his banjo with his brothers' fiddle music. Our grandfather John Sneed played the fiddle and sometimes played with dad, but he didn't know too many of dad's tunes, he played left handed. Dad was right handed. John Sneed spoke the Cherokee language fluently and at one time was interpreter for the Court in Bryson City when a trial involved a Cherokee because he spoke both Cherokee and English. He lived to be 87 and is buried in the Drama Cemetery. Dad lived to be 89 years old and is buried in the Cam Sneed Cemetery, where his brother Peco, along with Cam and their mother, Sarah Lovin Sneed, is also buried.

—Dakota Sneed Brewer, daughter of Manco Sneed.

(Transcription by Carmaleta Littlejohn Monteith, granddaughter of Peco Sneed and Armenthia Patterson Sneed. Reprinted here with permission of the Field Recorders' Collective, fieldrecorder.com.)

demonstration, and a skillet-throwing contest. The festival highlights the playing of two traditional Cherokee games: Cherokee stickball and a court-ship game called the Fish Game. Both games are no-holds-barred, full-contact sports. So while you are watching, always be aware that there are no boundaries and you may have to quickly dodge the action should it come your way.

Cherokee communities continue two long-standing musical traditions that are often represented at the Fading Voices Festival. The first is the old ceremonial songs of the Cherokee people, sung in the Cherokee language and accompanied by rattles and sometimes drums. Some of these songs provide the music for traditional Cherokee dances like the circle dance, which may have influenced mountain square and big-circle dancing. The

● Alfred and Maybelle Welch: Music Has Always Been a Part of Our Life

Alfred and Maybelle Welch live in Snowbird, a Cherokee community located in Graham County. They sing hymns in the Cherokee language, a tribal tradition that dates back to the early nineteenth century.

Alfred: My grandpa raised me. He was born around 1875. He raised pigs and kept some cattle too, what you call steers. He skidded logs with them. I was just a little boy then, but I had to work hard. I had to feed the hogs and cut wood. I'd get big trees down, chop them with an axe, then saw them with a cross cut. We had some cornfields on the mountainsides. They couldn't plow it cause it was too steep—they had to dig holes and plant the corn and beans.

Maybelle: We were basically raised the same way. We had to work hard. My dad was a farmer too, and a logger. During the lean times we had to raise hogs and stuff like that. We had a good upbringing. Our dad was a good person. We all went to church all the time. We were raised up in the church, and we were always singing. We kind of have different cultures because Alfred grew up in Big Cove near Cherokee. We both grew up speaking Cherokee, but his dialect is different. I've lived here all my life. It would take mountains to move me out of here.

   Alfred played guitar when he lived in Big Cove. His uncle used to have a guitar, but his grandmother wouldn't let him touch it. He tried to get it down off the wall and his grandma told him put it back. I think he was beginning to be interested in music back then.

Alfred: I was just trying to see how he made that sound. My uncle was a good guitar picker. He mostly played stuff from the *Grand Ole Opry* and songs from the *Cherokee Hymn Book*. My grandma used to sing those Cherokee hymns. She never had a song book though. She just had it memorized. Even her sewing machine was a Singer. [Laughs.]

Maybelle: My mom used to sing, but she wouldn't ever sing in public. She was always shy. From the morning after breakfast she would turn that radio on, and she would be whistling along. I heard every country song on that radio until I went to bed. Every country music artist, we knew them all. We'd sing along with them. Every Saturday or Friday night we always sat on the back porch. My parents would listen to the *Grand Ole Opry*. That's where I got my name: Maybelle, after Maybelle Carter. [Speaking to Alfred:] You listened too, didn't you?

Alfred: Yeah, we had a battery-powered radio. On Friday night it was time for the *Grand Ole Opry*. We didn't speak English. We talked Cherokee, so we had Cherokee names for all the singers. They made it sound the closest they could to English in Cherokee. We called Bill Monroe "Walosi." It means frog. I wasn't speaking English when I started school.

Maybelle: I think he was eighteen when he moved out here to the Snowbird area. Him and my brother used to sing together. He went off to Vietnam when he was what, twenty?

Alfred: I guess about nineteen, twenty, somewhere. I went in the army for a while and started right back at construction when I got out. I worked away from home most of the time. Road jobs, clearing right-of-ways, stuff like that. I worked all around Virginia, West Virginia, Georgia, Tennessee, South Carolina. All these states around North Carolina. It was hard being away, but that was the only work around.

Maybelle: We got together several years after he got back. I remember when he was off [working]. I was a "right-of-way wife" for a long time. I had to be a mother and a dad to both our boys. And I was working at the same time at the Snowbird Senior Center. Our son Hunter was one of the only children in his generation who could speak the Cherokee language. A lot of the music and a lot of the language have been revived within the last twenty years. I feel good that maybe something good came out of our singing. We have a choir at Buffalo Baptist Church right now that we're teaching [Cherokee], and they're doing a good job. They're singing the songs in Cherokee. Our mission is to do that, is to keep the Cherokee music—the Cherokee hymns—going so that younger generations can pick it up and run with it. They have [Cherokee-language] immersion classes now, and they're actually teaching some in the Robbinsville High School. They're bringing it to daycares here in Snowbird, too. Whenever our family gets together, we talk in Cherokee. We have two grandkids. They know when they come into this house they must speak Cherokee.

Music has always been a part of our life. We always sang at home and at church. For a while Alfred played bass and sang with the Snowbird Quartet. Later we had a larger family group that sang together. When we were younger, our son Hunter played for us, but he got married and he's got two babies. He's living on his own, and he kind of went on his own way. Most of the time nowadays, it's just me and Alfred. He plays guitar and we try to harmonize together. We also have a few gospel singings in the community every summer, where we bring in different groups. Anyone can come and sing along. There is one very old song we sing called the "Trail of Tears Song." When we do festivals or stuff like that, this is the last song that we do. It's special for us. This is the one that they sung on the Trail of Tears. I tell people to stand up in honor of the people who died.

Alfred: It's kind of like "Guide Me Oh Thou Great Jehovah," lead me, guide me, as I walk because I am weak and you are strong. You could tell they sang these songs because they asked God to help. That's one my grandma used to sing.

Maybelle: It says help me. Help me as I walk. You would imagine walking so many miles and you can barely make it. And the old people died along the way and the babies. It's just telling the Lord to help you make it. Help you make that Journey.

We're still going strong. We get asked to go everywhere. We get asked to do festivals, funerals, church services. We don't regret that it's just me and Alfred. If I'm not there, he's going to sing. If he's not there, I'm still going to sing. I'm going to carry on and he's going to carry on. We're older now. I don't know how long we can keep going, but we'll go as long as the Lord let's us go—and as long as we're doing the Lord's work. There's no stopping place for that. You just keep on going. That's where we are at now. We thank the Lord for everything we do.

other uniquely Cherokee tradition is Cherokee hymn singing, which co-evolved with the shape-note harmony singing tradition in both white and black communities across the region during the nineteenth century. Local churches, choirs, and quartets around Snowbird continue the practice of singing shape-note hymns in the Cherokee language, and groups like the Little Snowbird Baptist Church choir and the Welch family occasionally perform those venerable songs on the small stage at Fading Voices. Each month during the summer, singings take place at different locations around the Snowbird region. The largest singing happens in July at the Little Snowbird Baptist Church across the street from the Fading Voices Festival grounds. Visitors are welcome to camp out and join in the traditional Cherokee hymn singing and gospel music.

WHEN: Fading Voices: Saturday, Memorial Day weekend, 10 A.M. to 5 P.M.; Snowbird Mountain Singing: Friday and Saturday, second weekend in July.

WHERE: The grounds of the Little Snowbird Baptist Church, 1897 Little Snowbird Road, Robbinsville, 28771. From Robbinsville, take Atoah Road. Take a slight right onto Snowbird Road. Follow signs—you'll have to turn several times to stay on Snowbird Road. After several miles, the road forks into Big and Little Snowbird Roads. Take a left on

Little Snowbird Road and go 2 miles. The festival grounds will be on the right.

ADMISSION: Free

CONTACT: For Fading Voices, call the Junaluska Museum, 828-479-4727; for the Snowbird Mountain Singing, call Maybelle Welch, 828-479-6833

CHEROKEE COUNTY

JIMMY'S PICK N GRIN
Andrews

A painted portrait of the late Jimmy Jordan smiles out from a red barn backdrop behind the stage at Jimmy's Pick N Grin. Jimmy's son, Steve, and Steve's wife, Sue, founded this lively music hall, which is housed in a deceptively nondescript modern building in Andrews in Cherokee County.

Singer L. B. Solesby onstage at Jimmy's Pick N Grin.

Jimmy once played with the gospel singer Carl Story as well as with the local, legendary Snowbird Valley Boys. When Jimmy died, Steve dedicated the Pick N Grin to his memory, providing a family-friendly environment where people can enjoy mountain and classic country music.

Local musicians make up the house band, fronted by Steve Jordan, who sings and moves with ease between playing the fiddle and the guitar. The band's members vary from song to song as guest musicians come and go from the stage. A drum set and a steel guitar often augment the sound. These instruments may seem out of place to those who equate mountain music with old-time and bluegrass music, but in the years since World War II, country music has grown in popularity in western North Carolina. Many musicians play both bluegrass, which is usually all acoustic, and country, which often includes electrical instruments in the mix. At Jimmy's, the repertoire moves easily between the two genres, featuring songs and playing styles that date back to the 1940s through the 1970s. About every third song is an instrumental buckdance number. And when the band gets going on one of those, folks crowd onto the dance floor to clog and flatfoot. Some attendees prefer to line dance, two-step, or waltz, so the musicians strive to please the dancing needs of everyone. Many of the dancers wear elaborate and even glitzy outfits that often include cowboy hats, rhinestone-studded western shirts and skirts, colorful cowboy boots, and tap shoes. Check the website for special events like the annual Pickin' in the Valley Bluegrass Festival.

WHEN: Saturdays, 7 to 11 P.M.
WHERE: 220 Country Hearth Lane, Andrews, 28901. Take US 19/74 toward Andrews. Coming from the South, take a right on Locust Street, then take an immediate left onto Country Hearth Lane. Jimmy's is located next to the hotel.
ADMISSION: Fee, but children are admitted free
CONTACT: Sue and Steve Jordan, 828-361-6878
WEBSITE: www.jimmyspickngrin.com

JOHN C. CAMPBELL FOLK SCHOOL
Brasstown

The John C. Campbell Folk School at Brasstown was founded in 1925 as a collaboration between two progressive educators and an Appalachian community. Olive Dame Campbell, Marguerite Butler, and the people of Brasstown created a unique institution that seeks to bring people toward two kinds of development: inner growth as creative, thoughtful individuals and social development as tolerant, caring members of a community. Through-

An autoharp class at the John C. Campbell Folk School.

out its history, the Folk School has worked toward these goals through performing arts, agriculture, and crafts rooted in the traditions of Southern Appalachia and other cultures of the world.

The John C. Campbell Folk School has been listed in the National Register of Historic Places. The Folk School's twenty-seven buildings are the site of many services to the community, a variety of special events, and an internationally renowned instructional program. The 372-acre campus has fully equipped craft studios, a sawmill, meeting rooms, a covered outdoor dance pavilion, a nature trail, a craft shop, a vegetable garden, rustic lodgings, and one of the best dance floors in America.

On campus at the Keith House, the Folk School hosts weekly concerts, featuring local bluegrass and old-time bands, ballad singers, and gospel groups. The Friday-night concerts draw a responsive audience that's a mix of local residents, students enrolled at the school, and visitors. Concerts at the Folk School are enhanced by the intrinsic warmth of the Keith House, with its natural wooden floors, walls, and ceilings. The acoustics there are excellent.

The Folk School holds community contra and square dances with live music twice a month. There's also a Fall Festival at the school that showcases traditional music, dance, foodways, arts and crafts, occupational and home skills, and more. Attendance at the annual event, which the school has hosted for more than twenty-five years, numbers in the thousands.

Jan Davidson: I Really Wanted to Get a Banjo

Jan Davidson is the executive director of the John C. Campbell Folk School at Brass-town and a musician and writer. A native of nearby Murphy, North Carolina, he's been director of the folk school since 1992. Jan has a Ph.D. in folklore and museum studies.

I'm from Murphy, North Carolina. My folks have been there since the 1840s. Back then they were farmers in the valley between Murphy and Andrews, but the last few generations have been town people. One of my granddaddies was a storekeeper, and my other granddaddy was a salesman for a wholesale company. I grew up in downtown Murphy in an old house that was built by my grandmother's father, my great-granddaddy Robert Alexander Akin. He was a Confederate captain, and then after the war he was a schoolteacher.

That house has always been in our family. When I was a kid, there was a church on one side of it and a funeral home next to that, and then on the other side and across the street were filling stations. Those were the musical centers in towns like Murphy. In fact, there were four filling stations within an easy walk of our house, and they all played music. People came and played different types of music in each one. It was just great. It was *good* music.

My dad, who's still living—he's a hundred years old—was the Veteran's Affairs officer for six counties here in western North Carolina. He helped people get their GI Bill benefits and so forth. He

Photograph courtesy of Keather Weideman/John C. Campbell Folk School.

went to those counties every week, and in the summertime I'd go with him. I saw a lot of this whole end of the state, and I heard a lot of music. My dad knew I liked that.

When I first started listening in the 1950s, most of the guys tried to play like Flatt and Scruggs, but there were still a few old people around who did something that was obviously different from bluegrass. Once, I remember my father said he was going to see an old guy who had a banjo, a World War I vet named Caleb Mashburn. He'd had some health troubles, and his banjo didn't have but about three strings on it, so I took him some new strings and he started playing things like "Mamma's Darling Child," which most people call "Soldier's Joy" using a two-finger style. I worried a number of elderly people back then, asking them to play for me.

I never saw clawhammer played around here. Nobody around here did it that I know of. The way they played the banjo here was up-picking, like Pete Seeger's basic strum, which he learned from Aunt Samantha Bumgarner, who used to play a lot around Murphy.

When I was about thirteen, my daddy took me to Asheville to see a music show, and Frank Proffitt was in it. I really liked him. So I wrote him a fan letter, the only one I ever wrote in my life. And he answered it. I told him I really wanted to get a banjo just like he was playing. "I'm gonna get a job," I wrote. I was prepared to make the ultimate sacrifice to get a banjo. [Laughs.] So I did, I worked at the *Cherokee Scout* newspaper folding papers, and then when I was fourteen I went to work at WCVP (Western Carolina Vacation Playground) as a DJ. The guy who'd been doing the job had gone off to college, so I became the early-morning DJ. So I had to get up at four in the morning. We signed on at five. A thousand watts! It was me and the farmers and the milkman and the cops. The yawn patrol. So I did that for a while, and then Frank Proffitt sent me a banjo. He said, "It's got a crack in it, but you can have it if you'll pay the shipping." I've still got it. Then the guy who did the afternoon show went off to college, too, so I got that job, a teen show playing rock and roll records. I'd do the early-morning bluegrass show, go to school, and then do the afternoon rock and roll show.

While I worked at that radio station we had people like the Osborne Brothers come through here. Jim and Jesse were real popular, and they came here all the time. During that time I was playing commercial music on the radio and we'd change formats every couple of hours. Rock and roll, bluegrass, country—and live music, especially on the weekends. Church music. Whole congregations from places like Hanging

Dog would come in the studio and sing and have preaching. Sometimes the station would sponsor music shows at the gym, and those bands would come into the studio and play live. I worked there from 1962 to 1966. Then I went off to Chapel Hill.

I first came here to the Folk School as a small child at Christmastime. They had a great Christmas event here with a big tree and all that. That's the first thing I remember about coming here. Then

Jan Davidson, circa 1967, holding a mountain banjo made by Frank Proffitt. Photograph by Filmore Hunter. Courtesy of Jan Davidson.

we'd come up in the summertime and eat lunch here. The food was great. They always had homemade bread and fresh vegetables, so I remember that pretty well.

I first took a class here when I was in high school—wood carving. Then, later, when I was in college and I'd come home to Murphy, I'd go up to Brasstown and find the other college kids I knew who'd come home from school at the folk school dances. I always liked to see what was happening here.

During the late seventies the school started to get into local music more than it had before. There had never been a total connection between local music and the Folk School until the late seventies. I got hired to play the guitar here for a clogging event around then, and I've been involved with the Folk School ever since.

I'm really happy that there's this richness at the folk school in such a rural area. We have great concerts here; we have dances once or twice a week, a great classical concert series, jams on Sunday afternoon, and often more jams on Tuesday nights. What I like best about all this is that it's accessible to everybody and local people feel comfortable with coming here and participating. That's what I like to see.

WHEN: Concert series: Fridays, 7:30 P.M.; dances: usually (but not always) first and third Saturdays of the month, 8 to 11 P.M.; Fall Festival: first full weekend in October, 10 A.M. to 5 P.M. Check website for schedules and other events.

WHERE: 1 Folk School Road, Brasstown, 28902. Located off US 64, 7 miles east of Murphy. *From the west on US 64*, take a right onto Old Highway 64. Head into Brasstown and take a right at Clay's Corner onto Brasstown Road. *From the east on US 64*, take a left on Settawig Road, 8 miles west of Hayesville. Take a right at the T onto Old Highway 64 west. Take a left at Clay's Corner onto Brasstown Road.

ADMISSION: Concert series is free; fee for festival and other events

CONTACT: 828-837-2775 or 1-800-365-5724

WEBSITE: www.folkschool.org

CLAY COUNTY

CLAY'S CORNER NEW YEAR'S EVE CELEBRATION AND WEEKLY JAM SESSIONS
Brasstown

Clay's Corner is more than just a gas station, although it's that. It's also the self-proclaimed Opossum Capital of the World. The walls of the back room of the service station are plastered with opossum paraphernalia and

Clay Logan, the proprietor of Clay's Corner.

clippings from magazines and newspapers (including the *New York Times*) about the store's annual New Year's Eve event. On December 31, hundreds of people descend on the tiny crossroads community of Brasstown to revel in an Appalachian parody of the internationally televised New Year's Eve extravaganza in Times Square, New York City. Activities at Clay's Corner on New Years Eve begin around 9 P.M. and include plenty of bluegrass music, a *womanless* Miss Possum Pageant, and a smattering of fireworks.

The store's owner, comedian—and resident possum expert—Clay Logan, is also a music lover. On Friday nights throughout the year, bluegrass musicians can be found circled up and enthusiastically playing in the store's small back room. On some nights the room is packed with people from the John C. Campbell Folk School, which is within walking distance of the store. At other times there may be only a handful of locals and the players are from here and there. But it's always an open jam session, and anyone who wants to is welcome to join in the bluegrass, old-time, gospel, and classic country music that's played there. Acoustic instruments only, please. The music in the store is free and the playing begins around 7:30 P.M. in the evening and continues until 11 P.M., or whenever everybody gets tired and goes home.

WHEN: Jam sessions: Fridays, 7:30 P.M.; New Year's Eve: 9 P.M.
WHERE: Clay's Corner, 11005 Old Highway 64 west, Brasstown, 28902
ADMISSION: Free
CONTACT: 828-837-3797
WEBSITE: www.clayscorner.com

MACON COUNTY

JAM SESSIONS AT THE T. M. RICKMAN GENERAL STORE
Cowee

The place now known as Rickman's Store was constructed in 1895 by a man named John Hall. Thomas Rickman, who bought the store in 1925, operated it for over seven decades until his death in 1994. The building is located in the Cowee-West's Mill National Historic District, which was designated as such in 2007 to preserve the Cherokee, African American, and European American heritage of the area. The original Cowee was a Cherokee town. A pre-Cherokee mound site there dates to around 600 A.D. During the eighteenth century, the Cherokee town of Cowee was the political and economic capital of the Cherokee Middle Towns. Europeans made deals with

The T. M. Rickman General Store in Cowee, built in 1895.

the Cherokee to secure a desirable kind of white clay from local mines that was used to make fine porcelains. An African American church that once served one of the largest rural black communities in western North Carolina stands in Cowee, as do a number of homes and commercial buildings that date back to the 1800s. One of the few mountain schools built under the Works Progress Administration that still remains in use is located at Cowee.

A group called Friends of Rickman's Store, operating under the auspices of the nonprofit Land Trust for the Little Tennessee, hosts an open bluegrass and old-time jam session every Friday afternoon from late spring to early fall at the Rickman Store. The musicians sit in chairs out on the up-

The view from the porch at the Rickman Store, looking out over the Little Tennessee River valley. Photograph by Steve Kruger.

stairs side porch of the old store, overlooking the Little Tennessee Valley. Inside the old store, community volunteers are on hand with displays of vintage store equipment and furnishings. The work of local artisans, photographers, and writers can be purchased here as well. Beginning around Thanksgiving, the store is open on weekends and sells locally grown Christmas trees and wreaths. The store sometimes hosts additional mountain music performances and concerts as well, so check its website for details.

WHEN: Friday afternoons, May–October; check website or call for details; store is open 10 A.M. to 5 P.M.

WHERE: 251 Cowee Creek Road, 6 miles north of Franklin, 28734, off NC 28

ADMISSION: Free

CONTACT: 828-369-5595 or the Little Tennessee Land Trust, 828-524-2711

WEBSITE: www.rickmanstore.com

JACKSON COUNTY

MOUNTAIN HERITAGE DAY
Cullowhee

When Dr. H. F. Robinson was to be inaugurated as chancellor of Western Carolina University in Cullowhee during the fall of 1974, he requested that a barbeque and square dance be held to conclude the inauguration day's activities. The celebration proved so popular that the university promised to hold a similar event a year later. The university expanded the activities and presented the first annual Mountain Heritage Day in 1975.

Organizers did not anticipate the enthusiasm of residents of southwestern North Carolina for Mountain Heritage Day. The celebration has grown from a rather modest event featuring a few performers and crafts artists to a large, multifaceted festival showcasing traditional music, dance, occupational skills, crafts, and foodways. It is not uncommon for Mountain Heritage Day to draw 20,000 people, depending on the weather.

The two largest performance venues, the Balsam and Blue Ridge Stages, present a good mix of regionally known bluegrass, old-time, country, gospel, clogging, and smooth-dance groups. The music at the Balsam Stage tends to be more traditional and features local musicians from Jackson and the surrounding counties. The stages are located in a large grassy area, near over one hundred craft and food booths. The crafts are handmade, if not traditional, and the makers are usually on hand to converse with potential customers. The food is regional fare, including ham biscuits, cider, barbecue, Cherokee fry bread, and beans and cornbread. Contests take place throughout the day, including a chainsaw competition, beard and moustache contest, costume contest, canning competition, Cherokee stickball games, arts and crafts awards, and an antique car show.

Traditional Cherokee dancers perform at Mountain Heritage Day. Photograph by Mark Haskett. Courtesy of Western Carolina University.

The Tried Stone Gospel Choir performs on the Blue Ridge Stage at Mountain Heritage Day. Photograph by Mark Haskett. Courtesy of Western Carolina University.

Smaller performance venues and some first-rate crafts and occupational arts demonstrations are found near the Mountain Heritage Center located in the H. F. Robinson Building. The museum and research center collects, interprets, and disseminates knowledge about Southern Appalachia and its people. Craft and occupational traditions presented in past years include quilting, corn shuck doll making, basketry, and metalworking. The smaller Circle Tent is reserved for workshops and interview sessions. Shape-note singing gives attendees an opportunity to hear and join in on some of the oldest sacred song traditions practiced in the mountains. Entertainment for younger visitors can be found at the Children's Stage.

The Mountain Heritage Center itself is an attraction. A permanent exhibit, *The Migration of the Scotch-Irish People*, describes the links between the Scotch Irish who found their way to western North Carolina in the eighteenth century and their descendants. The center also preserves a large number of historical artifacts and conducts educational outreach programs with schools and community groups.

On-site parking for Mountain Heritage Day is limited, but free shuttles from outlying lots run throughout the day. Attendants who help park cars are highly efficient.

WHEN: Last Saturday in September, 8 A.M. to 5 P.M.; stage performances begin at 9:30 A.M.

JOHN ROMULUS BRINKLEY: GOAT GLAND DOCTOR AND BORDER RADIO PIONEER

Quack medicine, a failed gubernatorial campaign, and the spread of Appalachian music across the continent all have a role in the unusual story of John R. Brinkley. Brinkley was born near Sylva in Jackson County in 1885 and left the mountains in 1908 to pursue a career in medicine. Although he failed medical school, he eventually obtained a degree from "The Eclectic School of Medicine" in Arkansas. He developed a controversial treatment for male impotence: transplanting the sexual glands of goats into humans. He advertised his treatments over the first radio station in Kansas, where he narrowly lost a three-way gubernatorial race in 1932. Under increasing pressure from the U.S. government, which was cracking down on medical malpractice, Brinkley moved his operation to Del Rio, Texas, just across the border from Villa Acuna, Mexico. There he received permission from the Mexican government to broadcast a radio signal at 500,000 watts, making his XERA the most powerful radio station in the country at the time. Brinkley recruited country musicians to play on the station to help sell his curatives, including the Carter Family and two musicians from his hometown of Sylva, Samantha Bumgarner and Harry Cagle. Bumgarner also has the distinction of being the first woman to record string band music, which she accomplished in 1924. Bumgarner, Cagle, and the other musicians who played on XERA could be heard as far west as California and as far north as Canada. Although he lived an opulent lifestyle, Brinkley's wealth eroded after a barrage of lawsuits. He died penniless in 1942.

John Romulus Brinkley.
Courtesy of the Kansas
State Historical Society.

WHERE: Campus of Western Carolina University, Cullowhee, 28723
ADMISSION: Free
CONTACT: Mountain Heritage Center, 828-227-7129
WEBSITE: www.mountainheritageday.com

THURSDAY CONCERT AND JAM SESSION AT WESTERN CAROLINA UNIVERSITY
Cullowhee

The Mountain Heritage Center, located in the H. F. Robinson Building at Western Carolina University, hosts a concert series and jam session. On the first Thursday of each month during the school year, bluegrass and old-time acts from the southwestern mountain region play a free concert in the center's state-of-the-art auditorium, which seats less than one hundred people. After the concerts, the stage opens up for a jam session. The performing act joins in, offering a rare opportunity for audience members and fans to interact or play with the visiting musicians.

The center may be best known for organizing the annual Mountain Heritage Day, but it's also a year-round attraction. In its several exhibit rooms, visitors can learn about Appalachian culture, from Native American basketry to the story of the Scotch Irish pioneers to Decoration Day traditions.

WHEN: First Thursdays of the month (October–May), 7 to 8 P.M.; jam session, 8 to 9 P.M.
WHERE: Mountain Heritage Center Auditorium, Western Carolina University, Cullowhee, 28723
ADMISSION: Free
CONTACT: Mountain Heritage Center, 828-227-7129
WEBSITE: www.wcu.edu

A NOTE ABOUT THE
BLUE RIDGE MUSIC TRAILS PROJECT

The *Blue Ridge Music Trails of North Carolina* guidebook is a cultural tourism project of the North Carolina Arts Council, an agency of the North Carolina Department of Cultural Resources. This edition is jointly produced with the Blue Ridge National Heritage Area.

Funded through a generous grant from the North Carolina Department of Transportation, the project is a collaboration between the North Carolina Arts Council and the Blue Ridge National Heritage Area (www .BlueRidgeHeritage.com). We have combined expertise and resources— working with local arts councils and tourism development authorities—to achieve the goals and strategies that enable western North Carolina and the state to value our music heritage and promote it appropriately to benefit citizens.

Blue Ridge Music Trails is a place-based, creative-economies development project featuring western North Carolina's rich musical heritage. These unique music traditions already contribute significantly to North Carolina's economy and have the potential to bring greater benefits; music events create jobs, strengthen the tax base, draw visitors, and attract and retain people who live and work in North Carolina. In 2011, audiences were surveyed at only 26 of the more than 150 venues where Blue Ridge Music happens. They spent $18.6 million attending these music events, and 65 percent said they would have traveled to another community for a similar experience, resulting in a loss of $13.5 million to the region if the Blue Ridge music traditions did not continue.

Every 100 visitors to a Blue Ridge music event can be expected to support a direct economic impact of more than $4,000.

We appreciate the opportunity to share traditional music with residents and visitors and hope that this sparks an interest in your own creative life. We also invite you to experience other rich cultural traditions in North Carolina, including the exploration of literature, craft, historic Happy Valley, and African American music. The cultural trails portal (http://www .NCArtsTrails.org) is your starting point for finding out what's new, interesting, and, in many cases, lesser-known travel experiences in North Carolina. So don't forget to add http://www.NCArtsTrails.org to your travel radar.

A NOTE ABOUT THE
TRADITIONAL ARTIST DIRECTORY

The Blue Ridge National Heritage Area's online Traditional Artist Directory is a guide to many of the finest traditional craft artisans, musicians, dancers, and storytellers in the North Carolina mountains and foothills. The directory contains profiles for more than 500 artists and groups. Use this free resource to

- book an artist for a performance or presentation;
- plan a trip to an artist's studio or music event; or
- learn more about the region's traditional artists and heritage.

The Traditional Artist Directory is the only juried directory of its kind in the region. Artists are selected on the basis of artistic excellence, authenticity, and significance as practitioners of their respective traditions. The directory was compiled by the North Carolina Folklife Institute with assistance from many partner and sponsor organizations.

Visit the Traditional Artist Directory online at www.BlueRidgeHeritage .com/traditional-artist-directory.

ACKNOWLEDGMENTS

Blue Ridge Music Trails is a collaboration between the Department of Cultural Resources and the Blue Ridge National Heritage Area Partnership. Implemented by the North Carolina Arts Council with funding from a Federal Transportation Enhancement Grant awarded by the North Carolina Department of Transportation, Blue Ridge Music Trails celebrates western North Carolina's musical legacy and its influence on American music. In addition, the project builds on the economic benefits created with the launching of the initial project in 2003. All of the partners are deeply grateful to the musicians, dancers, and presenters who have collaborated with us to share the traditional music of western North Carolina with the world.

Blue Ridge Music Trails benefited immensely from the contributions of residents who served as our steering committee. These leaders urged the North Carolina Arts Council and the Blue Ridge National Heritage Area Partnership to expand this initiative from a guidebook revision to a comprehensive project where the rich music traditions are sustained and utilized in appropriate ways to improve the lives of residents; where traditional musicians thrive and feel supported in their creative lives; where visitors and residents alike can appreciate and enjoy the richness of the music; and where youth are provided with arts learning experiences that spark interest and innovation in the traditional music of the region.

We were honored to work with steering committee members Becky Anderson, community and economic development consultant and chair of the Blue Ridge National Heritage Area Partnership board; Patricia Beaver, Director, Center for Appalachian Studies, Appalachian State University; Alex Bernhardt, CEO, Bernhardt Furniture Company; Jan Davidson, Director, John C. Campbell Folk School; Phil Francis, Superintendent, Blue Ridge Parkway Division of the National Park Service; Tanya Jones, Executive Director, Surry Arts Council; Rob Pulleyn, crafts and fiber artist, publisher, and N.C. Arts Council board member; and Joe Sam Queen, architect and traditional dancer.

We sought the expertise and opinions of local arts council directors and tourism professionals. The knowledge of this group was crucial to the development of the regions: Marla Tambellini and Cate Marvill with the Asheville Convention and Visitors Bureau; Carol Price, McDowell County Tourism; Laura Boosinger, Madison County Arts Council; and Kay Miller, Haywood County Arts Council.

The Department of Cultural Resources enthusiastically supported the project as a way to position North Carolina's rich cultural resources and to utilize music traditions as a mechanism for sustainable economic growth.

Deputy Director Nancy Trovillion and Mary Regan, retired Arts Council executive director, are tireless in their support of the Blue Ridge Music Trails project. Marketing Director Rebecca Moore strategically shepherded the project through implementation with assistance from Ardath Weaver, Hal Earp, and Katherine Reynolds.

The Blue Ridge National Heritage Area Partnership, under the leadership of Angie Chandler, including Rob Bell and Jill Jones, have shown outstanding leadership in both conceptualizing and implementing the project. Leesa Sutton-Brandon, of the Blue Ridge Parkway, also deserves special acknowledgment for her vision and knowledge.

Thanks to David Perry, editor-in-chief at the University of North Carolina Press, and his colleagues, including manuscript editor Mary Carley Caviness, editorial assistant Caitlin Bell-Butterfield, and publicity director Gina Mahalek, for editorial and design expertise and insight.

Behind it all, from start to finish, was Wayne Martin, executive director of the N.C. Arts Council, and former director of the Folklife Program. Throughout this project his affection for the people and places that are the subject of this book established a pattern of personal sensitivity for all who were part of the process, and his insightful guidance remained the enjoining positive force that inspired everyone!

Most of all, thanks to the people of western North Carolina who play traditional music. This book commemorates their words, their communities, and their music-making over many generations.

North Carolina Arts Council

Listing all of the kind folks who have assisted me so much with the research, writing, and editing of this book is both a daunting and a rewarding task. Please forgive me if I have overlooked anyone who may have assisted in any way during the course of preparing this book.

The first to thank in so many ways and for so many things is Wayne Martin, executive director of the North Carolina Arts Council. His calm and knowledgeable assistance throughout our many years of collaboration has truly been a blessing.

Steve Kruger performed above and beyond all expectations and calls to duty in his tireless attention to the details and more that are included in this book. Steve was seemingly on the job 24-7. His contributions to this book were indispensable.

Cedric Chatterley continued to amaze us all with the incredible originality and incomparable clarity of his photographic images, always portraying the people and the places that are described herein with sensitivity and love.

I thank my wife, Cathy, for her assistance throughout, but especially for her help with travel logistics and navigation as we roamed around, over, and through many miles of mountainous highways and backroads.

My son, Luke Fussell, daughter-in-law, Kristin, and their daughters, Ryan Avery and Harper, generously shared their Avery County, North Carolina, home, which on numerous occasions served as our home away from home during the research and site visit phases of this project.

Jim Owen and Yvonne Isenberg opened the doors to Jim's ancestral Wilkes County, North Carolina, home and provided us with many interesting and valuable insights into the music history of western North Carolina.

Musicians and music scholars Chester McMillian, Nick McMillian, Kelley Breiding, Clyde Ferguson Jr., Dorothy Hess, Bobby McMillon, Christine Horton, Donna Ray Norton, Herb Key, Glenn Bolick, Clyde Ferguson Jr., Sheila Kay Adams, Uwe Krüger, Joe Sam Queen, Alfred and Maybelle Welch, Trevor and Travis Stuart, Kinney Rorrer, and Jan Davidson all generously submitted to lengthy recorded interviews from which the personal profiles in this book were created.

The many traditional musicians, venue managers, and community volunteers we encountered during the preparation of this book are way too numerous to mention individually. Thanks so much to all of you. You know who you are.

Fred C. Fussell
Columbus, Georgia

It's been a dozen years since I made photographs for the first Blue Ridge Music Trails guidebook. Since then, there have been a lot of high-tech advancements in the way our culture interfaces with entertainment. We have so many new gadgets to keep us occupied now. But I'm here to tell you that live music in the mountains and valleys of North Carolina feels as strong and important today as it did a decade ago—or a hundred years ago for that matter. I hope you use this book to find and experience truly great live entertainment.

I would like to thank all those who participated in the image-making process for this publication and the North Carolina Blue Ridge Music website. Your cooperation and enthusiasm for sharing will not be forgotten. I would also like to thank Wayne Martin, Steve Kruger, Fred Fussell, Sally Peterson, Lesley Williams, Rob Amberg, and June Thompson for their help, guidance, and friendship.

Cedric Chatterley

INDEX

Page numbers in italics refer to illustrations or illustration captions.

two-finger style, 108, 167, 226; up-picking, 226–27; Watson and, 108. *See also* String bands

"Barbara Allen," 124

Barbecue, *54*, 57–61, 65; pit-cooked, 57, 59

Barber Shop jam session (Drexel), 183–84, *184*

Barber Shop Preservation Fund, 183

Barn, The (Eden), *21*, 46, 49

Barn Dance (radio program), 189

Bascom Lamar Lunsford "Minstrel of Appalachia" Festival (Mars Hill), 150–51

Basie, Count, 176

Baugus, Riley, 211

Bean bread, 217

Beans, 53, 64

Beech Mountain, 5, *5*, 77, 111–12, 121

Bele Chere festival (Asheville), 143

Bethel, 209

Big-circle dancing, 13, 219

Big Country Bluegrass, 83

Big Cove, 220

Biltmore Forest School, 165

Biltmore house, 164

Bizarre Foods (TV show), 173

Black Banjo Gathering, 8

"Blackberry Blossom," 105, 109

Blackberry Road, 62, 63

Blackface comedy, 68, 69

"Black Mountain Rag," 109

Black Mountains, 121, 130

Blacksmithing, 61, 64

Blizard, Ralph, 209, 210

Blowing Rock, 56, 61–64

"Blue Blue Day," 175

Bluegrass, 8–9, 17, 18, 22, 23, 39, 44, 60, 61, 75, 96, 99, 120, 129, 131, 132, 141, 212; Americana music and, 71, 72; Asheville's importance to, 135, 136; banjo-fiddle combination and, 10; best venues for, 171; Cleveland County and, 167; community fes-tivals, 38, 42; Cradle of Forestry Songcatchers, 163; dancing and, 196; defining characteristics of, 10, 92, 171; Eden Barn concerts, 46, 49; Fairchild's banjo style of, 208, 211; festival of the year award, 183; fiddle playing style of, 41; live radio performances of, 19, 189; Maggie Valley Opry House show, 208, 211; Mountaineers and, 186; Mount Airy Fiddlers' Convention, 28–34; old-time music contrasted with, 41; Pickin' at Priddy's con-cert series, 43; Pickin' in the Valley festival, 224; record sampler, 74; Red, White and Bluegrass Festival, 171, 179, 183; Rickman Store jam session, 231–32; Royce Memorial Jam, 38, 43; Scruggs's innovation and, 167, 171, 185; Shuffler's gui-tar playing and, 178; Stokes Stomp, 42; three-finger banjo picking and, 10, 185, 186; Todd General Store jam, 100; Todd New River Festival, 101; trailblazers of the Blue Ridge, 92–93; Watson and, 66; Yadkin Val-ley Convention, 28, 52; Zuma Cof-fee jam, 148–50

Bluegrass at the Old Rock School (Valdese), 171, 177, 179

Blue Grass Boys, 92, 93, 135, *148*, 167, 189

"Bluegrass Festival of the Year" award, 183

Bluegrass Jam at Zuma Coffee (Mar-shall), 148–50

Blue Mountain Inn (Maggie Valley), 208

Blue Ridge Escarpment, 23, 65

Blue Ridge Mountains, 15, 26, 31, 56, 130; highest peaks, 121; iconic natural landmarks, 121, 128, 170; national forests, 139, 164–65; Swannanoa Tunnel, 144

"John Henry," 182
Johnson, Clyde, 32
Johnson, David, 84
Johnson, J. Laurel, *218*
Johnson, Junior, 57
Johnson, Phil and Gaye, 187, *188*
"Johnson Boys," 182
John's River, 180, 182
Jones, Grandpa, 17
Jones, Loyal: "Mountain Dance and Folk Festival: A Living Tradition," 142–45
Jones Farm (Lenoir), 65–66
Jones House Community Center (Boone), 103–4, 106
Jones House Concerts on the Lawn (Boone), 104, 106
Jones House Jam (Boone), 94, 104
Jordan, Jimmy, 223–24
Jordan, Steve, 223, 224
Jordan, Sue, 223, 224
Joyce Kilmer Memorial Forest, 199
Julliard Institute, 193
Junaluska, Lake, 195, 199, 212, *212*, 213
Junior Appalachian Musicians (JAM) program, 9, 94–95, 104, 209, 210–11, 216
"Just One Time," 175

Kaplan, A. W., 86
Karpeles, Maud, 4
Keith House (John C. Campbell Folk School), 225
Kennedy Center (D.C.), homegrown music series, 49
Kentucky, 9, 116
Key, Herb, *82*, 86; profile of, 81–84
King, *25*
King, Henry, 209
King Pup Radio Show, 187–88, *188*, 189
Kings Mountain, Battle of (1780), 171
Kings Music Center, 43
Kingsport (Tenn.), 133

Kingston Trio, 73, 77
Knott, Sarah Gertrude, 14
Knoxville (Tenn.), 167
Koch, Frederick, 14
Kona, 113, 119
Kona Baptist Church, 113, *114*, 116, 119, *119*; Silver Family Museum, 119
Krauss, Allison, 71
Krüger, Uwe and Jens, profile of, 73–75, *74*
Krüger Brothers band, 73–75

Lake Junaluska Conference and Retreat Center, 195, 199, 212–15
Lakes, 199. *See also key word for specific lake*
"Lamkin," 12
Landsberg, Joel, 73, *74*
Land Trust for the Little Tennessee, 231–34
Lankford, Jerry, 82
Lansing, 57, 95–97, 99
Lansing Creeper Trail Park, 97
"Last Date," 89
Laurel River, 2
LaVette, Mister, 67
Leadbelly, 73
Leaksville (later Eden), 43, 47
"Leaving Home," 47
Led Zeppelin, 71
Leeks, 215
Lenoir, 61, 62, 65–66, 67, 92, 109, 122, 123; as county seat, 56
Leonhardt, Gary W., 183
Library of Congress, 40, 49; Archive of Folk Song, 5
Lily Cotton Mill, 167
Line dancing, 195, 204, 206
Linn Cove Viaduct, 127
Linville, 125, 126
Linville Falls, *121*
Linville Gorge, 121, 128, 170, *170*
Liquor, homemade, 37, 57

CD NOTES

The *Blue Ridge Music Trails of North Carolina* CD is a sonic accompaniment to the text: a guide for the ears. Many of the artists featured here tell their stories in profiles found in the preceding pages. Other recordings were made by some of the region's most influential historic musicians, or represent distinctive Blue Ridge musical styles, such as the unaccompanied ballad singing tradition in Madison County and Round Peak string band music. "Swannanoa Tunnel," "Frankie Silver's Confession," "Otto Wood," and "Tom Dooley" are based on actual events that took place in the region. In the notes below, you will see page references where you can learn more about the artists, the songs, and the places they come from.

Some of the tracks are field recordings made in musicians' homes; others were recorded live at venues featured in the guidebook; but the majority of the songs were laid down in recording studios. The biggest labels in the music industry have released mountain music, but these days many Blue Ridge musicians record for smaller, independent record labels that operate regionally and are committed to producing quality traditional music. If you like what you hear, we encourage you to pick up some of the albums and compilations that these songs come from. Performers sometimes bring recordings of their music to sell at live performances. You can also order these albums online, often directly from the label or the artist. For a selected discography and bibliography of mountain music, visit our website at www.BlueRidgeMusicNC.com.

1. Trevor and Travis Stuart/"The Grey Eagle"
2. Bascom Lamar Lunsford/"Swannanoa Tunnel"
3. Ola Belle Reed/"I've Endured"
4. The Buckstankle Boys/"Rainbow Sign"
5. Etta Baker/"John Henry"
6. The New North Carolina Ramblers/"Cotton Mill Blues"
7. Dorothy Hess/"Drunkard's Dream"
8. Christian Harmony Singers at Saint John's Church/"Restoration"
9. The Watson Family/"Ground Hog"
10. Manco Sneed/"Georgia Belles"
11. Manco Sneed/"Snowbird Nation"
12. Elkville String Band/"Otto Wood"
13. Donna Ray Norton/"A Soldier Traveling from the North"
14. Lesley Riddle/"Honeybabe"

15. Flatt and Scruggs/"My Cabin in Caroline"
16. Glenn Bolick/"Sawmill Man"
17. George Shuffler and Laura Boosinger/"Down in the Valley"
18. Frank Proffitt/"Tom Dooley"
19. Pop Ferguson/"Black Cat Bone"
20. Tommy Jarrell and Fred Cockerham/"Rockingham Cindy"
21. Welch Family Singers/"Trail of Tears Song"
22. Christine Horton/"Come Take a Trip on My Airship"
23. Krüger Brothers/"Carolina in the Fall"
24. Etta Baker/"Peace Behind the Bridge"
25. Bobby McMillon/"Frankie Silver's Confession"
26. H. P. Van Hoy/"Some Closing Remarks"

1. Trevor and Travis Stuart/"The Grey Eagle"

(Old 97 Wrecords)

From *Mountaineer*

Courtesy of Trevor and Travis Stuart

Trevor and Travis Stuart (profiled on pages 209–11) grew up in Haywood County. They learned to play from the older generation of local musicians, including Byard Ray, the Smathers family, Ralph Blizard, and Red Wilson, the fiddler who taught them "The Grey Eagle." This lesser-known version of the tune, played in the key of C, was a favorite in southwestern North Carolina and southeastern Tennessee. A performance of this version of "The Grey Eagle" has opened the Mountain Dance and Folk Festival in Asheville (see pages 140–41) since 1928.

2. Bascom Lamar Lunsford/"Swannanoa Tunnel"

From *Ballads, Banjo Tunes, and Sacred Songs of Western North Carolina*
Courtesy of Smithsonian Folkways Recordings

Few individuals have played as large a role in the history of mountain music as Bascom Lamar Lunsford. Lunsford (1882–1973) (see pages 2–4) grew up in Madison County surrounded by traditional music. He was a teacher and a solicitor but also a tireless performer, collector, and documenter of traditional music. In 1928, he helped organize the Mountain Dance and Folk Festival, the longest-running folk festival in the country. He recorded this local work song in 1949 for the Library of Congress. The Swannanoa Tunnel is still in use in Buncombe County. It was built largely by convict labor in the late 1870s at the cost of hundreds of lives (see pages 144–45).

3. Ola Belle Reed/"I've Endured"

(Ola Belle Reed and David Reed/Midstream Music)
From *Rising Sun Melodies*
Courtesy of Smithsonian Folkways Recordings
Ola Belle Reed (1916–2002) wrote this song on her fiftieth birthday. Reed (see pages 96–97) was born in Ashe County. With her brother, Alex Campbell, and her husband, Bud Reed, she went on to establish the New River Ranch in Maryland, and Sunset Park in Pennsylvania, popular country and mountain music venues catering to fellow displaced mountaineers. During the 1960s, she became known in the folk revival for her strong voice and clawhammer banjo playing, as well as her original song writing, which drew on both her traditional background and her strong ideals. "I've Endured" and another composition, "High on a Mountain" have become standards in bluegrass and Americana music. She was awarded a National Heritage Fellowship in 1986.

4. The Buckstankle Boys/"Rainbow Sign"

From *The New Young Fogies*, vol. 1
Courtesy of the New Young Fogies Project
The Buckstankle Boys (Andy Edmonds on fiddle, Seth Boyd on banjo, Todd Hiatt on mandolin, and Wes Clifton on guitar) are a group of young musicians who play classic bluegrass and old-time music. All of the Buckstankle Boys grew up in the Blue Ridge around traditional music. Andy Edmonds played banjo and guitar with the legendary Surry County fiddler Benton Flippen. Wes Clifton is the grandson of Verlen Clifton, the mandolinist in the Camp Creek Boys. Like many other traditional musicians of his generation, Clifton has also played other genres of music, in his case punk and indie rock. This performance reflects the band's roots in Surry County: a bluegrass version of "Rainbow Sign," which was popularized in the old-time-music world by the Round Peak fiddler Tommy Jarrell.

5. Etta Baker/"John Henry"

Recorded by Wayne Martin, 1991
Etta Baker (1913–2006) (profiled on pages 181–82) first picked up a guitar at the age of three. She was born in Caldwell County into a prolific musical family and learned to play both the guitar and the banjo. Baker wasn't recorded until she was in her late forties, when she became one of the most influential finger-style blues guitarists. She played her slide-guitar version of "John Henry" in open D or E tuning.

6. The New North Carolina Ramblers/"Cotton Mill Blues"

From *Cotton Mill Blues*

Courtesy of Old Blue Records

This fine band features banjo player Kinney Rorrer (profiled on pages 45–47) and multi-instrumentalists Kirk Sutphin, Darren Moore, and Jeremy Stephens. Their name pays tribute to Charlie Poole's early influential band, the North Carolina Ramblers. Kinney Rorrer is related to Posey Rorer, who was a fiddler with Poole's band and is an authority on Poole's life and music. "Cotton Mill Blues" recalls the hard lives of southern textile workers in the early twentieth century. Poole, like many of the musicians of the day, worked in North Carolina mills, as did Wilmer Watts, who recorded "Cotton Mill Blues" in 1929 with his band, the Lonely Eagles.

7. Dorothy Hess/"Drunkard's Dream"

Recorded by Wayne Martin, 2003

Dorothy Hess (profiled on pages 102–3) spent long periods of her childhood in a children's hospital. Her mother taught her to sing old ballads and folk songs while she was lying in her hospital bed. "Drunkard's Dream" was printed in England in the nineteenth century and was popular across the United States, especially during the temperance movement that led to Prohibition in 1919.

8. Christian Harmony Singers at Saint John's Church/"Restoration"

From *Christian Harmony Singing at Saint John's Church*

Courtesy of Jane Spencer

The *Christian Harmony* hymnbook was first published by William Walker in 1867 (see page 156). Today, Christian Harmony remains the most commonly sung shape-note style in the North Carolina mountains. At most shape-note singings, a hymn begins with a song leader setting the key and then calling out the number of the song in the hymnal and the verses to be sung. The singers then sing the notes (do, re, me, fa, so, la, ti, do) of the melody one time through before singing the words. "Restoration" is found in many of the older shape-note hymnbooks. Another popular hymn, "Count Thy Fount of Every Blessing," is also often sung to this melody. The verses sung here were written by John Newton, who also wrote the words to "Amazing Grace," a hymn that first appeared with its now-famous melody in William Walker's *Southern Harmony* in 1835. This recording was made at the annual singing at the historic Saint John's Church in Rutherfordton (see pages 184–87). Jeff Farr leads the hymn.

9. The Watson Family/"Ground Hog"

From *The Doc Watson Family*

Courtesy of Smithsonian Folkways Recordings

Doc Watson (see pages 108–10), who passed away in 2012, is one of the Blue Ridge's best-known musicians. Mostly remembered for his virtuosity on the guitar, Doc could play a number of instruments and was a powerful singer. Watson plays autoharp and sings on this classic recording from 1963 that also showcases the family tradition he grew up in. He is joined by his fiddling father-in-law, Gaither Carlton, and his brother Arnold Watson on banjo. "Ground Hog" is a traditional song widely sung throughout western North Carolina, and many a ground hog has ended up as a head on a homemade banjo.

10. Manco Sneed/"Georgia Belles"

Recorded by Blanton Owen,1970

Courtesy of the Western Folklife Collection

The great Cherokee fiddler Manco Sneed (1885–1975) (see pages 218–19) was a student of his father, John Sneed, but also of the other great fiddlers of the region, especially Dedrick (J. D.) Harris. Traditional fiddlers of Harris and Sneed's generations in southwestern North Carolina were remarkable for using triplets and other complicated bowing patterns, and they had a repertoire that is unusual compared to that of current fiddlers. "Georgia Belles" and "Snowbird Nation" (Track 11) are examples of "modal" melodies played in G in standard tuning. The solo fiddling tradition represented here is the oldest instrumental style of music in the southern mountains.

11. Manco Sneed/"Snowbird Nation"

Recorded by Blanton Owen, 1970

Courtesy of the Western Folklife Collection

The origins of "Georgia Belles" and "Snowbird Nation" are unknown, but the latter may refer to the Cherokee community of the same name in Graham County. Another local fiddler, Bill Hensley, claimed the tune was created by Junaluska, a Cherokee leader from the Snowbird community.

12. Elkville String Band/"Otto Wood"

(Walter B. Smith/Universal Songs of Polygram International, Inc.)

From *Over the Mountain*

Courtesy of Mountain Roads Recordings

Otto Wood (1894–1930) was an outlaw whose exploits were followed, and admired, by the public. He was killed in a shoot-out with police in 1930. The song that told his story was first recorded by the Carolina Buddies only a year after his death. The Elkville String Band hails from Wilkes County, where Wood grew up and often sought refuge. Singer and guitarist Herb Key (profiled on pages 81–83) has repaired and built acoustic guitars for over thirty years and has also researched Wood's life. The fiddler on this recording, Drake Walsh (1930–2010), was the son of the influential early recording artist Doctor Coble "Dock" Walsh (1901–67). They are joined by current Elkville String Band bassist Bill Williams and the talented multi-instrumentalist Jeff Michael on banjo.

13. Donna Ray Norton/"A Soldier Traveling from the North"

Recorded at the Bascom Lamar Lunsford Festival, 2006
Courtesy of the Bascom Lamar Lunsford Festival
Madison County is home to one of the oldest unbroken ballad-singing traditions in the country. Today there are several younger singers such as Donna Ray Norton (profiled on pages 146–47) who are singing songs that have been in their families for generations. This risqué ballad originated in Britain and was collected in the nineteenth century as "The Trooper and the Maid." It was sung by many of the influential Madison County ballad singers and recorded by Dillard Chandler (1907–92). Donna Ray Norton learned the song from Sheila Kay Adams (profiled on pages 154–56). This version was recorded live at the Bascom Lamar Lunsford Festival (see pages 150–51) in 2006.

14. Lesley Riddle/"Honeybabe"

From the Mike Seeger Collection, Southern Folklife Collection,
University of North Carolina at Chapel Hill
Courtesy of Alexia Smith
Lesley Riddle (1905–80) (see pages 132–34) was born in Burnsville in Yancey County and spent his youth moving between his hometown and the cities of East Tennessee, where he played with other African American blues musicians like Brownie McGee. He later traveled with A. P. Carter, collecting songs for the Carter Family repertoire. Riddle learned this tune from his Uncle Ed Martin and added his own lyrics. The melody bears a strong resemblance to the "Cannonball Blues," which Riddle taught to Maybelle Carter. This recording of Riddle was made by the influential folklorist and musician Mike Seeger in the 1970s, long after Riddle had moved to Rochester, New York, and had mostly given up music.

15. Flatt and Scruggs/"My Cabin in Caroline"

(Lester Flatt and Earl Scruggs/Peer International Corp., Peer Music III, Ltd., Obo Scruggs Music, Inc.)

From *The Complete Mercury Recordings*

Courtesy of Mercury Records, under license from Universal Music Enterprises, a division of UMG Recordings, Inc.

In 1948, just a few years after they helped create the genre known as bluegrass, Earl Scruggs (1924–2012) (see pages 167–71) and singer and guitarist Lester Flatt left Bill Monroe's band to form their own group. Flatt and Scruggs's first recording session on Mercury in 1949 included this original composition. The song captures Earl's improvisational skills and the fiddling of Jim Shumate (see pages 92–93), one of the many influential early bluegrass musicians from western North Carolina.

16. Glenn Bolick/"Sawmill Man"

Courtesy of Glenn Bolick

Glenn Bolick (profiled on pages 63–64) is a potter and a musician and runs a sawmill at his home between Lenoir and Blowing Rock. He composed this song about the history of logging in his family, which goes back to his great-grandfather. "Sawmill Man" was included on a compilation of occupational songs called *Work's Many Voices*, produced by the folklorist Archie Green. This version was recorded live at the Jones House in Boone (see page 104) in 2010.

17. George Shuffler and Laura Boosinger/"Down in the Valley"

From *Mountain Treasures*

Courtesy of Copper Creek Records

A twelve-year-old George Shuffler learned "Down in the Valley" (also known as "Birmingham Jail") the same day he learned his first guitar chords. In an interview printed in the *Raleigh News and Observer* on October 21, 2007, he recalled, "I was barefoot, walking home with my dad afterward and playing my old guitar. I'd stop and play those three chords, G, C and D, because I was afraid I'd forget them. I'd do that, then run to catch up with my dad, stop and play some more. That evening, Mama was humming 'Birmingham Jail' and I seconded on guitar. She got so hoarse she couldn't talk."

During the 1950s and 1960s, Shuffler (see pages 178–79) toured and recorded with the Stanley Brothers, playing bass, guitar, and mandolin, and singing low harmony parts. (He plays bass and guitar on this track.) That group's singing style and Shuffler's distinctive cross-picking style of guitar playing became a definitive part of the bluegrass sound. After he left the road, he continued to play with family and friends around his home in Burke County. In 2003 he recorded with musician and singer Laura Boosinger, who also directs the Madison County Arts Council.

18. Frank Proffitt/"Tom Dooley"
Recorded by Frank and Anne Warner
Courtesy of the Warner Family
Tom Dula, a musician and Civil War veteran, was hanged for the murder of his lover, Laura Foster, in 1868. This rendition of what became North Carolina's most famous murder ballad (see pages 71–79) had a central role in the folk music revival of the 1960s. In 1940, Frank Proffitt sang the song for folklorists Frank and Anne Warner, who were collecting music in the Beech Mountain region of western Watauga County. The Warners' arrangement of Frank's performance was published in a songbook, which was the source for the Kingston Trio's famous 1958 recording, the first commercially successful recording of the folk revival era. This version was recorded a year later. Proffitt didn't benefit from the Kingston Trio's recording directly but enjoyed a brief career playing at festivals and folk clubs before he died suddenly at the age of fifty-two in 1965. In addition to being a musician, Proffitt made dulcimers and wood-rimmed "mountain banjos" (see pages 111–12), one of which he plays on this song. More of Proffitt's songs, as well as those of other musicians from western North Carolina can be heard on two volumes of music recorded by the Warners, *Her Bright Smile Haunts Me Still* and *Nothing Seems Better to Me*, available on AppleSeed Records.

19. Pop Ferguson/"Black Cat Bone"
From *Big Boss Man*
Courtesy of TAM Records and Clyde Ferguson Jr.
Clyde "Pop" Ferguson recently celebrated his seventy-fifth year playing music. He learned the guitar while growing up in North Wilkesboro. The son of a holiness preacher, he played in a family group for tent revivals and learned the blues in secret from the radio and from a disfigured street musician in Lenoir named Max Moore. After a few years in the military, Clyde traveled around the country, making a living mostly from playing music. During that time he transitioned from the finger-style playing he learned as a young man to a more urban electric sound. After a long hiatus, he began playing with his son Clyde Jr. (profiled on pages 67–69), a music teacher and bassist living in Caldwell County.

20. Tommy Jarrell and Fred Cockerham/"Rockingham Cindy"

Field Recorders Collective
From *Round Peak*, vol. 1
Courtesy of Ardena Moncus and Diane Alden

Tommy Jarrell (1901–85) and Fred Cockerham (1905–80) were two of the best-known musicians to play in the Round Peak style of old-time string band music (see page 23). Round Peak music is characterized by its driving rhythm and the complex interplay between fiddle and banjo. Cockerham's distinctive clawhammer style on the fretless banjo and Jarrell's voice and powerful fiddling shine through on this distinctively Round Peak version of an old standard, "Cindy." This field recording was made by Ray Alden, one of the early documenters of Round Peak music and a founder of the Field Recorders Collective.

21. Welch Family Singers/"Trail of Tears Song"

From *In Memory of Jeffery "Ryalee" Adam Welch*
Courtesy of the Welch Family

The "Trail of Tears Song" is a Cherokee hymn, also found in the wider southern hymn tradition as "Guide Me, O Thou Great Jehovah." Alfred and Maybelle Welch (profiled on pages 220–22) learned the song from elders in their community, who said it provided strength to the Cherokee people as they endured the hardships of the forced removal to Oklahoma in the 1840s. Unlike most of the Welches' repertoire, which includes many songs sung in the Cherokee language, the "Trail of Tears Song" is sung in unison (not harmony), and without instrumental accompaniment. They are joined by Vincent Wesley, who sings the bass vocal part.

22. Christine Horton/"Come Take a Trip on My Airship"

Recorded by Wayne Martin, 2007.

The piano is not often thought of as an Appalachian instrument, but at one time plenty of piano players in the Blue Ridge played string band music. Christine Horton (profiled on pages 88–89) grew up providing the music for square dances in Ferguson, North Carolina. Her father and her grandfather were both old-time fiddle players. Here she plays an interesting instrumental version of a curious Tin Pan Alley song published in 1904, popularized as a string band song by Charlie Poole. The words, written at the dawn of powered flight, describe a suitor's offer of a romantic trip "to visit the man in the moon."

23. Krüger Brothers/"Carolina in the Fall"
(Uwe Krüger/Double Time Music)
From *Up 18 North*
Courtesy of Double Time Music
Jens and Uwe Krüger (profiled on pages 73–75) discovered traditional Appalachian music growing up in Switzerland. They came to the mountains of North Carolina to visit the music's source, and found a new home. Today they are world renowned for their instrumental virtuosity and their innovative approach to bluegrass, but they remain fixtures in the local music of Wilkes and Caldwell Counties. Uwe Krüger's "Carolina in the Fall" tells that story, and it's one of the band's most popular songs.

24. Etta Baker/"Peace Behind the Bridge"
(Snake Lady Music)
Recorded by Wayne Martin, 2000
From *Banjo*
Courtesy of Snake Lady Music/Music Maker Relief Foundation
Etta Baker (profiled on pages 180–81) is known primarily as a blues guitarist, but when Baker was born in 1913, most of the music played in her family and in the John's River community of Caldwell County was "country music," played on the fiddle and banjo. Baker learned "Peace Behind the Bridge" from the Crisps, a white family that lived nearby. The story goes that the tune was inspired by two men who had to hide under a bridge to avoid detection by a group of sinister riders. She is accompanied by folklorist Wayne Martin on the fiddle.

25. Bobby McMillon/"Frankie Silver's Confession"
From *Lords and Merry Maids All*
Courtesy of Ivy Creek Recordings
In 1833, Frankie Silver was hanged for the gruesome murder of her husband, Charlie (see pages 114–20). A ballad sung from her perspective became popular in the surrounding area and is sung here by Bobby McMillon (profiled on pages 122–24), a ballad collector and singer, who is also a member of the Silver family. He sings two versions of the ballad. He learned this one from his great-aunt Lounette Hopson who lived in the Toe River valley, close to where the murder took place.

26. H. P. Van Hoy/"Some Closing Remarks"

From *Thirty-Seventh Old-Time Fiddler's Convention at Union Grove, North Carolina*

Courtesy of Smithsonian Folkways Recordings

This recording of Union Grove Fiddlers' Convention founder H. P. Van Hoy (see page 50) was made in 1961 by folklorist Mike Seeger. It is not uncommon for a fiddlers' convention to be emceed by a well-known local resident. These colorful talkers often open and close the festival and announce the competitors as they come onstage.

Behind the scenes at venues up and down the Blue Ridge, people donate their time and their property to help foster a place for the tradition to grow, often for little or no monetary gain. We thank them, and we thank you for listening. — Steve Kruger

All tracks were mastered by Jeff Carroll at Bluefield Mastering.